1994

The Craft of Justice

University of Pennsylvania Press
Law in Social Context Series

A complete list of the books in this series appears at the back of this volume.

The Craft of Justice

Politics and Work in Criminal
Court Communities

Roy B. Flemming,
Peter F. Nardulli, and
James Eisenstein

upp

UNIVERSITY OF PENNSYLVANIA PRESS   Philadelphia

Library of Congress Cataloging-in-Publication Data
Flemming, Roy B.
    The craft of justice: politics and work in criminal court communities / Roy B.
Flemming, Peter F. Nardulli, and James Eisenstein.
        p.   cm.—(Law in social context series)
    Includes bibliographical references and index.
    ISBN 0-8122-3187-2
    1. Criminal justice, Administration of—Social aspects—United States.   2. Criminal
justice, Administration of—Political aspects—United States.   3. Criminal courts—
United States.   I. Nardulli, Peter F.   II. Eisenstein, James.   III. Title.   IV. Series.
KF9223.F43   1993
345.73'01—dc20
[347.3051]   91-25106
                                                                                                        CIP

TO TONI

Who knew when to rumba and when to waltz
while we lived in Michigan,
but after our move to Texas had to learn when to do the
two-step

Contents

Acknowledgments

This book concludes a research project that was conceived in the fall of 1978 and received funding a year later. The project was designed to compare nine felony criminal courts in three states. Thousands of felony cases were sampled, and several hundred interviews were conducted; the data collection and fieldwork consumed the better part of three years. This project constitutes one of the most comprehensive and intensive social scientific investigations into America's criminal courts in the past thirty years. A list of reports, books, and articles based on the data from this project is presented in Appendix B. With the exception of the interview transcripts, the project's data have been archived at the Interuniversity Consortium for Political and Social Research, P.O. Box 1248, Ann Arbor, Michigan, 48106-1248.

Research of this scope and complexity could not have been undertaken without the generous support provided by the National Institute of Justice and the National Science Foundation. Grants 79-NI-AX-0062 and 81-IJ-CX-0027 came from the National Institute of Justice. The National Science Foundation grants were designated SES-83-08989, SES-83-09609, and SES-83-08705.

Several people in the National Institute of Justice provided wise and useful guidance and encouragement, particularly Carolyn Burstein, Debbie Viets, Linda McKay, and Cheryl Martorana. We are also deeply indebted to Felice Levine at the National Science Foundation for her support at the later stages of this endeavor. Our advisory panel participated actively and productively in the early stages of the research and made a number of excellent suggestions. The panel consisted of James Gibson, Thomas Church, Milton Heumann, George Gish, Magnus Seng, and Clifford Kirsch. Obviously, despite the important contributions from these various sources, we alone are responsible for the viewpoints and findings reported herein.

We are also grateful to Wayne State University, the University of Illinois, and Pennsylvania State University for their support. We are indebted, as well, to a number of specific individuals who worked at our research sites.

The following people provided invaluable assistance in collecting the case data in Michigan: Jan Johnson, Janet Van Tiem, Peter Kalawert, Donna Larson, Elizabeth Lenihan, Michael Draving, Laura Skiragis, Rolf Heubel, Steven Rosenberg, Sharon Hansen, Stephen Roach, Scott Mahoney, and Robert Sydlow. Meg Falk, a graduate student at Wayne State University, ably performed a variety of tasks relating to all phases of the field research. Evelyn Cloutier Lappan devoted many hours to preparing and sorting the Michigan Q-sort data, clipping newspaper articles, and a number of other important chores. Carol Wesson, Nancy Michaels Kaminiski, and Linda Laird provided typing assistance.

In Illinois, David Chambers, Keith Emmons, Michael Bass, and John Carroll provided important services as graduate assistants. Arthur Jameson and Robert Illyes were invaluable as computer consultants. Assistants Karen Wilson, Kathy Wilson, Carol Freund, Karla Kraus, Tammy Turner, and Darlene Riccuito performed far beyond reasonable expectations. Ann Nardulli contributed untold hours to sorting and organizing the Q-sort data. Students Jan Powell, Frank Saibert, Ann Fohne, Laurie Edgar, Rick Morris, Scott Rubermeyer, Rich Hampton, Lisa Lindsay, David Bowers, and David West very ably collected the case file data. Florence Edmison and Laurie Mitchell typed the interview transcripts. Special thanks are due Samuel K. Gove, Director Emeritus of the Institute of Government and Public Affairs at the University of Illinois, for his support for this project.

In Pennsylvania, thanks go to Mark Kessler, who served as the principal research assistant; Rich Feiock, Jeff Webster, Paula Carta, Tony Filippello, Terry Kline, and Mindy Morrison for a fine job collecting the case file data; Diane Colonna, Colleen Young, Chuck Kimmel, and Leslie Castaldi for performing a variety of chores; Louise Foresman for her heroic labors in organizing the Q-sort; Martha Waldman for assistance during the later stages of the project; Chris Hopwood for doing just about everything; Bob Rutchick for computer assistance; Bonnie Grove, Mary Jane Johnson, Audrey Smith, Lee Carpenter, Elena DeLuca, and Jan Walther for a fine job typing data forms, reports, drafts, letters, and so forth, often on short notice; Marva Hillard for an outstanding job in the difficult task of transcribing interviews; Greta O'Toole for competently handling all budget preparation and financial administration; and Irwin Feller, Director of the Institute for Policy Research and Evaluation at Pennsylvania State University, for his support.

At Texas A&M University, Marcia Bastian performed her customary miracles in preparing various drafts of this manuscript. We owe her special thanks for her help and cooperation in getting this book word-processed and for preparing the table and figures.

While it may seem obvious, it must be understood that the original project and particularly this book would never have been completed if it had not been for the cooperation and participation of the judges, attorneys, court personnel, and many others who gave generously of their time and insights. Without their honesty, frankness, and direct-ness, this book, which relies so greatly on the interviews to describe the craft of justice in America's criminal courts, would not have been possible. For this reason, every effort has been made to cloak the identities of the courts and individuals in anonymity.

Finally, readers should know that the entire project was a joint enterprise. No single individual could have undertaken research of this magnitude. A fortuitous blend of individual skills enriched the final product substantially.

Portions of Chapter 2 first appeared in slightly different form in "The Political Styles and Organizational Strategies of American Pros-ecutors: Examples from Nine Courthouse Communities," *Law and Policy* 12(January 1990):25.

Introduction: Craft and Communities

Legal Pluralism and American Criminal Courts

State trial courts in America are highly diverse. No one court looks or acts exactly like another. Indeed, even courtrooms in the same courthouse may differ from one another in significant ways, as with sentencing in criminal cases. This should come as no surprise. The American political system, and its principles virtually guarantee these results. Federalism decentralizes the legal system, and the continuing legacy of Jacksonian democracy further assures localized patterns of criminal justice. The consequence is legal pluralism.

This book, using the ideas of craft and court communities as conceptual compasses, explores the "plural legal orders" of nine medium-sized felony courts located in Illinois, Michigan, and Pennsylvania.[1] The structures and processes of criminal justice in these nine courts reflected relationships between the inhabitants in these communities and emerged out of the interactions of the participants in the courtrooms. The characteristics of these relationships—status, influence, dominance—were shaped by local political incidents, by the specific histories of the courts, by disputes and competing ideas, and by the actions of prosecutors, judges, and defense attorneys. The craft of justice as practiced by these actors refers to how they went about their work as well as to how they politicked within the court community. Legal pluralism evolved through the purposive adaptive behavior of attorneys and judges within the diverse institutional relationships of the court communities.

1. A review of the literature on legal pluralism from which the quoted phrase is taken can be found in Sally Engle Merry, "Legal Pluralism," *Law and Society Review* 22(1988):869.

Craft of Justice: A Metaphor for Behavior in Courts

I think it's easier, frankly, to defend a criminal case than any other case . . . legal skill-wise. I think it's the toughest job, human skill-wise.

*   *   *

In this business, it's credibility from the day you walk into that cell to talk to your client to the day you talk to the jury and to when you talk to the judge. If you don't have credibility, you don't have nothing.

*   *   *

Harry was a man who knew the system. And, taking nothing away from Harry, when it was rumba time, he rumbaed. When it was waltz time, he waltzed. Sometimes we young attorneys were waltzing when we should have been rumbaing. We can all learn from the Harrys in our courts.

Criminal courts are legal institutions. The criminal law is their business, and the law is made up of rules. Yet these rules do not dictate with precision and force how legal professionals must dispose of felony cases. No law books provide detailed instructions telling attorneys how to negotiate guilty pleas or when they should file motions. No legal treatises explain to judges the best way for reducing backlogs of cases. Prosecutors cannot consult hornbooks that describe exactly when to file one felony charge rather than another.

As a consequence, when attorneys and judges talk about their work and how they perform it, what they say can be described as a discussion of craft. When defense attorneys explain how thay practice criminal law in their local courts, as the lawyers just quoted did, they place less stress on legal knowledge as the key to success than on other factors. For example, they point to the importance of knowing how to deal with people, stress the value of a reputation for credibility that elicits respect and cooperation from others, and then underscore the need to know in detail how courts as social and political organizations operate so that they know when they should waltz and when they should rumba. As another of these attorneys put it, the practice of criminal law is difficult because of the "human skill-wise" demands it places on its practitioners.

Prosecutors and judges discuss their jobs in similar ways. To cite one instance, a New York trial court judge wryly confessed in his autobiography that years on the bench had persuaded him of the sageness of a British jurist's definition of a good judge. The jurist stressed the importance of personal qualities in his definition before adding, almost as an afterthought, that if the judge "has some knowledge of law it will help." The trial judge commented, "As a practicing lawyer I used to smile at [this] observation; but I no longer discount its underlying wisdom."[2] Schooling in the law is a prerequisite for those who labor in trial courts, but it is not the be-all and end-all for a successful career. A law degree and admission to the bar are tickets to the well of the courtroom, yet as another criminal defense attorney in one of the nine courts said, "The law is a backdrop, but if you use too much law, you're probably gonna lose."

The fact that courts are varied and that the law does not adequately or sufficiently explain why these differences occur has been well established by the past twenty years of empirical research.[3] Much of this research has focused on individual actors in order to understand how courts work. Studies abound that seek to explain differences in the behavior of judges and lawyers by looking at their backgrounds, attitudes, or conceptions of their roles in court.[4] Another body of research investigates the dynamics of the guilty plea process, a somewhat

2. Autobiographies by state trial judges are few and far between. The quotation is from the autobiography by Bernard Botein, *Trial Judge* (New York: Cornerstone Library, 1952), 3. A more recent example is Judge Robert Satter, *Doing Justice: A Trial Judge at Work* (New York: American Lawyer Books/Simon and Schuster, 1990). Biographies of trial judges are no more common. For one example, see J. Woodford Howard, "Judge Harold R. Medina: The 'Freshman Years,'" *Judicature*, 69(October–November 1985):126.

3. The literature is very large. Useful discussions of theoretical developments can be found in Peter F. Nardulli, ed., *The Study of Criminal Courts: Political Perspectives* (Cambridge, Mass.: Ballinger Publishing Company, 1979), and in the more recent review by Herbert Jacob, "Decision Making in Trial Courts," in John B. Gates and Charles A. Johnson, eds., *The American Courts: A Critical Assessment* (Washington, D.C.: CQ Press, 1991), 213–33.

4. For an assessment of the literature on judges, see James Gibson, "From Simplicity to Complexity: The Development of Theory in the Study of Judicial Behavior," *Political Behavior* 5(1983):7–49. As for defense lawyers, three seminal pieces should be consulted: David Sudnow, "Normal Crimes: Sociological Features of the Penal Code in a Public Defender Office," *Social Problems* 12(1965):255; Abraham Blumberg, "The Practice of Law as a Confidence Game," *Law and Society Review* 1(1967):15; and Jerome Skolnick, "Social Control in the Adversary System," *Journal of Conflict Resolution* 11(1967):52. A review of the research done in the wake of these studies can be found in Roy B. Flemming, "If You Pay the Piper, Do You Call the Tune? Public Defenders in America's Criminal Courts," *Law and Social Inquiry* 14(Spring 1989):393. The prosecuting "styles" of assistant prosecutors are analyzed in Lief Carter, *The Limits of Order* (Lexington, Mass.: Lexington Books, 1974). For a recent analysis of how the "crime control" and "due process" views of chief prosecutors influence their policies regarding guilty pleas, see Alissa Pollitz Worden, "Policymaking by Prosecutors: The Uses of Discretion in Regulating Plea Bargaining," *Judicature* 73(April–May 1990):335.

broader orientation that takes into account the negotiating interactions among the major actors.[5] A third and smaller number of studies takes an even broader perspective, one that centers on the court "system" and views judges, prosecutors, and defense attorneys as organized sets of functionally interdependent actors.[6] In this perspective, the varied behavior of individual actors regarding guilty plea negotiations and sentencing is explained with respect to courtroom work groups that differ in their stability and familiarity as a result of policies adopted by the "sponsoring organizations" that assign these actors to the court-rooms and send them work.

Each of these perspectives leads to searches for particular pieces to a very complex puzzle. The notion of "craft" is intended to draw these pieces together so that at least the outlines of a solution will emerge. The craft of justice refers to how chief prosecutors and their assistants, chief judges and their colleagues, head public defenders and their assistants, and private defense attorneys pursue their individual ca-reers, go about their tasks in the courtrooms, organize themselves for collective purposes, and interact politically in the institutional realm of the courthouse. Their craft is both practical and political; it refers to learned and adaptive knowledge that guides practitioners in getting things done within the courthouse.

The value of craft as a metaphor for describing behavior in criminal courts stems from the well-established finding that rough classifica-tions of defendants—their behavior and cases—foster the use of rela-tively simple decision rules that in turn lead to patterned behaviors in courts that resemble routines.[7] In contrast, attorneys like to say that "all

5. A valuable summary of the "plea bargaining" literature can be found in the special issue devoted to this topic in *Law and Society Review* 13(Winter 1979). See also Milton Heumann, *Plea Bargaining: The Experiences of Prosecutors, Judges, and Defense Attorneys* (Chicago: University of Chicago Press, 1977), and Douglas W. Maynard, *Inside Plea Bargaining: The Language of Negotiation* (New York: Plenum Press, 1984).

6. Abraham Blumberg, in *Criminal Justice* (Chicago: Quadrangle Books, 1967), used this approach to analyze a large metropolitan court. A court in a much smaller, Mid-western city was studied in this way by David W. Neubauer, *Criminal Justice in Middle America* (Morristown, N.J.: General Learning Press, 1974). Feeley employed an "open systems" perspective in his study of a misdemeanor court in New Haven. See Malcolm M. Feeley, *The Process Is the Punishment: Handling Cases in a Lower Criminal Court* (New York: Russell Sage Foundation, 1979). Eisenstein and Jacob adapted key ideas from organiza-tion theory to develop their comparative analyses of three big city felony courts. See James Eisenstein and Herbert Jacob, *Felony Justice: An Organizational Analysis of Criminal Courts* (Boston: Little, Brown and Company, 1977).

7. With respect to how practitioners construct classifications of cases, the path-breaking article is Sudnow's "Normal Crimes." As for the use of basic decisions rules used by public defenders when deciding whether to go to trial or file guilty pleas, see Lynn Mather, *Plea Bargaining or Trial* (Lexington, Mass.: D. C. Heath, 1979).

cases are different" and that they "never say 'never'." If this were true, then the law as it is practiced in courts would be analogous to arts such as painting or sculpture in which every effort is aimed at creating a unique piece of work. In courts, however, there are practical and normative restraints to such efforts. As a practical matter, legal professionals find it convenient and expeditious to play down what is unique and to emphasize the familiar so that solutions to problems are not continually reinvented. From a normative perspective, doing justice also encourages routinization so that "likes are treated alike"—that is, so that similarly situated defendants are treated similarly.

Yet court routines are not so highly structured or the behavior of judges and attorneys so rote, as to justify the popular impression that criminal courts resemble mass-production factories. As a prosecutor who was upset over a court's refusal to provide more trial time for criminal cases protested, "I'm not here to run a drill press." The idea of craft recognizes that over time and through repetition practitioners discover that what at first appeared to be separate, distinct problems requiring different solutions have enough in common that a single solution is satisfactory for most of them. This process of simplification, however, is never complete, because of the diversity of the problems and because of continuing changes in the nature of the problems. Ambiguity and uncertainty remain as obstinate, inherent qualities of the workplace. Moreover, courts are collective enterprises in which conflict and cooperation coexist. Thus disagreements over whether a case is "typical" and warrants "typical" treatment do not disappear even though courthouse routines are well established. Because routines incorporate satisfactory, not optimal, solutions to problems, and since the routines themselves are likely to reflect partial resolution of conflicting interests, conflict may erupt even over the routines themselves.

At one level, then, craft is a metaphor for patterns of behavior that are generally, but not always, governed by rules of thumb and by the lessons learned by legal professionals as they develop their careers and go about their daily tasks within the court. It is also a metaphor that is intended to link these "micro-level" behaviors with the "macro-level" processes that occur within the courthouse. While most research has focused on how attorneys and prosecutors negotiate guilty pleas and on how judges sentence convicted criminals, studies of this kind ignore the organizational and institutional decisions of chief prosecutors, judges, and the defense bar that influence the content of courtroom routines. A related function of this metaphor is to incorporate within a single concept the fact that attorneys and judges are not groups of homogeneous individuals. Prosecutors and public defenders

TABLE 1. Aspects of the Craft of Justice.

	Orientation	
Focus	Internal	External
Work	Building a career	Succeeding in court
Politics	Leading the organization	Constructing institutional relations

work within organizational settings that may be hierarchical. Courts have chief judges and often have administrative divisions. The craft of those holding positions of formal authority will differ from the craft of those who do not. The different aspects of craft also recognize and highlight the importance of courtroom and courthouse relationships as influences on the behavior of lawyers and judges. Table 1 presents these various aspects of the craft of justice.

This table identifies four aspects of craft: building a career, succeeding in court, leading the organization, and constructing institutional relationships. These aspects can be distinguished from one another according to whether they are focused on the work or the politics of the actors and whether the orientation of a particular aspect is internal or external to the group of which the actor is a member. While only four aspects of craft are presented here, it should be clear that the content of these crafts will vary with the position and role of particular actors. For example, the organizational craft of chief prosecutors and chief judges will not be identical. It also should be noted that these aspects are not isolated from one another; they are related and influence one another in various complex ways. Thus the career craft of assistant prosecutors overlaps in some measure with how well they succeed in the courtrooms, and the substance of their courtroom craft may be substantially influenced by the way the chief prosecutor practices the organizational craft needed to run the office and by how the prosecutor feels about the office's institutional relationships with the court and the defense bar.

Attorneys and judges build careers in the courts. They earn their livings there and attain professional stature through their work in them. For many attorneys and judges, the local criminal court will satisfy their professional ambitions. For others the court may be a way station or stepping-stone on the path to establishing a private practice or gaining a seat on a higher court. Regardless of their ultimate goals, however, they must first learn through experience what it means to be a trial prosecutor or public defender, how to judge, or how to establish a legal practice. Courtroom prosecutors and defense lawyers who are just starting their careers have to learn the rudiments of their profession at the same time they are developing reputations for being competent trial attorneys, an important part of the credibility needed for their careers. In many instances, this is a "sink or swim" experience; the attorneys and judges learn their craft by practicing it. For private attorneys, another facet is learning how to reconcile the economic realities of operating a law office with the interests of their clients. Judges undergo several changes in how they conceive of their role over the span of their careers on the bench.[8] The content of this aspect of craft is a compound of law school socialization and how it shapes views of the law, the lessons of experience in practicing law and their effects on what attorneys and judges feel is the practical application of law, and the personal views of the individuals.[9]

The craft of succeeding in court pivots around relationships in the courtrooms and the skills needed to dispose of cases. The outcomes of criminal cases are jointly produced through the interactions of prosecutors, defense attorneys, and judges. Courtroom craft refers to how these actors manage these ongoing relationships and how they construct processes to dispose of cases. For judges, this is largely a matter of developing ways of moving cases and of monitoring guilty pleas. For attorneys and prosecutors, courtroom craft is knowing the routines that govern the handling and disposition of cases as well as the informal rules of etiquette that influence how exceptions to these routines will be handled. The significance of courtroom work groups resides in the possibility that differences in routines and etiquette may exist within the courthouse. For attorneys and prosecutors, knowledge of such differences is critically important to the practice of their respective crafts. Thus, knowing how to rumba and waltz is not enough; attorneys must also know the dance preferences of their partners and when they are willing to try a new step to a slightly different tune. Courtroom craft, then, is a matter of mastering the relationships and processes of courtroom work and knowing how to use this knowledge in both routine and nonroutine cases.

The work that is done in courtrooms, however, is inextricably entangled with organizational and institutional relationships within the political realm of the courthouse. These parts of the puzzle have most often been overlooked in studies of criminal courts, but they cannot be

8. These changes are identified in studies by Lenore Alpert, Burton M. Atkins, and Robert C. Ziller, "The Transition from Advocate to Arbiter," *Judicature* 62(1979):324, and by Paul B. Wice, "Judicial Socialization: The Philadelphia Experience," in James A. Cramer, ed., *Courts and Judges* (Beverly Hills, Calif.: Sage Publications, 1981), 149–72.

9. See, for example, Carter's discussion of the different responses of assistant prosecutors to the ambiguity and uncertainty surrounding criminal cases and the resulting differences in the styles adopted by the assistants. See Carter, "Prosecutors' Backgrounds and Expectations," in *The Limits of Order*, 45–73 *passim*.

ignored when thinking about craft within the courthouse. For example, the autonomy of courtroom work groups depends in substantial measure on the policies of the organizations that "sponsor" the appearances of the participants in the courtrooms. Work group autonomy is not inevitable, it evolves out of the policy choices of the bench, bar, and prosecutor.[10]

Organizational craft in the courthouse involves leadership and the potential for collective action. It takes different forms in the prosecutor's office, on the bench, and in the defense bar because of inherent differences in the structures of these organizations. The resources of the three major actors differ. The prosecutor's office locates executive authority in one position. In contrast, courts are much more likely to be decentralized and nonbureaucratic. Executive authority is limited, often shared with other judges, and the chief or administrative judge who is the titular head of the bench is often elected by the bench. The defense bar, which is made up of differing numbers of public and private attorneys, depending on the locality and its public policies, is the least bureaucratic of the three major actors in the courthouse.

The significance of organizational craft for understanding courts residues in whether organizational leadership, policies, and structure can define or limit the discretion exercised by organizational members working in the courtrooms. In general, the potential for such control is greater in the prosecutor's office than it is elsewhere, if the chief prosecutor chooses to exploit this resource. In the absence of effective control, the likelihood of policy diversity within the sponsoring organizations increases.

The prosecutor's office, bench, and bar through various means must allocate time, resources, and cases among their members. These decisions often are made to satisfy internal needs or constraints (one aspect of organizational craft is maintaining morale within the sponsoring organization), and yet these decisions inevitably have external consequences for others in the courthouse. For example, time is a limited resource, and for attorneys working on a fee basis, time is also money. Thus, how the bench schedules court appearances has a direct bearing on the work of prosecutors and attorneys. There is no assurance that the court's policy will be convenient to others; indeed, the bench may have adopted the policy solely for its own benefit. While coordination may be desirable, no means exist to ensure that it will happen; if a consensus does not exist among the sponsoring organizations, coercion is not possible. Accordingly, relations among the bench, bar, and prosecutor's office within the political realm of the courthouse are

---

10. Eisenstein and Jacob, *Felony Justice*.

made up of ongoing mixed-motive situations characterized by varying degrees of conflict and cooperation.

Mixed-motive relationships are at the core of institutional craft. The leaders of sponsoring organizations can parlay the positional and organizational resources they have at their disposal to effect changes in policies that they perceive as disadvantageous to their organization or groups. However, prosecutors, judges, and defense attorneys may not be equal players in this game.

Prosecutors have several potential advantages over courthouse rivals. Their position affords them electoral political clout. As elected officials, they can lay claim to mandates from citizens for their policies. As partisan officials they are free to use the symbols of law-and-order politics. As elected executives who represent the state and its citizens in prosecuting crime, they are not expected to be neutral or passive in performing this task, although they have certain ethical responsibilities to seek justice.[11] Judges are barred by ethical canons from speaking out publicly about crime and justice in ways that would make them direct political competitors of chief prosecutors. Still, the legal authority and formal role of judges give them status within the courthouse, at least as individuals. They are not necessarily pushovers for aggressive prosecutors, especially if the judges have partisan connections that can be used to thwart the career aspirations of chief prosecutors. Unlike judges, criminal defense attorneys cannot fall back on their formal status within the courthouse as a resource. Defense lawyers are shackled by the stigma attached to their clients. They are usually the weakest competitors for influence within the courthouse. For defense attorneys, the central tenet of their institutional craft may be "getting along by going along."

The craft of justice as a metaphor is intended to organize descriptions of criminal court behavior according to how actors in the courthouse learned to do their work and how they perform their tasks. Craft is used to tie together the dimensions of work and politics in the court. However, the contents of the various aspects of craft will vary with the position and role of the actors. Equally important, from a comparative perspective, the craft of justice will greatly reflect the contexts within which it is practiced. A second metaphor that will be used when describing the relationships in courts that establish these contexts is that courts can be viewed as if they were "court communities."

11. See, for example, the short discussion in Sanford H. Kadish, Stephen J. Schulhofer, and Monrad G. Paulsen, *Criminal Law and Its Processes,* 4th ed. (Boston: Little, Brown and Company, 1983), 142–43.

Court Community: A Metaphor for Relationships in Courts

The court community provides the professional setting and the political arena for the craft of justice.[12] Various kinds of relationships emerge from the functional interdependencies that bind participants in the criminal disposition process. These relationships arise out of the simple fact that the courthouse is a workplace for people with common occupational backgrounds. Over time, as experiences in dealing with one another accumulate, norms and common understandings develop; a sense of being a distinct group with its own language, particular ways of looking at things, and manner of doing its work come together to form a local culture. The emotional undercurrents of this culture are revealed by the courthouse grapevine, which carries news, gossip, and rumors about what is going on in the community. Beyond this informational function, the grapevine plays a central part in the development of reputations within the community, and because of this the grapevine becomes a means of enforcing norms.

Membership in the courthouse community generally leads to a sense of identification with the community. Inhabitants of the community want to feel a part of it and with few exceptions seek its acceptance. Partisan ties, career interests, and dependence can reinforce these bonds. In addition, internalization of courthouse customs and traditions by new members of the courthouse community perpetuates the work habits and craft of the community and its status structure as well. Support for the dominant local norms and ways of doing things frequently leads to a kind of boosterism or community pride. This communal identification and internalization of courthouse norms muffles expressions of opposing views. Adversarial discourse is often governed by courthouse etiquette and courtesies encouraging cooperation.

This feeling of attachment, however, is necessarily fragile. Its bonds stretch across institutionally separate roles that have distinct legal and functional responsibilities. Attitudes and interests generally vary accordingly. Prosecutors and defense attorneys, for example, are not interchangeable parts. They are members of separate organizations and "citizens" of the courthouse community. Tension exists between the two memberships that may be resolved one way or another, de-

---

12. The value and components of the "courthouse community" as a metaphor in understanding trial courts is discussed in more detail in James Eisenstein, Roy B. Flemming, and Peter F. Nardulli, *The Contours of Justice: Communities and Their Courts* (Boston: Little, Brown and Company, 1988) "Trial Courtrooms as Organized Workgroups," 19–39.

pending on the leadership and social organization or cohesiveness of their "home" organizations.

Court communities, then, may be harmonious or conflictual and riven by disputes and disagreements. Mixed-motive relationships of all kinds are plentiful in criminal courts; members of the community may find as much benefit in conflict as they do in cooperation, depending on the situation. Opportunities for cooperation or conflict continually occur during the handling of cases and arise out of the formal, legal relationships within the courthouse. Outside the courtrooms, in the court's political realm, cooperation and conflict as perceived by the major actors have their own rewards and costs, and what may be seen as an advantageous action by one may not be seen that way by another. The balance between cooperation and conflict fluctuates over time within court communities and varies from one community to the next.

Every court community develops a "technology" for disposing of its felony caseload. This technology is a complex set of ways through which the community processes its work. The community's technology is the joint, but not necessarily coordinated, outcome of policies adopted by the court community's sponsoring organizations. The prosecutor's office, the bench, and the defense bar must decide how to allocate their personnel to particular tasks, decide how to divide time for particular kinds of work, and choose how to allocate workloads. No formal, legal rules govern these decisions. More important, no one sponsoring organization has the authority to compel another to assign its work or personnel in particular ways. It is often the case that what seem from the outside to be mundane, humdrum administrative decisions look very different from inside the community because they vitally affect the interests of everyone in the community. Since everyone has a stake in these decisions, disregard for these interests sets the stage for conflict.

The courthouse community also has a status and influence structure. In a formal sense, judges occupy a special status within courtrooms and the courthouse, a status that elevates them above prosecutors and defense attorneys. Less formally, this status hierarchy may be turned around. The bench as a whole may be held in low regard by prosecutors and attorneys. The judges may fail to work efficiently or refuse to apply the industry needed to complete cases in a timely fashion. Judges also may find they cannot agree among themselves about how the court should be run. Whatever the reason, the bench's status may fall, and, often as an accompanying result, its influence within the courthouse will decline. Similar kinds of problems can occur within the prosecutor's office or the defense bar with corresponding effects on their status and influence within the court community.

Status and influence are variables within the courthouse community. They are not constants. More important, status and influence may become motives for change within the courthouse community if dissatisfaction leads to efforts to improve status or to increase influence. Prosecutors unhappy with the status of their offices seek to change this condition. Similarly, judges who are displeased with what has happened to the bench's position within the courthouse or who feel the bench is threatened by policy changes made by the prosecutor or perhaps by the defense bar can also take action. The critical factor in these efforts may be the strength and type of links actors in the court community have to major allies in the court's political environment. Court communities are not isolated, autonomous bodies. They are vulnerable to external pulls and pressures as well as to unexpected shocks and disturbances, especially through the electoral process, all of which lead to unsought disruptions in relations within the court community.

The court community, therefore, is a segmented, occupational world inhabited by prosecutors, judges, and defense lawyers who create various kinds of order through negotiation and conflict in the courtrooms and within the courthouse. The central characteristics of these orders—the court community's status and influence structures, its technologies for processing cases, its grapevine, and its norms governing interpersonal relations—evolve through the actions and interactions of courthouse participants. The conduct of negotiations and conflict reflects the craft of justice as practiced by the key participants. Most of the time, this craft reproduces and reinforces relations within court communities because the aspects of craft centered around career and courtroom work are iterative, experiential, practical skills based on knowing what should be done and when. Uncertainty and conflict are generally avoided.

Learning About the Craft of Justice in Court Communities

The craft of justice varies markedly among America's criminal courts. For example, in some courts, defense attorneys with few exceptions routinely ask that preliminary examinations of the charges lodged against their clients be held, while lawyers elsewhere just as regularly pass up this opportunity.[13] Prosecutors' offices scarcely resemble one

13. Compare the habits of public defenders in Los Angeles with those of defenders in Connecticut, as described, respectively, by Lynn Mather, *Plea Bargaining or Trial* (Lex-

another with regard to how strictly they evaluate cases when they decide whether or not to file charges and what these charges should be. Some impose high standards and prosecute only cases for which the offices consider the likelihood of a jury trial victory (if the cases were to go that far) high. Others set much lower thresholds, feeling that evidence of probable cause warrants prosecution.[14] Bail decisions in criminal courts also vary widely. One court may require stringent bail conditions, leading to more pretrial detention and forcing defendants to pay higher costs for their release from custody. In another court, bail officials may follow more lenient policies.[15] The craft of moving cases in courts also varies widely in the United States, with corresponding differences in the length of time courts take to dispose of their caseloads.[16] And, finally, the style and manner with which members of court communities handle cases and the severity of sentences they mete out to defendants contrast sharply among courts.[17]

Diversity in the craft of justice is a major obstacle to understanding America's criminal courts. Patterns and regularities in these practices undoubtedly exist, but they are difficult to discern from the current literature. The lion's share of studies focus their attention on one actor (judges, for example), or they concentrate on one stage of the criminal disposition process (say, sentencing), or, if they have a broader perspective, they are case studies of single courts. Comprehensive, comparative studies are few in number.[18] Even these few studies are limited to a handful of courts located in big cities or large metropolitan areas (for example, Minneapolis and Pittsburgh, or Chicago, Detroit, and Baltimore).

ington, Mass.: Lexington Books, 1979), and Jonathan D. Casper, *American Criminal Justice: The Defendant's Perspective* (Englewood Cliffs, N.J.: Prentice-Hall, 1972).

14. Compare the different philosophies and policies in New Orleans, Kansas City, and Boulder, Colorado, described by Joan E. Jacoby, *The American Prosecutor: A Search for Identity* (Lexington, Mass.: Lexington Books, 1980).

15. See the comparison of Baltimore and Detroit in Roy B. Flemming, *Punishment Before Trial: An Organizational Perspective of Felony Bail Processes* (New York: Longman, 1982).

16. See the many comparisons in Thomas Church, Jr., *Justice Delayed: The Pace of Justice in Urban Trial Court* (Williamsburg, Va.: National Center for State Courts, 1978).

17. From among several studies documenting these differences, see the contrast between "good government" Minneapolis and politically "traditional" Pittsburgh in Martin A. Levin, *Urban Politics and the Criminal Courts* (Chicago: University of Chicago Press, 1977).

18. Least common are studies that are both comparative and longitudinal. For what may be the only example of this rare species, see the analysis of Georgia's felony courts covering the period from 1976 through 1984 presented by Martha A. Myers and Susette M. Talarico in *The Social Contexts of Criminal Sentencing* (New York: Springer-Verlag, 1987).

This book rests on an empirical foundation built with data collected from trial courts of general jurisdiction located in nine medium-sized counties in three states. This is one of the largest and most complete research efforts in the past thirty years. A key concern was the selection of the nine courts. Medium-sized counties ranging in population from roughly two hundred thousand to nearly one million were chosen, for both practical and theoretical reasons. As a matter of practicality, limited time and resources inevitably constrain research. If smaller courts are chosen, more courts can be studied with a given amount of resources. The other benefit is that studying smaller courts expands what is known about America's criminal courts. A lingering question about studies of large city courts, such as those in Los Angeles, Chicago, and Manhattan, is whether their size makes them unique and hence unrepresentative of most of the criminal courts in the United States.[19] In 1987, there were 1,328 circuit-level courts with jurisdiction over felony cases in the United States, but 67 percent of these courts had three or fewer judges, and only 8 percent had more than fifteen. The remaining 25 percent had between three and fifteen judges; the courts in this study fell within this size range.[20]

A sampling of medium-sized courts also expands the array of political environments from which the courts can be chosen. One of the strongest presumptions about American courts is that they reflect their political environments. Many of the differences between the criminal courts in Minneapolis and Pittsburgh, for example, were held to be reflections of the cities' political cultures. A tradition of "good government" and "reform" in Minneapolis, in contrast to Pittsburgh's history of "traditional, machine-oriented" politics, led to different ways of processing cases and very different sentencing patterns.[21] Urban reform tends to be strongly related to the economic characteristics of local communities; middle-class communities with small ethnic or minority populations are more likely to practice a reform style of politics than industrial, blue-collar communities with large ethnic and minority populations.

Accordingly, the social and economic characteristics of local communities within the three states were determined to make sure the sampled courts were sufficiently different for any environmental effects to

---

19. A detailed discussion of the relationship between size and the characteristics of criminal courts can be found in Eisenstein, Flemming, and Nardulli, "Contours of Justice: Criminal Courts in the United States," in *Contours of Justice*, 259–90.

20. These tallies are based on calculations using information from Kamla J. King and Judith Springberg, *BNA's Directory of State Courts, Judges, and Clerks: A State-by-State Listing*, 2nd ed. (Washington, D.C.: Bureau of National Affairs, 1988).

21. Levin, *Urban Politics and the Criminal Courts*.

become apparent. Three communities were selected from each of three states—Illinois, Michigan, and Pennsylvania—for a total of nine courts. For each state, there was a suburban county located on the fringes of a metropolitan city, an "autonomous," largely middle-class county located away from major metropolitan areas, and an industrial, typically economically declining county, usually with a large minority population. The nine sites formed three triplets of similar communities.[22]

The fieldwork for the larger project from which this book is derived started in 1980 and did not end until 1982. Many visits during these years to gather data and conduct interviews involved "hanging around" and "poking and soaking" into the milieu and life of each courthouse.[23] While locating the offices of lawyers, sitting in the anterooms of judges' chambers, waiting for an assistant prosecutor to finish a telephone conversation, catching brief chats with probation officers in the corridors of the courthouses and lunch-table talks with public defenders, we were led to many small and not so small discoveries that accumulated into a feeling for the social life, work rhythms, and evolution of the communities.[24] This knowledge was a bonus that came out of the complicated and time-consuming nature of the study's basic research design.

A "triangulated" research strategy guided decisions about the collection of data and information.[25] Different kinds of data were gathered to gain as firm an empirical understanding of how the nine courts operated as possible. For example, information from court records was needed to check the comments and opinions of courthouse regulars about the operation of their courts, or to confirm defense attorney

22. Further information about the nine communities is presented in Appendix A. A more detailed description of how the communities were selected is presented in Peter F. Nardulli, James Eisenstein, and Roy B. Flemming, *Tenor of Justice: Criminal Courts and the Guilty Plea Process* (Urbana: University of Illinois Press, 1988).

23. Fenno describes and explains "poking and soaking" in Richard F. Fenno, Jr., *Home Style: House Members in Their Districts* (Boston: Little, Brown and Company, 1978), 249–95.

24. Richard F. Fenno, Jr., "Observation, Context, and Sequence in the Study of Politics," *American Political Science Review* 80(March 1986):3.

25. Norman K. Denzin, *The Research Act: A Theoretical Introduction to Sociological Methods,* 2nd ed. (New York: McGraw-Hill Book Company, 1978). See also Sam D. Sieber, "The Integration of Fieldwork and Survey Methods," *American Journal of Sociology* 78(May 1973):1335; Robert K. Yin, *Case Study Research: Design and Methods* (Beverly Hills, Calif.: Sage Publications, 1984); and William Foote Whyte, *Learning from the Field: A Guide from Experience* (Beverly Hills, Calif.: Sage Publications, 1984). A valuable assessment of the case study is presented by Lawrence B. Mohr, "The Reliability of the Case Study as a Source of Information," *Advances in Information Processing in Organizations* 2(1985):65.

claims about hard-nosed prosecutors with actual case outcomes or the attitude scores of prosecutors.[26] Environmental, political, and historical information about the local communities was culled from census documents, voting records, public files, and newspapers. In addition to these background data, three basic kinds of information were needed.

First, the records of the courts and prosecutors' offices were mined for case-level information on more than 7,400 felony defendants.[27] These data provided the basis for identifying major activity patterns in the nine courthouses. Questions about delay in the courts, the preliminary hearing and motion decisions of defense counsel, the charging policies of the prosecutors, the outcomes of the guilty plea process and trials, and other related concerns were answered through these data.

The second source of information was provided by members of the court communities who filled out questionnaires about their careers and backgrounds. In addition, they answered questions that were later used to measure their attitudes regarding the sentencing and punishment of criminals, the importance of administrative efficiency in the courts, and due process matters. Further information was collected about the reputations of prosecutors and defense lawyers and how they evaluated each other in terms of their trustworthiness, trial competence, and accommodativeness or responsiveness. Judges were ranked by prosecutors and attorneys according to the judges' concern about the state of their dockets, their activity and informality on the bench, their predictability, and their accommodativeness.[28] These data made it possible to identify attitudinal and reputational patterns within courtroom work groups or triads of attorneys and judges to determine the effects of these patterns on sentences in guilty plea cases.[29]

For this book, the third source of data—interviews with 306 members of the courthouse communities—was most important. The interviews with these attorneys and judges were loosely structured, which allowed

26. For a complete discussion of the rationale for a comparative, integrated research design, see James Eisenstein, Peter F. Nardulli, and Roy B. Flemming, "Explaining and Assessing the Pretrial Process: A Comprehensive Theoretical Approach and Operationalized, Multi-Jurisdictional Application" (Paper presented at the Annual Meeting of the Law and Society Association, San Francisco, Calif., 10–12, May 1979).

27. The sampling procedures used in each court and the array of case-based data are discussed in further detail in Nardulli, Eisenstein, and Flemming, *Tenor of Justice*, 73–78.

28. Details about these procedures and operationalization of key measures and indicators are in Nardulli, Eisenstein, and Flemming, *Tenor of Justice*, 61–73 and appendices I and II, 385–99.

29. See the "best case" analysis in Peter F. Nardulli, Roy B. Flemming, and James Eisenstein, "Unraveling the Complexities of Decision Making in Face-to-Face Groups: A Contextual Analysis of Plea-Bargaining Sentences," *American Political Science Review* 78(December 1984):912.

the interviewees to expand on topics when they wished. Moreover, as the workings of the court and relations within the courthouse became clearer, the semi-structured interview procedure made it possible to raise issues or phrase questions that probed more deeply for the perceived implications of recent events or past incidents.[30] Furthermore, some respondents became "informants." They divulged incidents or revealed relationships that, while well known within the courthouse community, could have become embarrassing if they had become more widely known. In some instances this was a matter of letting off steam and perhaps settling old scores. In others, it was an effort by the informant to make sure that the underpinnings of how the court worked were understood. In either case, insights into the court emerged that a more structured interviewing format might have blocked.[31]

This book relies greatly on these interviews. Whenever possible and as much as possible, attorneys and judges were allowed to describe in their own words their relationships with one another and how they performed their work. The hoped-for advantage of this approach is that it will portray the craft of justice in convincing, down-to-earth terms that make the excitement and challenge of this craft palpable. These extracts let attorneys and judges describe what real life and work are like in the courthouse. What they had to say is interesting; it deserved a hearing.

Orientation and Assumptions of the Book

This is the final book of a trilogy based on a large-scale, complex study of nine criminal courts. The two previous books, working within a common conceptual framework, presented different but complementary perspectives of the nine courts. The first book, *The Contours of Justice: Communities and Their Courts*, develops the metaphor of "court communities" and compares the courts at a macro-level of analysis. The second, *The Tenor of Justice: Criminal Courts and the Guilty Plea Process*, quantitatively assesses the statistical impact of variables at the individual, contextual, and environmental levels of analysis on the guilty plea processes in the nine courts. This book, the third in the trilogy, builds on the findings of the first two. However, it is more

30. As Rosenthal suggests, there are times when "it is more productive to attend to what is on other people's minds than to ask questions about what is on one's own mind." See Alan Rosenthal, *Legislative Life: People, Process, and Performance in the States* (New York: Harper and Row, Publishers, 1981), 6.

31. Fenno's tip, "Go where you are driven; take what you are given; and, when in doubt, be quiet," was useful advice when occasions for unexpected revelations arose. See Fenno, *Home Style*, 264.

qualitative and less macro-oriented, places less stress on comparing specific courts than in using them to illustrate aspects of the craft of justice, and is more concerned with illuminating how courts work than in explaining the outcomes of cases. With regard to the latter emphases, much of the research in criminal courts concentrates on determining what factors affect dispositions and sentences in criminal cases. However, despite the fact that it takes this tack, *The Tenor of Justice* also notes that "limiting research on criminal courts to case outcomes would be like limiting research on Congress to votes."[32] There is much to be learned about criminal courts besides the search for explanations of case outcomes. The present volume looks at criminal courts from a slightly different angle to reveal aspects of behavior that have been ignored or overlooked.

This book rests on the basic findings of the first two books. In a sense, the following general conclusions serve as the assumptions for this book.

• The court community is particularly important in understanding courts in medium-sized jurisdictions, because courtroom workgroups have relatively less autonomy in these courts than in larger courts. Courtroom diversity depends much more on the social and political dynamics of the courthouses in medium-sized courts than in large courts. Because of the importance of the court community, it becomes an important arena for the interplay of institutional interests.

• Guilty pleas dominated court proceedings in these nine jurisdictions, but the pleas were not characterized by concessions in charges and sentences. Reductions in primary charges were infrequent, and dismissals (or *nolle prosequi*) of related or secondary charges were generally symbolic in their impact. Going rates or patterned relationships of the charge, record, and sentence governed the sentencing process. The process, however, is not entirely consensus-oriented but a blend in which concessions play a smaller but still significant part in some cases.

• The specific features of the guilty plea process in each court directly reflected such "contextual" characteristics as those dealing with the practices, personnel, and politics of the sponsoring organizations. In contrast, no broad, systematic pattern could be established that linked the characteristics of individual actors (e.g., their background, attitudes, or role conceptions) to case outcomes in the

32. Nardulli, Eisenstein, and Flemming, *Tenor of Justice*, 368.

courtrooms. The leadership of individual actors and the organization of collective action, however, are the means through which contexts are created and maintained.

• Environmental factors, such as local crime rates, media attention to the courts, or the county's sociopolitical system, have very little direct effect on guilty plea outcomes or sentencing in the short run. Much more important is the effect of state penitentiary capacities on sentencing severity. Local political factors, however, may be more relevant to other aspects of court community behavior, such as prosecutor charging policies, than to case outcomes.

This book is divided into three parts of two chapters apiece and ends with a concluding chapter. Part 1 focuses on the craft of prosecution. It begins with a chapter that identifies and analyzes the "courthouse styles" of the nine prosecutors and the organizational strategies they followed in accordance with these styles. A central theme of this chapter is that style and strategy are in large part a reflection of the chief prosecutors' views regarding the status of their office within the courthouse community, an "internal" orientation rather than an "external" one. The next chapter explores in more detail the organizational craft of leading a prosecutor's office and then proceeds to describe the career and courtroom craft of assistant prosecutors.

Part 2 is devoted to the craft of judging. The first chapter investigates how bench policies reflect the social organization of the judges. Two themes weave through this chapter: (1) Policy diversity within a court is likely to be the result of noncollegial relationships between judges; and (2) decisions about seemingly mundane administrative matters, such as the type of docket or the calendar, raise complicated problems of equity and efficiency for judges, threaten the stability of judicial collegiality, and influence the court's status within the courthouse. Accordingly, the craft of chief judges in leading their brethren is a subtle process, because their authority rests on their ability to earn the trust of their colleagues. The next chapter explores in more detail the courtroom craft of judges and the varied ways in which they run their courtrooms as they try to move cases, police guilty pleas, and do justice.

Part 3 looks at the craft of defense. The chapter on the political craft of defense develops the notion that the defense attorney tends to be the weakest actor in the institutional triad that constitutes the core of the courthouse community. Social, economic, and political ties of various kinds define the boundaries of adversarial behavior for the defense bar. The next chapter looks at how defense attorneys work within and around the routines of their courts. The central point of this chapter is that the key to the defense attorney's craft is knowing how, when, and with whom to stretch courthouse norms in nonroutine cases.

The concluding chapter, after summarizing the findings of the preceding chapters, draws together the various strands of the craft of justice to present a classification of the nine court communities. This classification highlights the pluralistic quality of American trial court communities. A complex, varied pattern emerges when the institutional policies and political practices that make up the craft of prosecution, judging, and defense are combined for the nine courts. Beneath this complexity, however, there is one fundamental dimension of great significance to understanding criminal court communities: the likelihood that the prosecutor's office will dominate the status and influence the structure of a court community. This chapter also probes a related issue centering on the stability or durability of the structure of these communities.

The craft of justice in America's trial courts is a fascinating puzzle. This book presents a systematic, ambitious, empirically well-grounded effort aimed at identifying the shapes of the major pieces to this puzzle and at showing how they fit together to reveal how criminal courts in the United States operate and how they may change. By letting the people who work in these courts voice their views and comment on their craft, this book offers an inviting opportunity to see criminal courts from the vantage points of these insiders.

Part I
The Craft of Prosecution

Chapter 1
The Political Craft of
Chief Prosecutors

Introduction

Institutional inequality among prosecutors, judges, and defense attorneys is common in the real world of trial courts. Status and influence are integral features of court communities, and differences in status and the ability to exert influence matter in shaping what happens in the courthouse and courtrooms.

When challenging the institutional status quo of a court community, chief prosecutors hold several advantages over their rivals. Prosecutors virtually own the politically potent symbols of "law and order" politics.[1] Judges cannot openly play this game, and defense attorneys, tainted in the public view by the people they represent, are politically disqualified. Moreover, district attorneys frequently build independent power bases within or outside the local party that can be used as stepping stones to higher office or the bench, or as a means of getting their way within the courthouse.[2]

The functional role of the district attorney (DA) within the courthouse is another important resource. Control over charging and the screening of cases governs the flow of cases into court. By tightening or loosening this spigot, DA's can decrease or increase the volume of cases

1. For analysis of the law-and-order politics that draws on a cultural-symbolic perspective, see Stuart A. Scheingold, *The Politics of Law and Order: Street Crime and Public Policy* (New York: Longman, 1984).

2. Political mobility is not inevitable, nor do prosecutors always seek higher office. Local customs and the size of the prosecutor's office seem to make a difference. See, for example, Herbert Jacob, *Justice in America* (Boston: Little, Brown and Company, 1984), 96–100; James Eisenstein, *Politics and the Legal Process* (New York: Harper and Row, 1973), 20–25; and James J. Fishman, "The Social and Occupational Mobility of Prosecutors: New York City," in William F. McDonald, ed., *The Prosecutor* (Beverly Hills, Calif.: Sage Publications, 1979), 239–54.

flowing into the courts as well as change the kinds of cases and their mix of charges. In effect, they shape courthouse work rhythms and the workloads of judges and defense lawyers. Of greater importance are the prosecutors' attitudes regarding "plea bargaining." Their policies define the discretion of trial assistants over nontrial dispositions. The chief prosecutor's preferences about the content of these dispositions (e.g., whether they should include reductions in charges or agreements about sentences) dramatically affect how cases are typically handled within courthouses.

Last but not least, the chief prosecutor can better exploit the organizational potential of the DA's office. Prosecutors face fewer constraints in molding organizations that will follow their policies. Judges balk at restraints on their autonomy. Whether elected or appointed, judges cannot be fired or easily removed from office and thus make poor building material for constructing a bureaucratic apparatus. Chief public defenders, like chief prosecutors, are heads of offices. Nevertheless, public defenders usually recoil from the idea that their assistants should comply with policies that ensure uniformity in handling cases. The private defense bar generally lacks both the cohesion and the incentives to act collectively. In contrast, prosecutors have more freedom and less compunction in restricting the autonomy of their assistants. Both as elected politicians and executive officials, prosecutors can be formidable figures within court communities. The question that emerges is, "When are prosecutors most likely to exploit these advantages?"

Courthouse Styles: Insurgents, Reformers, and Conservators

With a handful of exceptions, almost all chief prosecutors with responsibility for prosecuting felony crimes are elected officials in the United States.[3] This electoral link between the office and the local community has attracted considerable interest in how environmental factors or political incentives influence prosecutorial policies.[4] Far less attention

3. The exceptions are Alaska, Connecticut, Delaware, New Jersey, and Rhode Island, where they are either appointed or members of the state attorney general office.

4. Jacoby makes the strongest claim regarding the impact of environmental factors on prosecutors' functions. At one point she remarks, "The single most powerful influence on the prosecutor, his role, and the operations of his office is the nature of the population he represents, its resources, and the consequent social and cultural patterns it develops," and at another she claims, "Much of a prosecutor's exercise of power is constrained by an external environment over which he has little control but to which he must respond." See Joan E. Jacoby, *The American Prosecutor: A Search for Identity* (Lexington, Mass.: Lexington

has been paid to how relations within court communities affect the style and strategies of prosecutors.[5] While prosecutors clearly have external relationships that are important to them, the focus of this chapter turns inward to highlight how relations within the courthouse are also important incentives affecting prosecutorial style and policies.

Prosecutors pick courthouse styles based on strategic concerns over status within the court community and on the prosecutors' personal views about politics.[6] The first consideration centers on whether prosecutors are dissatisfied with their office's relationship with the bench and the defense bar. The second rests on the prosecutor's view of the utility or expected value of conflict in changing the office's status and influence in the courthouse; challenges to the status quo carry costs that are compared to the perceived chances of successful challenges. Figure 1.1 outlines how these factors affect the prosecutor's choice of courthouse or political styles.

The chief prosecutors in the nine court communities can be characterized as having one of three political styles: courthouse insurgent, policy reformer, or office conservator.[7] Insurgents were most dissatisfied with the status quo and were prepared to do battle in order to

---

Books, 1980), 47, 276. It is clear this view is overdrawn and too simple, as the following studies suggest. With respect to charging policies, compare George F. Cole, "The Decision to Prosecute," *Law and Society Review*, 4(February 1970):313, and David W. Neubauer, "After the Arrest: The Charging Decision in Prairie City," *Law and Society Review*, 8(Spring 1974):495. For the effects of electoral changes and shifting campaign alliances on prosecutorial policies, see Herbert Jacob, "Politics and Criminal Prosecution in New Orleans," in James R. Klonoski and Robert I. Mendelsohn, eds., *The Politics of Local Justice* (Boston: Little, Brown and Company, 1970), and Stuart A. Scheingold and Lynne A. Gressett, "Policy, Politics, and the Criminal Courts," *American Bar Foundation Research Journal* 1987(Spring–Summer 1987):461. In a study comparing two California prosecuting offices, Utz, in sharp contrast to Jacoby, points out, "A key to variations in the exercise of prosecutorial discretion . . . lies in the prosecutors' own conceptions of their professional role and responsibilities." See Pamela J. Utz, "Two Models of Prosecutorial Professionalism," in William F. McDonald, ed., *The Prosecutor* (Beverly Hills, Calif.: Sage Publications, 1979), 99–124.

5. Portions of this chapter are drawn from an earlier article that includes more detailed information about each of the nine counties. See Roy B. Flemming, "The Political Styles and Organizational Strategies of American Prosecutors: Examples from Nine Courthouse Communities," *Law and Policy* 12(January 1990):25.

6. The relationship between leadership or courthouse style and organizational strategy outlined in this chapter borrows loosely from Mohr's status-driven model of the centralization of authority in organizations. See Lawrence B. Mohr, *Explaining Organizational Behavior* (San Francisco: Jossey-Bass Publishers, 1982).

7. There are some similarities between insurgent and reformer styles and Utz's distinction between the "adversarial" and "magisterial" models of prosecution she found in San Diego and Alameda counties, respectively. See Utz, "Two Models of Prosecutorial Professionalism." *15/ 2 16*

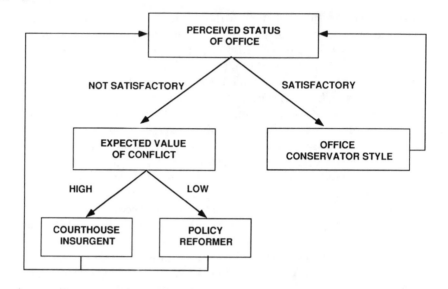

Figure 1.1. A decision model of prosecutor courthouse styles. (From Roy B. Flemming, "The Political Styles and Organizational Strategies of American Prosecutors: Examples from Nine Courthouse Communities," *Law and Policy* 12[January 1990]:25. Reprinted by permission of Blackwell Publishers.)

change it. Policy reformers sought to improve the status of the prosecutor's office but shunned open conflict and employed more subtle strategems. Office conservators accepted the status quo. Prosecutors who chose to be office conservators were most likely to perceive the status of their office as satisfactory.

Courthouse Insurgents: Challenging the Institutional Status Quo

Two chief prosecutors, both conservative Republicans in predominantly Republican, suburban counties, were courthouse insurgents. Each expressed deep dissatisfaction with the status of the prosecutor's office within the court community and were dismayed with what happened in the courtrooms as a result. Both had a taste for conflict and neither hesitated to challenge the courthouse community in the pursuit of their goals.

Both DAs accused their predecessors either of being under the bench's thumb or of being too slow, too reluctant to stand up to judges and defense attorneys. The first prosecutor pinned the blame for the office's plight on the local Republican party, accusing it of being cavalier about whom it nominated for prosecutor. The second pointed a finger at the bench for taking advantage of politically feeble DAs to make prosecutors do the judges' bidding.

According to the first courthouse insurgent:

> The bar had a soft deal because [the prosecutor] was a former public defender. He's now a judge. But he'd been a public defender, and he ran the office like a public defender. They never went to trial. His last year in office they had 18 felony trials. This past year we had 126.

Worries about stepping on sensitive toes did not bother this prosecutor. Politics, he claimed, was simply a "very rough game." As he bluntly advised, "You've got to be willing to kick, and punch, and scratch, and shove, and be obnoxious. Otherwise you'll be a doormat. That's not my style." His low standing with the defense bar did not concern him. As he admitted, "I am very disliked by the bar." Nor did he lose sleep over his tattered relations with the GOP. He minced no words as he described how he was viewed by the party's chairman and, in turn, his feelings about the chairman: "The county chairman of the Republican party doesn't like me. He's never liked me. He'll probably never like me. The feeling is mutual."

From the perspective of the second courthouse insurgent, as described by the DA's close friend and chief lieutenant:

> The historical problem we faced was that the judges basically controlled the prosecutor. The court considered the prosecutor's office as its adjunct and really controlled it, basically because we had politically weak prosecutors, prosecutors who did not want to disturb the ship. Now they have a prosecutor who takes them on, who is not afraid to publicly criticize them. . . . We have attempted to restore the separation of powers between the executive and judicial branches.

Another office administrator sketched the outlines of how relations between the bench and the prosecutor's office had changed.

> When I first became an assistant prosecutor, the arrogance of the judges was such that the prosecutor reflected their view on just about everything. He was predictable in how he would behave vis-à-vis the judges, because they were the real power. He never offended them. He did things that suited their needs, like being concerned about their dockets. . . .

In the past, judges called assistants to their courtrooms in a demanding way, maybe three or four times over the course of a day. But they allowed defense attorneys to be tardy. The judges just interrupted the prosecutor's day whenever it suited them. . . . Now they treat us more like lawyers rather than like county employees who are there to do something that will please them.

This insurgent and his first assistant assumed high political profiles within the county and sought to reshape the local Republican party. For example, at one point the first assistant accused two black county commissioners of being "puppets of organized crime" because they voted against funds for the prosecutor's pet project, an organized crime strike force. The prosecutor also put his considerable electoral weight behind the election bids of selected county commissioners. He battled the Republican party's moderate wing at both local and state levels to recast the GOP so it would fit the "New Right" mold. He saw himself as pitted against an "establishment" that, in his words, included "the opinion people, the party leadership, the bar association, the judges, the people that really control the community and the courthouse."

The kickoff to this broader political effort was the prosecutor's campaign pledge to ban plea bargaining. After his election, the courthouse bristled with tension. His first assistant remembered the court community's reaction.

There was a lot of antagonism with the bar. . . . There was a lot of antagonism even with the assistant prosecutors early in the game. . . . The judges, of course, absolutely didn't like it because they had someone powerful taking them on. They couldn't destroy him. So they had to deal with him, and they weren't used to that.

After their elections, both prosecutors adopted policies, such as banning or restricting plea bargaining, and instituted organizational changes that were designed to alter their offices' roles within the courthouse.

The first insurgent turned his office inside out and embarked on a campaign to change the office's subservient relationship with the defense bar, public defenders, and judges. He took a broom to the office. He swept out the part-time staff, handpicked new assistants with crusader-like attitudes about prosecuting criminals that put them at odds with defense attorneys, and then severely restricted plea bargaining latitude within the office. "Of course," he admitted, showing no sign of concern, "the defense lawyers were screaming." Without a second thought or worry, he rubbed the chief public defender the wrong way by taking away his offices in the courthouse.

He's never forgiven me for taking over his offices when we ran out of space. Before the county board, he asked me, "Where do you suggest I go?" What a dumb thing to ask. I told him, "New York has a nice ring to it."

Judges were fair game, particularly lower court judges, whom the insurgent prosecutor described as "scum on the top of the pot." Several judges angered him when they refused to impose state-sanctioned fees on defendants who went to trial in order to defray the costs of prosecution. As he described the incident:

You would have thought we were taxing the judges personally. One of the more obnoxious ones has failed to levy about $2,000 in these fees. So I'm going after him personally. Besides, he's an arrogant little prick. You can't let anybody push you around or you'll get killed in this system.

The insurgent's staff reflected his contentious style, as their comments about judges and attorneys indicate.

We've got some judges who, in my opinion, don't follow the law, don't administer justice fairly, don't give the people a fair trial.

*   *   *

The judges don't follow the law and they don't realize the seriousness of the crime and they don't take the victims into consideration often enough in their sentences.

*   *   *

The defense bar thinks we're very unreasonable because if they don't like our offer we make them go trial. We're not here to keep them in business and to please their clients. I think they resent that.

*   *   *

They'll come in and say, "It can't be a $500 fine because my fee's coming out of the bail bond." But we're not here to help them collect their fee.

*   *   *

A small number of the bar, a lot of them former assistants who do a lot of criminal defense work, tried to discredit our office, but it blew up in their face. . . . They have a lot of clout, though, and are very friendly with most of the judges, who are much closer to the defense bar than us.

Like this DA, the second insurgent also fought a battle over space in the courthouse, except that the opponent was not the public defender, but the bench. After the state created additional judgeships for the county, existing offices in the courthouse had to be converted into new courtrooms to accommodate the bench's expansion. This provoked, according to one combatant, a "space war."

One day the judges issued an administrative order telling us to get out. We just told them where to get off. When we took that hard line, they finally sat down and started talking. Judges are a unique animal. They serve higher ends than the rest of us and they wear different-colored costumes. They take themselves too seriously sometimes.

Open, overt antagonism between the bench and prosecutor diminished with time, to be replaced by what another observer called "guerrilla warfare." An office insider looked back over these years and concluded:

The stature of the prosecutor has risen significantly vis-à-vis the bench. We're at least their equal in political muscle, if not their superior. . . . We can pick out any judge now and just rag him forever. . . . The public seems to take our word as gospel. They are certainly more than ready to accept attacks on the bench. . . . And the judges are very sensitive to that. . . . I know this for dead stone fact. I have had many a judge tell me directly to either "Get him off my back" or "Well, you know we're not going to do that because he'll do this." He's dynamite as far as they're concerned. None of them want him on their back unless they're absolutely reckless, careless, or in their last term.

Courthouse Reformers: Coaxing Changes in Institutional Relations

In constructing or rearranging relations in court communities, style counts as much as substance. The manner in which goals are pursued affects the quality of relations and creates an atmosphere or tone within the courthouse. The bristling tensions that insinuate themselves into everyday encounters in court communities with insurgent prosecutors are absent when prosecutors adopt a reformer style.

Like insurgent prosecutors, courthouse reformers tighten up their offices' guilty plea policies, encourage more assertive attitudes among their assistants, seek to increase their staff's professional caliber, and try to develop innovative approaches to prosecutorial work. They do not shrink from trying to alter their relationships with judges, but what distinguishes reformers from insurgents is a more cautious and conciliatory approach toward changing the status of their offices or when exerting influence.

Three prosecutors had reforming political styles. Two were Republicans from autonomous, middle-class, largely Republican counties; the third was a Democrat elected in a working class, Democratic community. These prosecutors shared a common feeling that open, continuous conflict was counterproductive and that there were better ways of achieving their ends. Nevertheless, the line between reform and insurgency could be blurry. For one reformer, for example, judicial opposition led to reconsiderations about crossing this line. Another reformer provided an illustration of how a prosecutor could work behind the scenes to further policy ends.

In one of the middle-class counties, the circuit bench collapsed into disarray when relations among the judges worsened during fights over bench policies. As the court's performance deteriorated and its prestige ebbed away, the prosecutor's well-polished image as an innovative administrator shone even brighter. Indeed, the office's status within the community was such that former assistants won judicial seats or gained contracts to represent indigent criminal defendants, while key administrators from the office, basking in the glow of the DA's reputation, moved into high-ranking county government jobs. In a nutshell, the prosecutor's office held center stage in courthouse and county politics.

The chief prosecutor did not rest on his laurels. He was no shrinking violet. "I don't like to be a responder," he said, explaining, "Many times I like to be the initiator; then you have more control. That's why in lots of things, I'm at the front end." He also felt that while occasionally he had to be "a burr under the saddle," he had to be discreet. For one thing, he worried, "I'm uncomfortable with any system where the prosecutor is *the* most important person." For another, he stressed, "I very, *very* firmly believe that many people win the battle but lose the war. I've seen it happen all too often."

There's great ego satisfaction in saying: "I'm the prosecutor, God damn it! This is the way it's gonna be!" Okay, so you win that battle. But you've got a whole lot of people out there who're gonna kick the shit out of you the first chance they get. That doesn't help you, the office, or the criminal justice system.

There are two ways to accomplish change. One is to challenge people. That will probably get you change—short-term and grudgingly. Or you can embark upon a long-term process, which is what I'm persuaded to do. I don't think lipping off does any good, like some of my brethren do.

The circuit court's problems nevertheless prompted the prosecutor to fend off suggestions that office policies might be the cause of the bench's difficulties. "On occasion, when a case is dismissed for lack of a speedy trial," he remarked, "I've been known to tell the media that it is not my responsibility to schedule cases." Still, he did not attack the bench or particular judges, although the court's sagging status made the judges easy targets.

In the other autonomous county, the DA's office traditionally had had partisan, part-time attorneys who wheeled and dealed to dispose of cases. This custom changed with the arrival of the new prosecutor who rode into office with the backing of the city's power brokers and Republican party. The new chief introduced his reforms gradually. He proceeded cautiously, nurtured a nonpolitical reputation, and ultimately gained such popularity that he would have been a shoo-in for a third term if he had not retired from the office.

This reformer's recollections of his early years illustrate his low-key style. At the same time, they indicate that he was prepared to take action when he found bench practices or particular judges objectionable.

There were a lot of holdovers in the office. I made it a point not to fire anyone, because it would look political. There were lazy people. Some had drinking problems; some were incompetent. . . . Many of the bad people (though less than I wanted) left on their own before I could talk to them.

The world was different then. Everything was "don't make waves." It was very common for one judge in contested traffic cases to give *ex parte* continuances. Cases would be continued until [the prosecutor] dismissed the case. I'm not suggesting corruption in the normal sense. Anyway, I went to the chief judge and told him to get that son of a bitch out of traffic court. I made a public issue out of it, got the support of the police, and concentrated on it almost daily. There was lot of controversy about it.

Defense attorneys back then also would come in and threaten assistants with going to trial. Which is incredible! So, over a period of time, I got some excellent assistants who were really gutsy in terms of standing up to people, but not obnoxious. . . . I had a number of meetings with the judges when I first came into office. I told them things would be different, that plea bargaining would still exist, but our sentencing recommendations would be much higher, and so I expected a lot more trials.

Toward the end of his last term, the state's attorney joined forces with the only major daily newspaper in the county to defeat a circuit court judge running for another term on the bench.[8] In a previous outing, the judge had picked up 83 percent of the ballots; another victory seemed like a sure bet. For this reason, the DA did not fight in the open to oppose the judge. He hesitated to risk his nonpolitical reputation and his credibility in the courthouse through a public challenge.

The prosecutor's cordial relations with the news media paid off. He had made a point in the past of having "a large number of conversations with the news media off the record" because he believed that "within limits, the more they know, the better off you are. . . . Otherwise they think you are hiding something from them." He fed information about the judge to the newspaper that was so specific and authoritative that the judge could not easily refute the paper's charges. The judge lost the retention election, polling only about 51 percent of the vote, far below the mark he set the last time he ran, and less than the 60 percent he needed to keep his seat on the bench.

The third policy reformer felt that ineptness and inefficiency had plagued the district attorney's office under the former prosecutor. He claimed that the office had dropped to the point where it had "very little respect in anyone's eyes, including the bench." His plans, however, clashed with the docket policies favored by the court's chief judge. The judge refused to give the new prosecutor more court time and declined to rearrange the scheduling of trial terms. His obstinacy annoyed the new district attorney.

8. Information for this section draws from the account by Paul Lermack, "The Retention-Election System: Some Generalizations and a Case Study" (Paper presented at the annual meeting of the Southern Political Science Association, Gatlinburg, Tenn., 1979).

I'm not here to run a drill press. We can't do quality things because this office is always stuck in a clerical bind. . . . The court's schedule drains our resources and traps most of our time in an illogical sequence that doesn't serve anyone's convenience but the bench's. . . . The [chief] judge devised the system and takes some public pride in it. . . . I keep lobbying him. But he's irrational, inconsistent, and erratic. He intimidates a lot of people. I've learned that if he barks at me, I have to bark back. It's kind of dangerous, I suppose, but I'm past that.

The DA's disagreement with the judge brought to the surface the larger issue of the office's status within the courthouse.

Local court rules have always been promulgated by the chief judge without consultation. . . . This county historically, in my view, has had a district attorney who is *not* the autonomous figure he is elsewhere. . . . I've decided I have to be autonomous from the bench.

This reformer, however, dodged open confrontations with the chief judge. Instead the DA mounted an indirect campaign to win support for his position from the bar and among allies on the bench.

I don't criticize the judge directly. . . . But I don't see what's wrong with a little public pressure at this point. . . . With the other judges I'm trying to play on any built-in hostilities, jealousies, or rivalries to win them over. The court administrator sees things pretty much like I do, and we're personal friends, political allies, and members of the bar's rules committee. I've gone before the bar association.

Courthouse Conservators: Living with the Status Quo

Prosecutors satisfied with the status quo or lacking the appetite to challenge it find the conservator style politically comfortable. Conservators avoid stepping on toes. They do not topple apple carts in their rush to make changes. If policy changes do occur, they generally involve minor tinkering that as often as not comes at the requests of others.

Four prosecutors from very different counties chose this passive, reactive posture. Three Republican prosecutors—one from a suburban county, another from a blue-collar community, and the third from an autonomous middle class county—were conservators from the moment they entered office. The fourth was a Democrat in an industrially declining, heavily Democratic community who ventured forth with a reforming style when he first took office but soon withdrew under heavy political fire to safer conservator territory.

This converted conservator felt that the police had betrayed him when he tried to tighten up his office's charging policies. "We met tremendous police resistance," he recalled, adding, "I strongly sense they're going to be happy to see me go." He also received little support from the local media. Throughout his term, the local newspaper published editorials which he felt were "brutally unfair" to him. Finally, he lost his party's support after he refused to follow the entrenched custom of "lugging" county employees by having them contribute a percentage of their salaries to the Democratic party. His fall from grace accelerated after he also decided to ignore the equally long-standing tradition of fixing traffic tickets. Ultimately, his staff felt he buckled under the pressure. His frustration was evident as he talked about his first and only experience in public office.

> If you want to keep your sanity, you have to find the parameters to "To thine own self, be true." You do the best you can. But you know what? Somebody is going to be bitching at you and chewing at your ass for four years. Not that I knew this going in.

The other three prosecutors offer more typical examples of the conservator style, especially their willingness to bend to judicial wishes.

In one county, the DA, who at the time was an assistant in the office, embarrassed the Republican party leadership by winning a hard-fought victory over a primary opponent backed by the GOP. The opponent was the chief public defender who called in years of political debts to purchase the party leaders' backing. As the DA recalled later on:

> The party screening committee gave the public defender just about all their votes. [The public defender] worked on all the committees, all the campaigns. I went to the yearly dinner—that was it! My announcement caused a large amount of friction in the courthouse. This office was like a fortress. No one would talk to us because we were running against the party. It was against the rules. . . . There was a lot of pressure on the staff; threats and gossip that the new guy would fire everybody. But we stuck it out.

Although he fought a bruising battle for the post, the DA's ambitions for the office were modest; he wanted to preserve the office's integrity and to maintain its continuity with the past. As his first assistant explained, "I think most of the people in the campaign knew [the DA] would be the best to carry on the same philosophies of [his predecessor]. Maybe a lot of us didn't want any change." Indeed, few policies were changed. In fact, few existed in the first place. Significantly, the push to have the district attorney review his assistants' guilty pleas came from one of the judges. The *status quo ante* reigned in this court community.

Continuity also ruled in the suburban county where the new prosecutor, who had been supported by the GOP establishment, kept the office's preexisting staff intact after his victory. He fashioned some guidelines regarding guilty pleas, but they were flexible, symbolic gestures—signs of a changing of the guard, not a revolution. Moreover, when filling staff vacancies, party affiliations and political contacts were checked, as they had been in the past, because the prosecutor chose to, not because the Republican party demanded it. According to one assistant, "I'd say a lot of people in this office got their job either because they're political or they know someone who's political." Most important, the DA tolerated the court's traditional dominance of the courthouse community.

An office administrator recalled how the previous district attorney's assistants were chastized if they embarrassed judges. Pressure from the bench came from two sources. First, several judges who had been district attorneys held strong opinions about the office and they were not shy about expressing them. Second, with several former DAs on the court as proof for their supposition, many members of the court community believed the office was a toehold for climbing onto the bench (a goal the new DA did not rule out). As a member of the office staff pointed out, "If I need a judge's okay to get on the bench, he has some power, all right? That conflicts with prosecutions at times. . . ."

The chief prosecutor was mindful of these considerations.

> I think half the judges are frustrated district attorneys. They all have opinions on how this office should be run, and at one time or another they're all going to try it. . . . You've gotta be firm. They can't run your office. But it's give and take. . . . If you start a war with a judge, make sure it's an appropriate case, because they can slow down the list [docket] and clog up your system. So don't start a war over a shitty case. . . . You can't tell a judge to pound sand up his ass. You gotta be nice, but you gotta be firm.

The conservator in one of the declining industrial counties simply stated that he would not get into "pissing matches" with judges. He preferred a low profile in the courthouse. A county commissioner unfavorably compared relations between the commissioners and the prosecutor with those the board had with the circuit judges. His comments provide an indication of the prosecutor's withdrawn style: "The prosecutor has not been sociable with the board. Everybody's friendly with the judges. Everybody's buddy-buddy with each other. The prosecutor isn't."

The DA ran his office with a light hand; his policies were elastic, and his assistants felt they could be bent and stretched with impunity. The chief had little interest in innovation; his only federally funded program came at a circuit judge's prompting. "Let me tell you the truth," he confessed. "The only reason we have it is that Judge ———— talked me into it. I didn't have the slightest intention of going after it, but he thought he could get a research clerk as part of the grant, and he did."

The Organizational Craft of Chief Prosecutors

Organization is the prosecutor's major policy tool. The form or shape of the office, however, is not entirely a reflection of the prosecutor's feelings about the status of the office within the court community and the value of conflict; there are constraints that limit how this tool can be crafted. The organizations the chief prosecutors created emerged from concerns over loyalty, office size, and policy needs. Given these concerns, the shapes of the offices and how they were used depended on each prosecutor's style within the courthouse.

Loyalty and the Political Logic of Hierarchy

Political candidates for chief prosecutor often spring up from the office ranks. In eight of the nine counties, the DAs had worked as assistants at one time or another, and in four of them the DA went directly from being a first assistant or trial division chief to the head of the office. The threat of palace coups, then, is not an idle one. For example, a trial deputy, after being fired by his boss, turned the tables on him by defeating him when he ran for reelection. A prosecutor's administrative cadre of first assistants, deputy chiefs, and trial chiefs normally includes at least one politically ambitious pretender to the throne. The temptation to move up to chief prosecutor can be quite strong. One first assistant made no bones about his ambitions.

> I have personal aspirations. I want to be prosecutor one day, and I want to go on from that to either Congress or the judiciary. . . . I've been asked to run for judge. Probably every law firm in town has offered me a job at one time or another. I've already turned down a U.S. attorney job.

Electoral invincibility was the most obvious way of blocking internal opposition.[9] In one county, for example, a previous prosecutor was nominated by both political parties and ran unopposed for his last two terms before retiring. Personal and professional indebtedness also made assistants reluctant to turn against the person who entrusted them with authority and promoted their careers. Head prosecutors, furthermore, could use their clout to help underlings win some other public post, as happened in another county, clearly a political boost potential challengers might consider too valuable to squander.

Finally, chief prosecutors asked close professional, political, or personal friends to serve as their next-in-command, assuming not unreasonably that they would be loyal to them and their interests. Because of the typical division of labor between a DA and the second-in-command, this tactic produced an added benefit. First assistants usually handled the office's day-to-day operations, while the chief prosecutor performed various political and professional duties outside the office. This inside-outside arrangement demanded mutual trust. First assistants put the prosecutor's policies into action. The risk of politically costly mistakes or embarrassments was always present. The prosecutor's life was made much simpler if he was confident his next-in-command instinctively protected his interests and pursued them capably.

Size and the Administrative Logic of Hierarchy

The number of full-time attorneys (or their equivalents, as a couple of offices had part-time staff) ranged from six to fifty-one in the nine offices with five of the offices clustered between ten and eighteen.[10]

9. Surprisingly little is known about the average tenure or turnover of elected prosecutors. Jacob reports that Boston's DA stayed in office from 1952 through 1978. Herbert Jacob, *The Frustration of Policy* (Boston: Little, Brown and Company, 1984), 121. The Dallas County District Attorney spent thirty-six years in the office, apparently the longest tenure of any prosecutor in the country. Brian W. Wice, "Randall Adams Case Provides Reminder of Dallas' DA's Flaws," *Texas Lawyer* 4(1989):25. Whether big city prosecutors, such as those of Boston or Dallas, have longer stays in office than do prosecutors in smaller jurisdictions is an open question. In the nine counties in this study, no prosecutor in the recent past had held the office for more than three four-year terms. In one of the counties, the DA at the time of the fieldwork was the first to have been reelected to a second term since the early 1950s.

10. It should be noted that the vast majority of prosecutor's offices are quite small. According to Jacoby, in 1976, a few years before the start of this project, offices as large as those in Los Angeles, with 605 assistants, Cook County, with 341, the Bronx in New York City, with 151, or Houston, with 109, occupied a very small band on the spectrum of

Administrative problems occur more frequently as offices grow in size. Coordination and supervision become more difficult, and formal mechanisms begin to replace informal ones.[11] For example, the bigger offices with fifty-one and forty assistant prosecutors were centralized, hierarchal, and formally supervised. As one of these chief prosecutors remarked, "This is getting to be a pretty sizeable operation. It won't work with indoctrination. . . . I can't watch over fifty assistants, but I can make sure that policy is adhered to." Smaller offices were loosely structured and less formal. The effects of size should not obscure the importance of whether the prosecutors wanted to enforce specific policies, however. Bureaucracy evolved out of political styles and their related policy needs as much as from the problems associated with increasing size, as the following examples contrasting a conservator and an insurgent prosecutor suggest.

In one office of middling size with twenty-five attorneys, a clear-cut hierarchy defined the lines of formal authority and division of labor. Yet the office was not firmly ruled from the center, nor were its assistants closely or rigidly monitored. According to one assistant, "I can't think of anybody in the office that's been called on the carpet for too easy a guilty plea." An administrator reported that he told assistants, "You're not going to have somebody looking over your shoulder." The office's intermediate size was not the reason for its relative lack of bureaucratization. The chief prosecutor did not have clear-cut policies, and as a conservator he was prepared to live with the office more or less as he found it. This was not the case with a second prosecutor who was unwilling to leave things alone after his election victory.

This insurgent DA faced a sullen staff when he took over the office. The attorneys greeted him like a "conqueror," his first assistant recalled. The two decided wholesale reorganization was needed. "When we walked in here," the first assistant continued, "this place was com-

---

office sizes. See Jacoby, *The American Prosecutor*, 62. Approximately 76 percent of the roughly two thousand eight hundred county prosecutor's offices in 1976 had staffs smaller than four persons (including the DA), while 21 percent of the offices had staffs between five and forty-nine assistants (roughly the size range of the offices in this study). A mere 3 percent of the offices had more than fifty employees. This information is from the National Criminal Justice Information and Statistics Service, *State and Local Prosecution and Civil Attorney Systems*, (Washington, D.C.: U.S. Department of Justice, March 1978), 2.

11. A considerable literature exists regarding size and organizational structure. For reviews, see John R. Kimberly, "Organizational Size and the Structuralist Perspective: A Review, Critique, and Proposal," *Administrative Science Quarterly* 21(December 1976):571, and Henry Mintzberg, *The Structuring of Organizations* (Englewood Cliffs, N.J.: Prentice-Hall, 1979).

plete chaos. It didn't really have any division chiefs, and each assistant was his own prosecutor. . . . We put in division chiefs and established some criteria." A senior prosecutor compared what it was like before, and after the new DA made these changes.

> There was a much looser orientation before with more stress on the individual prosecutor. You had almost unlimited discretion to do just about anything in a case. . . . This office is now much more centralized in terms of its control. The individual prosecutor has much less discretion, if any. We have a policy manual, and that determines how "x" number of cases are going to be handled.

Organizational Strategies: Case Studies and Sketches

Within the flexible constraints imposed by size and loyalty, the prosecutors impressed on their offices their political styles. If the office's status and influence did not concern prosecutors, little or no energy was spent on forging a bureaucratic tool. On the other hand, if they were important, the time and effort put into creating a compliant bureaucracy might be well spent. Table 1.1 displays the general characteristics linking the courthouse styles with the prosecutors' organizational strategies.

This table identifies three organizational strategies: bureaucratic weapons, efficient firms, and reactive clans. Courthouse insurgents carved bureaucratic weapons out of their offices.[12] Policy reformers, on the other hand, designed efficient firms. What distinguishes these two forms was the reformers' emphasis on their responsibility for making sure that cases moved through the courts as quickly as possible. Conservators showed no interest in bureaucracy, inaugurated few policies that had to be monitored and enforced, gave their assistants considerable courtroom discretion, and were comfortable with nonhierarchical offices that resembled clans.[13]

An Archetypical Bureaucratic Weapon

Bureaucratic weapons are not merely bureaucratic; their usefulness does not reside exclusively in the control their administrative struc-

---

12. The label, "bureaucratic weapon," is liberally borrowed from the title (but not necessarily the analysis) of Philip Selznick's book, *The Organizational Weapon: A Study of Bolshevik Strategy and Tactics* (New York: McGraw-Hill, 1952).

13. This is another liberal borrowing, in this instance from W. C. Ouchi, "Markets, Bureaucracies, and Clans," *Administrative Science Quarterly* 25(1980):129.

TABLE 1.1 Courthouse Styles and Organizational Strategies.

	Courthouse Insurgents	Policy Reformers	Office Conservators
Administrative Characteristics			
Centralized leadership?	Yes	Yes	No
Hierarchal structure?	Yes	Yes	No
Subordinate monitoring?	Formal; close monitoring	Formal; close monitoring	Informal; little monitoring
Policy Features			
Charging standard	Lax	Tight	Lax
Guilty plea guidelines	Strict	Strict	Flexible
Office Attitudes			
Value of punishment	Very high	High	Variable
Importance of efficiency	Low	High	Low
Organizational Strategy	***Bureaucratic weapon***	***Efficient firm***	***Reactive clan***

Adapted from Table 1 in Roy B. Flemming, "The Political Styles and Organizational Strategies of American Prosecutors: Examples from Nine Courthouse Communities," *Law and Policy* 12(January 1990): 25. Reprinted by permission of Blackwell Publishers.

tures offer chief prosecutors. Bureaucratic weapons also include lax charging criteria and strict guilty plea policies that put pressure on defense attorneys and judges. Furthermore, these offices develop cultures that sharpen the cutting edge of this tool by inculcating among deputy prosecutors the critical importance of punishment.

Two of the suburban prosecutors developed bureaucratic weapons during their terms in office. One of these DAs created a virtual archetype of this organizational strategy. The office reflected the chief prosecutor's style. His assistants strongly favored criminal punishment and expressed little concern over the efficient handling of cases. These attitudes contributed to an office climate that defense counsel found extremely distasteful and which put the office at odds with the court.

Defense attorneys complained that the chief prosecutor instilled mistrust of them in his assistant prosecutors. This mistrust, they sensed, went so far as to question their integrity and even their legitimacy. Private attorneys in particular accused assistants of being heavy handed, of lacking the empathy needed to appreciate human problems, and thus of being incapable of doing justice. A former assistant for a previous DA castigated the office for looking at things in black and white terms.

They cannot make the distinction, in my opinion, between innocence and not guilty, and there is a distinction. An innocent man never committed the crime; a not guilty one cannot be proved without a reasonable doubt. They say he's either innocent or he's guilty. There's no middle ground. There's no "not guilty."

I was in that office. I was taught, and I taught everybody that I ever trained, that I was there to do justice. I wasn't there to punish people. . . . The problem starts at the top and works its way down. They have no concept of justice. . . . Absolutely none!

The office's screening criteria were porous, its charging practices aggressive. The office winnowed out only a small proportion, less than 10 percent, of the cases brought to it by the police. It added to this a predilection for charging multiple counts whenever possible; 65 percent of the sampled cases had more than one count. This loose policy was then combined with an extremely stringent guilty plea policy that limited the discretion of deputy DAs. This combination aroused even further the ire of defense attorneys.

All felony court assistants prepared memoranda ("pros memos") outlining the strengths and weaknesses of their cases. Once a week they met with the DA and his administrative chiefs, who sat as an "Indictment Committee" to discuss how the cases would be handled. At this time "bottom lines" regarding plea offers (count drops, charge reductions, if any, or sentence recommendations) were set, and assistants could not go below them without permission from committee members. Significantly, the committee challenged the court's sentencing habits or going rates, as one assistant pointed out:

The Indictment Committee tries not to make offers commensurate with what the judges are going to give. Our position is that there's a line below which we will not go. If the judge wants to do it, then it's on the judge's head. If the judge wants to give a bad guy a break, then let him do it. We're not gonna be a party to it.

This policy put pressure on defense counsel and judges. It was also time-consuming and slowed the pace of cases through the court. Neither consequence bothered the chief prosecutor.

Defense attorneys complained bitterly about the office's policies. Multiple charges led to symbolic plea bargaining; additional, superfluous counts were dropped, but substantive concessions were rare. Attorneys also accused the office of levying charges with minimum prison sentences in otherwise weak cases in order to stop defense counsel from entering "blind pleas."

Knowledgeable lawyers put blind pleas—that is, guilty pleas accompanied by neither charge concessions nor sentence recommendations—before judges who understood that these pleas signalled disagreement with the DA's bottom line. As an assistant prosecutor pointed out with respect to public defenders:

> Because they handle so many cases and they're assigned to one judge, they know what they can get out of their judge. They know what a case is worth. Nine times out of ten they'll get a better deal by pleading a guy blind in front of their judge rather than accepting our offer. . . . The judges just go lower than we do.

By including charges with mandatory minimum sentences, the office tried to curtail this "backdoor" tactic. Some private attorneys reported they received stiff bottom lines and felt they were on the office's "shit list," a feeling exacerbated by the indictment committee's inaccessibility to defense attorneys. Many more criticized the bottom lines as too rigid. As one attorney put it, "Take it or leave it. That's what the bottom line is. That's not too bad, except there are cases where they don't take values, human values, into consideration."

An Archetypical Efficient Firm

On paper, efficient firms look like bureaucratic weapons. Reform prosecutors, however, place greater stress on efficiency. They counterbalance the insurgent's emphasis on punishment with a self-conscious concern over the prosecutor's responsibility for moving cases expeditiously through the courts. The chief prosecutors foster attitudes that, despite tightly structured offices and clearly stated policies, encourage office views that stress the importance of efficient case handling. Moreover, they are more flexible in their dealings with judges and defense attorneys. Bureaucracy and policy are not used as blunt instruments of prosecutorial strength to assault courthouse sensibilities and interests.

Chief prosecutors in two of the autonomous counties molded their offices into efficient firms and with a couple of exceptions were very similar. Both offices, of course, had high regard for the importance of efficiency in the courts, a distinguishing feature of this organizational strategy. Both centrally checked or approved all negotiated pleas. One office, however, went further than this by requiring "on the nose" pleas in which defendants pled guilty to the primary felony in serious cases.

In accord with this goal, the second office vigorously weeded out nearly four of every ten warrant requests because of their low conviction probabilities and diverted two out of ten when the offense was minor and the defendant a first offender. Over a five-year period prior to this research, the office approved warrants for only 43 percent of the felony cases the police submitted to it. The office shunned additional charges; only 16 percent of the sampled cases had more than one charge, the lowest proportion among the nine offices. The prosecutor paid a political price for his policies. When he ran for reelection, he lost the support of the city's police union. Still, he won handily. He gave two reasons for his policies: courthouse efficiency and public credibility.

> Would I issue warrants on less than a reasonable probability of conviction standard? Would I go down to bare probable cause? No. Because then I'd be wasting the court's resources, which are already overtaxed. But doing otherwise also means you'd be back in the same old rut again, and everyone'd say, "They're starting to plea bargain again. They'll take a plea to a misdemeanor on a felony."

This prosecutor felt that his policy of "on the nose" pleas required some form of quid pro quo. His goal was to maximize the proportion of guilty pleas to the primary charge. In pursuit of this end, he extended various enticements to defense attorneys.

> The defense attorney's got to get something for his client. He just can't go in there and lay down and roll over dead. . . . You've got to give him something. You've got to give the defendant something. And so we give them bond recommendations, sentence recommendations, restitution, no restitution, six months in jail, two days in jail, expungement of their record, a whole host of things.

In order to ease cases through the courts, the prosecutor's office also opened its files to the defense. Open files made it possible for attorneys to determine the reasonableness of bottom lines, plus they made it easier for them to decide whether to hold preliminary hearings or to file motions. An experienced defense attorney pointed out:

> We read their entire file. Now that does two things. With a clear evaluation of the case from the outset of the proceedings, it does away with the necessity of having to file discovery motions. It also clears up a lot of preliminary examinations that we used to have for discovery purposes only. . . . So, a lot of times, you don't need the prelim.

Reactive Clans in Four Conservator Offices

Four prosecutors did not structure their offices around clear-cut policies; instead they produced "clans." Rather than drawing up elaborate organization charts and writing thick policy manuals, these prosecutors relied on consensus, informal adjustment, and flexible, informal guidelines to lead their assistants. As with the other organizational strategies, clans took on the courthouse styles of the chief prosecutors.

The four offices had little need for elaborate bureaucracies. Only one of them kept a close eye on plea negotiations, and this came at the behest of the judges; it was not a policy innovation by the DA. The other three prosecutors placed few restrictions on their deputies' discretion. As one of these conservators put it, "I try to delegate a lot of authority."

This outlook shaped hiring decisions in one office. By recruiting people who shared his view, the DA hoped he would not have to look over their shoulders to be sure they followed orders. He wanted "people that work by themselves" who had "independent minds" and a "conservative philosophy" because "I don't try to run their cases." He signaled to assistants that they were on their own. "The one speech I give everybody," he reported, "is, 'Listen, I'm not going to make you an attorney. If you want to be a good trial attorney, you have to do it yourself. . . . It's up to you to learn the trade.'" Deputy prosecutors got the message. As one described his boss, "Very seldom does he say 'Do this' or 'Do that.'"

Assistants in other clans described their offices in similar ways. For example, one remarked, "As far as this office goes, it's up to us. It's completely ours." For many assistants the lack of policy guidance meant they had to depend on each other to maintain some degree of consistency. One assistant complained, "We have to talk amongst ourselves to keep some continuity, because with no law laid down from the top, we have to do it horizontally." That a prosecutorial clan reflects a chief's views about how the office should be run is clear from one DA's comments. As he explained, "You can't have hard-and-fast policies. Every case is different." He then added, "I try to encourage as much discretion as possible. . . . They're young professionals, not clerks."

Flexible plea policies were consistent with the lax charging policies of the clans, which relied on the less demanding standard of probable cause rather than whether cases would stand up during jury trials. One of the chief prosecutors described his warrant policy in the following way: "If there is probable cause, there's virtually no warrant we will refuse. But if it looks like it's gonna be a real suicide mission and there's some half-assed misdemeanor that'll fit it, we'll probably charge it there." These views created problems for the prosecutor within the courthouse.

The DA was acutely mindful of a predecessor's fate after he clamped down on warrant requests. According to a member of the office's inner circle:

> [An earlier DA] turned down an awful lot of warrants. . . . And it pissed off the cops. He started to run for reelection and found he had no support from the Fraternal Order of the Police and dropped out of the race. . . . The memory is there in everyone's mind. If you get on the wrong side of the cops, they'll screw you.

Thus, this clan's charging policies were lax because the prosecutor did not want to alienate the police. In order to keep their support, he suffered criticism from the press, bench, and bar. The newspaper complained of "widespread" plea bargaining by the office that "cuts across all crime categories without any significant difference based on the seriousness of the crime." In an election eve editorial, the paper urged voters not to reelect the DA because he would provide only "four more years of honest, competent, but status quo administration." A circuit court judge recalled that he warned the prosecutor about the problems his policies created.

> "You over issue," I told him. "And then you get a plea to one and drop four. The public, as far as they're concerned, think you've dropped four delivery cases against a guy. That's killing you. And it's killing us administratively. We're having a difficult time because of that keeping up with our civil docket."

A Proactive Clan in a Reformer's Office

A clan, like other organizational strategies, ultimately reflects the political style of the chief prosecutor. In small offices, a clan may be reactive or proactive, depending on how the prosecutor wants to use the office.

The four prosecutors with conservator political styles established reactive clans, but a fifth prosecutor with a reforming orientation imbued his clan with a proactive view. Consistent with his campaign theme, "It's Time to Get Tough," the prosecutor replaced the office's old staff with a handful of full-time assistants and then hired several experienced lawyers as part-time assistants to serve as his "big guns." He assumed a dominant leadership role. But, instead of bureaucracy, he relied on close professional and political ties with his staff to govern the office.

One assistant explained: "He knows me and I know him. . . . I think we think alike, we act alike, and we have probably similar attitudes. . . . So consequently we really don't have any problems." Continual conversation in the office's nerve center, its conference room, gave the prosecutor the information he needed about his assistants' activities and problems. According to another assistant, "[The DA] very much stays in the conference room and just sort of sits there and sees what's going on and asks, 'Why did you do this?'"

Summary

The courthouse community is a political arena. The functional interdependencies that require ongoing interactions among courthouse actors are characterized by varying degrees of cooperation and conflict. The stakes in these interactions are often institutional, because courthouse communities have status and influence structures that transcend their courtrooms. Chief prosecutors have several advantages in changing these structures. As elected officials they can develop independent power bases out of the reach and control of the courthouse community. They also hold executive powers that can be deployed in a centralized fashion that judges and the defense bar normally cannot duplicate. The prosecutor's decision to exploit these advantages depends on how the district attorney perceives his position vis-à-vis others in the courthouse and the benefits and costs of the status quo. This decision also depends on the prosecutor's taste for conflict versus cooperation.

Prosecutors satisfied with the status of their offices within the courthouse community adopted a conservator style. Conservators were unlikely to exert strong administrative leadership. As a consequence, their offices resembled clans; they were nonhierarchical, loosely arranged groups in which assistants wielded discretion without being hobbled by policies. Conservator prosecutors, finally, did not use their offices to battle the courthouse community and thus did not need to mold these tools into political weapons.

Prosecutors dissatisfied with the status of their offices faced a more complicated problem. If they perceived threats to their office's stature, felt that actual declines in the office's performance had occurred, or disagreed with courthouse practices that hindered the office's effectiveness, the prosecutors had to decide whether the risks and costs of political conflict would exceed its benefits.

In making this decision, prosecutors considered at least two things. One was their perceived chances of winning if they challenged the status quo. The other was the prosecutor's appetite for conflict within the courthouse. The former reflected the prosecutor's assessment of the local political situation, particularly the strength of the bench, its ties to a locally dominant political party, the defense bar's involvement in local politics, plus the prosecutor's own relations with the police. Attitudes about conflict reflected the prosecutor's personality and temperament. Thus, depending on how prosecutors weighed the expected value of tilting a lance against the courthouse, they adopted either a courthouse insurgent or policy reformer stance.

Insurgents took their offices and recast them into bureaucratic weapons. Policy-reforming prosecutors created offices that were like efficient firms. As with other kinds of organizations, size influenced to a degree the bureaucratization of prosecutor offices. The office culture, however, reflected the prosecutor's political style. Courthouse insurgents and policy reformers were likely to produce different kinds of "committed polities," while offices led by conservators were more likely to drift with environmental pressures.

Chapter 2
Leading Prosecutor Offices and the Courtroom Craft of Assistant Prosecutors

Introduction

Organizational strategies must be implemented. The administrative policies and "nuts and bolts" used by chief prosecutors to lead their offices were essential elements in the implementation of their strategies. However, they were also vital in the construction of court communities. The ways in which chief prosecutors allocated work among assistants, for example, were not merely internal office matters but decisions with important consequences for the frequency and stability of interactions between the chiefs' staffs and judges and attorneys. Involved in this process were questions of efficiency and equity, rewarding and punishing performance, and the social structures of the prosecutors' offices. The assistants' "courtroom craft" reflected on the one hand these constraints and incentives and on the other hand the need to develop working relations with judges and attorneys.

The "Nuts and Bolts" of Leading Prosecutors' Offices

The nuts and bolts of administration involved several issues. Assistants, of course, had to be assigned cases. But, in addition, they had to be assigned to workplaces, their activities had to be monitored, and their performance had to be rewarded or sanctioned through promotions and salary raises. Solutions to these problems shaped work patterns in the courtrooms and the disposition of cases. They also contributed to the tone and spirit of the offices. Case assignment policies were particularly important, because they created the contexts of the assistants' daily work. Case assignments also created opportunities for the office hierarchy to reward or punish trial assistants.

Assignment Problems in Prosecutors' Offices

Prosecutors face two basic decisions when assigning work to assistants: they must decide whether to establish continuous versus discontinuous prosecution and whether to assign assistants to judges or to cases. With regard to the first decision, the DA can have assistants follow cases from arraignment in lower court to their conclusion in the upper court. This is continuous or "vertical" prosecution. Alternatively, the prosecutor can divide the office staff so that some assistants handle cases only during their early phase in the lower court while others take over the cases when they reach the upper court. This alternative is discontinuous or "horizontal" prosecution.

The second decision centers on whether to assign trial assistants to judges or to cases in circuit court. With the first option, deputies work before the same judge and handle any cases assigned to that courtroom. With the second, assistants are assigned to cases and work before whichever judge is responsible for disposing of a particular case. This means that assistants during the course of a trial term will appear before several judges. Table 2.1 shows the work assignment policies adopted by the nine prosecutors.

Six of the prosecutors assigned their staffs to cases, while three assigned assistants to judges. One county followed a continuous or "vertical" assignment practice. The other eight offices used various horizontal methods of allocating their staff. A simple example will illustrate this method. In one of these counties, one set of assistants worked in the lower courts, conducting preliminary hearings for felony cases (as well as handling traffic and misdemeanor cases), while another, smaller group assigned to circuit court took the cases to final disposition after they reached this court.

Chief prosecutors adopted this two-tiered, horizontal policy for similar reasons. New assistants could earn their spurs in the lower courts without unduly jeopardizing the outcomes of felony cases. Horizontal prosecution also minimized scheduling problems and prevented the conflicts that would have arisen if assistants had worked in both lower and upper courts. Finally, it meant that more experienced deputies represented the office in circuit court.

The lone exception to the practice of horizontal prosecution was in an office that had started with this policy when circumstances forced the DA to reconsider his choice. After several senior assistants resigned, leaving the office shorthanded in circuit court, the DA decided to switch to continuous prosecution. He reasoned that this was preferable to boosting the workloads of the remaining circuit court veterans or prematurely promoting lower court assistants to fill the vacancies.

TABLE 2.1. Prosecutors' Work Assignment Policies.

	Assignment Policies	
Nature of Prosecution	Judge	Cases
Continuous/vertical	0	1
Discontinuous/horizontal	3	5

With this change, assistant prosecutors took cases at their start in lower court and stayed with them until they were finished.

This change was feasible because the lower courts were located in the same building as the prosecutor's office and the circuit court. The proximity of the lower courts eased scheduling, consultation, and supervisory problems that continuous representation would have created had the lower courts been scattered about the county. A second consideration was the morale of the relatively inexperienced staff. The DA felt that keeping two tiers of assistants would have created artificial distinctions that would have disheartened some members of his staff. As he explained, continuous or vertical prosecution gave everyone a chance to work in circuit court:

> I think everybody wants to be a circuit court attorney. . . . So it's motivation. I think you have to give them a chance to try something. The office is so circuit court oriented that if I didn't, I'd have second-class assistants.

A senior prosecutor pointed to the switch's other advantages. In his view, assistants learned more about their cases and were in a better position to know how they should be handled.

> They get a feel for the witnesses. They know the case. They have a much better feel for the case than if someone is assigned to it later on and has to read a transcript and doesn't know the personalities involved. They know that the victim may look great on paper but on the stand look like shit. They come in and tell us. We can make a sensible solution. . . . In my mind, that's the best way to do it. To learn a case, I want an assistant to take it all the way through.

As for the second decision, regarding whether to assign assistants to individual judges or to particular cases, three district attorneys allocated their personnel among the courtroom judges. The other six offices assigned their deputies to cases, so that during the course of a day or week each prosecutor might appear before several judges, according to which judge had responsibility for each case. All prosecutors justified their decisions on the basis on efficiency and effectiveness. However, a basic concern over assigning trial assistants to judges was the fear that the judges would co-opt the prosecutors assigned to them. This concern lay behind the decision of one insurgent to have his assistants reassigned to cases. The other insurgent made a different choice that created a more complex working environment for his trial assistants.

Match Game Number 1: Assigning Assistants to Cases

Six prosecutors assigned individual assistants to cases, and five of them typically made the assignments after the defendants had been arraigned in circuit court. No prosecutor randomly assigned felony cases among assistants; instead, they had to decide which assistants would prosecute what kinds of cases. A division of labor or specialization sometimes emerged. For instance, female assistants were often asked to handle sexual assault cases. In some offices assistants worked in special units and handled cases involving organized crime, white collar offenses, or career criminals. However, most of the circuit court prosecutors were generalists. The actual burden of assigning assistants to cases typically fell on the shoulders of the trial division or circuit court chief or of the office's first assistant.

Whenever a prosecutor's office assigns assistants to specific cases, it must match the assistant's skills with the nature of the case and, if possible, with the judge and attorney. Equity and office morale were exceptions to this general rule. As one first assistant explained, "The only exceptions will be where I feel that an assistant didn't get enough trials last term." He sought to make sure that assistants had equal opportunities to try cases during trial terms, which he felt was necessary for *esprit de corps*.

The situation described by the following trial chief was typical. His assignments generally hinged on matching the skills, experience, and personalities of assistants with those of the attorneys and judges.

> You know the assistants' abilities, what kind of cases they have had in the past and how many. . . . You also have to know the defense counsel, so that you don't stick someone with an attorney who's just going to overawe them. . . . We also have to match [the assistant] a little bit with the judge; some judges can be quite overbearing. . . . You've got to match all three. Then you've got to figure out who's available. Sometimes it's just not possible to have an ideal match.

You don't want to put a guy in over his head, either in regard to the facts of the case or the counsel against him. It's usually not so much goodness or badness; the real thing is how cantankerous he is. Like you get some attorney who's a real pain in the butt and you're in front of Judge X. It takes a lot of effort to try a case in front of this judge because he won't ride herd on the defense. Where maybe the same case in front of Judge Y, he'll just shut the guy up. If you've got an experienced assistant, he knows how to handle X and he can roll with the punches.

The problem as I see it is the screwy things that come up. Sometimes there are unique situations that arise due to nonsensical motions and nonsensical conduct by the defense. If the guy isn't experienced, he's liable to lose his poise and lose track of what the hell he's trying to do, or, worse yet, play right into the defense's hand.

As in most other courts, the kinds of cases assistants received obviously depended on how well and how quickly they learned their craft. As their skills grew, they were given more serious or complicated cases. According to a senior prosecutor:

The general rule is you would like to give them a heavier diet of larcenies before you move them into breaking and entering, which is related but a little more complex, and simpler assaults before more complex ones.

If an assistant turned out to be a "slow study," this prosecutor reported that the assistant would be given a "steady diet of the same kind of crime" until he or she knew it "like their own home address."

Match Game Number 2: Assigning Assistants to Judges

Three offices placed their assistants before particular circuit-level judges to handle whatever cases were sent to the judges' courtrooms. In two of the courts with only two or three judges presiding over felony matters, the prosecutors felt that with so few judges handling cases there was little reason to have prosecutors moving from one courtroom to another.

In the third county, however, with fourteen judges often under prosecutorial fire, the reasons reflected a political concession by the DA. According to the first assistant, the office simply followed a tradition that he and his chief had decided not to challenge. At the same time, the first assistant argued that this policy was justifiable for reasons of efficiency and effectiveness.

> It's a historical legacy, okay? That's the way they were doing it before. If we had to make a new decision, we'd still go that way. . . . Mechanically, it's too difficult to go the other way [i.e., assign cases to prosecutors]. You would have prosecutors tripping over one another. This way, when a prosecutor gets the case he starts off at arraignment in circuit court, he has to argue bond, and then there are motions that are filed. He has to be in that courtroom on a consistent basis.

The court administrator in this county randomly assigned felonies to individual judges, who were then responsible for each case until they were disposed of. Thus, with few exceptions, each trial assistant handled virtually everything, from relatively simple assaults through property crimes, drug cases, and first degree homicides, that appeared before the judge to whom he or she was assigned. This put a premium on the office's ability to pick trial assistants with the experience and skills needed to prosecute a wide array of felony matters, since the office could not bottlefeed assistants and pamper them while their courtroom craft developed.

The solution to this matching problem blended politics, the assistants' docket skills, and personalities. For example, assistants were supposed to be reassigned every year to a new judge. However, as a well-informed administrator in the office noted, one prosecutor stayed in a politically well-connected judge's courtroom for several years.

> Well, in the case of Judge ———, I doubt there will be a change, because the judge, to the extent that his responsibilities allow him to, has been very helpful to the prosecutor's office. So we are very responsive to his personal requests.

The assignment problem was complicated by the fact that many of the judges expected their courtroom prosecutors to manage their dockets. As a tacit *quid pro quo* for its strict guilty plea policy, the prosecutor promoted and appointed assistants with a knack for handling dockets efficiently. The first assistant explained it was not always possible to find an ideal match. With some judges, the trial assistants felt their assignment was the equivalent of hardship duty. According to a high-ranking attorney in the office:

> Judge ——— has really peculiar ways of handling things, and some assistants don't get along with him and have a tough time. . . . We

might make a change, because we're also responsible for the mental health of our prosecutors, and if you think a guy's shell-shocked, you make a change.

But let's say a judge comes to us and says, "I don't like this prosecutor." Sometimes we move them and sometimes we don't. We don't let them control us. . . . If the judge doesn't like a guy because the guy is following our policies, then we'll say, "Well, not right now."

If there is some genuine personality problem, we realize it happens and we are not going to be completely obstinate about it. . . . There are some prosecutors that are excellent trial lawyers but horrible managers of dockets. We try to handle that by giving them a judge that controls his own docket.

The following recollections of an assistant vividly illustrate what could happen when assistants and judges clashed. In this instance, the office reassigned the assistant, but not until matters had plunged to a very low point.

I was assigned to Judge ——— for about a year. Judge ——— and I did not hit it off. I thought we would do very well together. I thought his interests were not that different from the prosecutor's office. He's not a left-wing, super-defense judge by any means. He *is* a wheeler-dealer, though. And, frankly, I'm adverse to wheeling and dealing.

It was just a personality clash. The judge, in my opinion, is a very forceful man. He's very persistent. When he's on to something, he just never lets up. He's just as persistent as can be. He can be very charming when he wants to be. But he can change his moods. He can be in chambers and be as charming as can be—if you're doing what he wants you to do. But the minute you don't do what he wants you to do, he will just cut you to pieces. He'll do it publicly, before your peers.

After a while—it's not conscious, just subconscious—you make a mistake. You're under such pressure that you make an error in judgment. We've had a couple of guys on this staff who've gotten into very serious trouble in Judge ———'s court. I don't think it's simply coincidence. The judge can do that to you. He didn't do that to me, but I was under such pressure that he would have in time.

One example: he'd pick cases and just dismiss them. The judge would say, "Call your witnesses." And I'd say, "Judge, I need three hours to get them." And he'd say, "Case dismissed." Then he would castigate you: "Didn't you know this case was set for trial?"

In a desperate attempt on my part to deal with that, I once sub-poenaed twenty-two cases to appear during the trial term. The next thing I know I get called on the carpet. I didn't realize what I had done, but I had subpoenaed every single detective from one of the police departments. They had no detectives left and their chief was bitching. I was just desperate.

Match Games and Governing Assistant Prosecutors

Most assistants become prosecutors because they want to learn how to try cases. One assistant succinctly expressed the views of many others regarding their jobs.

It's not a "plum to hang around at" job, but it's a plum if you want to learn how to be a trial lawyer. It's great training. And after two years you cut out, and then you're making some money.

The kinds of work, cases, or judges that chief prosecutors assigned to their assistants were a means of rewarding behavior and assuring conformity to office views. Failure to measure up to the chief's expectations meant either no promotion from or reassignment to humdrum, routine cases, so that assistants would realize their dreams of being a felony trial prosecutor had come to an end. More subtly, status and prestige within the office depended on work assignments. Admission to the "inner circle" of one clan, for example, rested on whether the chief thought an assistant had the right stuff. One DA minced no words as he described his position.

If you want to be a screw-off and handle minor cases, fine. That's your business, because somebody has to do the diddly-shit cases. It's up to them. I don't chew anybody's ass out. I tell them in the beginning, "If you don't have any gumption, you won't get good assignments. Period!" The noncompetitive person will never be in the inner circle here. There is no formal structure, but I think the guys out there know who I listen to and who I don't.

Case assignments, as in other offices, were the currency of status in this clan. Some prosecutors handled serious, challenging cases, such as homicides, sex cases, and major offender cases, more often than others. "After that," one assistant claimed, "it's sort of like we're all equal—we all do the garbage equally."

Offices that assigned trial deputies to judges lost the use of case assignments as rewards. One of these offices retrieved some of this loss through "special assignments." Cases that, because of their complexity, publicity value, or political ramifications, had special significance to the office were parceled out to prosecutors to break the day-to-day routine and to recognize performance. As the trial division chief explained, special assignments publicly acknowledged an assistant's worth to the office and served as a means of encouraging certain kinds of behavior.

> Special assignments bring public recognition very often. Seeing your name in print is good for the family. Grandma and Grandpa get off on that. . . . Some people just get out of bed in the morning thrilled by that. For the guys that like that kind of stuff, they'll take that before they'll take six figures in income.

> In getting a special assignment, you have to have good relationships with me and you have to have good relationships with the first assistant. . . . I make recommendations partly on the basis of a guy's native skill as a thinker and a lawyer, but mostly on the grounds of how hard they work in preparation for trial. That's the real key for me. The "finessers" don't get to me, and I tell them so. It's the beavers that get the work around here. And when they get the work they get the recognition, and then they get the rewards.

When trial assistants expected special assignments and did not receive them, it was seen as an indication of the office's disfavor.

Courtroom assignments also could be used to reward or punish assistants. As one trial assistant stated about the court in which he worked, "There are a number of judges with whom the environment is either conducive to sleep or to hysterical screaming." In this same court, another assistant pointed out that "everyone knows that the prosecutor in front of Judge ——— has got it pretty tough." Until the judge complained about the constant turnover of prosecutors in his courtroom, the office assigned newly promoted assistants to this difficult judge (perhaps as an initiation rite), as well as trial assistants whom the office no longer wanted to stay in the office. The previously quoted assistant explained further:

> The prosecutor that was in Judge ———'s court before me quit and the prosecutor before that quit. . . . It's known as the "brown helmet"

assignment. It's the worst assignment in the office. I came up at a time when someone else quit and I got the judge.

"Policy Enforcers" in Prosecutors' Offices

If office policies are to have any authority in the courtroom, they must be enforced. This responsibility generally falls on the shoulders of the first assistant or trial division chief. Because these individuals play such important roles in the day-to-day operation of the office, the tone of the office is often set by them. In one office headed by an insurgent DA, the first assistant fired a courtroom prosecutor "within ten minutes" for breaking the rules the chief had installed regarding guilty pleas, and other dismissals followed. As the first assistant recalled the first incident:

> It was a marijuana case. . . . [The assistant] felt it was in the best interests of the case to take a plea. He was called into the office. He had an opportunity to explain the circumstances. Then he was fired. . . . Other prosecutors—not too many—have been fired for similar violations. Our policy is not just a piece of paper.

The effect of these dismissals on the office's climate was evident in the assistants' descriptions of what it was like to work there. One assistant, for example, pointed out, "Everybody functions around here on the presumption that if you plead a policy case, somebody will find out about it." A colleague agreed, saying, "The administration likes to create a feeling of paranoia in you to make sure you're toeing the mark." And a third prosecutor lamented, "Everybody runs scared a little bit because they call you on the carpet if they think you're giving away the store." Moreover, the first assistant did his job with what trial assistants felt was disarming ease. An assistant described him as the office's "hatchet man."

The first assistant's heavy-handed actions, according to one experienced prosecutor, meant, "You practice defensive law. It's not 'Let's discuss how to handle this case,' but 'Why can't you do this? Why did you mess up?' " Another assistant's mixed feelings about the second-in-command were typical.

> He's not somebody I want to socialize with, but he's got to run a large office and keep up a tough law-enforcement image. Maybe you need someone like him just to ride herd, and he's good at riding herd. I wouldn't want to cross him. I want to do things right because I don't want to be called into that office. You'd come out bleeding; y'know,

he's a tough little guy. So I guess I respect him, but he keeps his distance, as if to say, "I am the boss and you are the flunky."

In the office of one of the reformer prosecutors, the trial chief served as enforcer. The DA had once played this role, and, as the following comments indicate, he had very clear views about the purpose and function of the trial chief as policy enforcer.

One of the basic tenets of negotiation is "Never send anybody to negotiate who has the ultimate authority to make decisions. . . ." That way the people who negotiate always have the option of saying, "Well, hey, I'm still your friend and I like you, and we gotta continue to negotiate, but let me take it back to the bastard who. . . ." We have assistants who use that as an effective tool.

That's why the judges are screaming at me all the time about ———, who's my trial chief. Because he's always the one that my assistants report, "Hey, we tried but ——— says, 'No.'" So the guy who works in front of the judges continually is still the judges' friend. He's still the friend of the defense bar, and he can still continue to work with them. It's the people at the management level that become the foils of their wrath . . . and that's fine.

For a while I had that position. It bothered me, but I did it. Now ——— has it. He's my lightning rod. There's no question about it. The defense bar dislikes him. The judges dislike him. . . . It's a negotiating tool: "I'm a nice guy. It's ——— who's the asshole."

Policy enforcers were more than a means of implementing the chief prosecutor's wishes. They deflected anger and opposition to policies away from the trial deputies and toward someone else in the office hierarchy. This escape valve released the tension between assistants and the judges and defense attorneys. It also meant that the chief prosecutor could stay out of daily negotiating problems until he was called on to listen to appeals. This aloof posture kept chief prosecutors out of the daily fray; it preserved their authority and allowed them to perform benevolent acts as the need arose.

Courtroom Craft: The Work of Trial Prosecutors

Trial Assistants and Office Policies

Assistants in offices with strict guilty plea policies expressed ambivalent feelings about these constraints. For many deputies, clear-cut policies made their dealings with attorneys or judges easier when they disagreed over cases or when the deputies preferred not to discuss a matter. Some disliked haggling and cut it short by reciting office policy. The views of several assistants in different offices reflected these feelings.

> More often that not, I just make the offer that I've received from the Indictment Committee. I don't like to negotiate. I don't like to play around. But if I know the attorney I'm negotiating with is gonna bitch and complain, I'll start high. . . . I hate bickering. I want to make an offer, and if they don't like it, I'd rather just go to trial.

* * *

> I personally like it because I can simply say to attorneys: "You can tell me anything you want to tell me, but this is the Indictment Committee's offer. You can beg, plead, cajole, and threaten, but this is it. No matter what you say, this is the offer."

* * *

> I've had the judge lean on me and talk to me about dismissals or pleas to lesser charges. It's very easy to truthfully say to him at that point, "Judge, my hands are tied. If I wanted to do that, and I'm not sure that I do, I couldn't. Let's just not get into a screaming match over it." Having a policy like that solves the problem.

* * *

> A judge will turn to me and say, "Mr. Prosecutor, don't you feel embarrassed? You're a professional, just like defense counsel, but he can discuss what to do with the case and you just sit there like a dummy, saying, 'Policy, policy, policy. I can't do it.'" I would prefer not to have policies, although they do make my job easier. You can sit back and say, "Don't give me any grief. I can't do anything about it."

* * *

> Most defense attorneys want to come away with something for their clients. So when it comes to policy cases, you don't waste time negotiating. In that sense it perhaps cuts down on some of the games that go on.

By claiming their hands were tied by office policies, assistants avoided conflict with judges and forced attorneys to make up their minds without the benefit of concessions. On the other hand, policy restraints put assistants in a bind when they felt that doing justice or solving unanticipated problems required an exception to the policy rules.

At this point, after almost three years of doing this, I wish I had a little more discretion right at the end. There are certain times, and they're not that often, when I would like to be able to do something with a case right at the last minute. . . . But I don't undercut the DA's policies. I don't believe I've ever done that intentionally on any case since I've been here.

Most assistants had learned to live with office policies, even though at times they voiced qualms or reservations about their lack of discretion. One reason for their acquiescence (aside from the threat of being dismissed, demoted, or reassigned) was that opportunities for trial work made up for the lack of discretion in dealing with guilty pleas and its accompanying frustrations. A veteran trial assistant stressed this point.

My main thing is that I'm a trial lawyer. As long as I get to try my case, I'm happy. I've been working for this administration for a number of years, and in all that time they've never told me how to try a case. I am let alone. I do it my way. That's my area. Their area is to have a uniform system of prosecution. They do that through policy memorandums, through discussions. . . . So that's their area. My area is trial work and I'm left alone. . . . Those are the positive things. The negative thing for me would be that there are some cases where I can't make some reduction or some disposition. And those are frustrations. But you take the good with the bad.

Other attorneys added that they recognized that their interests and their bosses' responsibilities were not always synonymous. Their bosses, as elected public officials, had a right to impose policy priorities on their staff. Moreover, attorneys knew when they were hired that they would have to adhere to policy.

You'll find people here that are somewhat irked, as I am, at times, by having my professional judgment second-guessed or by not having the discretion I think I should have. But I knew that when I started here. It's not that [the DA] doesn't trust me or is in some way out to affront me. It's just that he feels that's the best way he can serve the public.

Still, there are costs attached to enforcing office policies. As feelings of being watched and of having professional judgments questioned and overruled mount, and as resentment over not being allowed to handle cases as circumstances dictate accumulates, policies can exact a toll.

In one insurgent office, bureaucratization and stiff policy enforcement led to a flurry of resignations. "It was probably the high-water mark of reaction to the tone of administration around here," an insider remembered. "Experienced people got fatigued by all the petty bullshit. . . . They just said, 'I'm tired of being growled at,' and they left." Until this time, the office had tried to hire experienced attorneys. It decided to change this practice and began to look for lawyers fresh out of law school. The office reasoned that neophytes would be more malleable and willing to follow established policies. The first assistant explained, "We don't care whether they are liberal or conservative. The question is whether they feel comfortable working in an office with strict policies. We want them to follow those policies."

Working Around Policies in an Insurgent Office

Assistants who worked in offices with strict policies were often put in difficult situations. Denied the latitude to negotiate on cases that were weak or improperly charged, assistants had to find ways in the courtrooms of circumventing their bosses' policy restrictions when they were handling cases that they felt were inappropriate to try, but which they could not dismiss or *nolle prosequi* without jeopardizing their position in the office or incurring the wrath of the office's policy enforcer. Moreover, many assistants felt their credibility with judges and attorneys suffered when they were forced to confess their impotence to do anything that would help dispose of cases that they themselves agreed were "dogs" or "garbage cases." Thus pressed, the assistant DAs learned how to discreetly dispose of exceptions to their chief's policy rules. The comments of deputy DAs in an insurgent prosecutor's office, while reflecting something of an extreme case, nevertheless illustrate the more general problems faced by other assistants in coping with restrictive guilty policies.

Lax charging practices exacerbated the assistants' difficulties. When cases were inappropriately charged or weak but the assistants were prohibited from reducing the charges or from negotiating sentence recommendations, the assistants could lose their cases. Weak cases also embarrassed deputies before judges who were not reluctant to tell them what they thought of cases the office brought to court. The following assistant's remarks were typical.

You get cases that are impossible to try. Some of the judges stay their judicial distance and you just try the cases. But other judges call you up to the bench and say, "What the hell are you doing? Why is this crap in my court? Why am I trying this crap? I want some answers." . . . I had a case where I had a guy breaking into and entering his own house but it was a divorce matter and the house was still completely titled in his own name and there was no divorce agreement. . . . We finally withdrew, not dismissed, the warrant. The judge would have killed me if I'd wasted his time on something like that. Those are the kinds of policy situations that make everybody run scared all the time.

Poorly charged or weak cases were not fun. As one assistant groaned, "It's just humiliating when you get something that just falls to pieces in court. . . . We lose our credibility. Nobody believes us. We've just no credibility." The assistants' plight carried little weight within the office. An office administrator argued, "We can either look at the hole in the doughnut and never write a warrant or we can look at the doughnut itself." The prosecutor in charge of issuing warrants objected to complaints from assistants that they were forced to prosecute "dogs" or weak cases. "Some of our circuit staff," he countered, "sometimes are not willing to go that extra inch just because they see a minor little technicality that may present a problem."

"Rolling over" on motions was one way of getting out of this cul-de-sac, although this could be risky, because it left a "paper trail" that the office's policy enforcer could trace. Nevertheless, when circumstances warranted it, an assistant might make a *pro forma* argument or objection for the record to a defense motion in order to get rid of a weak case.

One method is rolling over on motions. You've got a policy case, but your witnesses are worse dope dealers than the defendants. Or there are a lot of equities. Or your case is weak. A motion to suppress the evidence is brought, or something like that, and the judge rubber stamps it.

Another prosecutor hinted that judges encouraged defense attorneys to file motions in certain cases. "They wouldn't get the idea if certain judges around here didn't grant them," this assistant discovered. "Not all of them will, but —— will, —— will, and so does ——."

In this court community, assistants were assigned to particular judges. Many times they found themselves near the brink of violating office policies with judges who would extend a helping hand if asked. Some approached their judges openly. Others, like the following assistant, let his judge draw his own conclusions about the prosecutor's preferences.

I have not yet gone to the judge if it's a policy case and said, "Judge, get me out of this." I try to be scrupulously honest with him, though, and if he asks me about the strengths or weaknesses of a case, I will always, you know, be very honest. But if he asks me whether I want to prosecute it or not, I don't think I have the discretion to give that answer.

Deputies also came close to ignoring the spirit, if not the letter, of the DA's prohibition against sentence bargaining. Each of them worked in front of their particular judge long enough to know the judge's sentencing habits. In many instances, defense counsel asked about probable sentences. As one assistant put it, "Attorneys say, 'Will the judge give him anything instead of probation?' And I say, 'I don't foresee anything other than that, but that's not an agreement or promise.'"

Another occasion for slipping the office's policy harness occurred during the judges' sentencing conferences, which they held in chambers prior to the formal proceedings in the courtroom. These off-the-record conferences involving the judges, defense attorneys, and probation officers opened up other opportunities for assistant prosecutors. By agreeing to mute their opposition to the attorneys' pitches, the prosecutors offered incentives for pleas without openly breaching office policies. If a prosecutor also had particularly strong relations with the judge, this incentive gained in value.

> *Prosecutor:* I've had defense attorneys say to me, "Will you promise that you'll make sure the judge doesn't give more than what we've talked about?"
>
> *Interviewer:* Can you deliver?
>
> *Prosecutor:* Sometimes. Well, the judge will always ask me in chambers what kind of recommendation I'm gonna make. Some judges will let you, some won't. My judge likes recommendations.
>
> *Interviewer:* If I were a savvy attorney, should I assume your recommendation makes a big difference when I plea bargain in nonpolicy cases?
>
> *Prosecutor:* Even on a policy case, okay? When I remain neutral on a case, I'm telling the judge that I know he will do the "right" thing. . . . If he decides to burn the attorney too much, I'll just tell him I don't think what he's doing is fair.

A final factor, which was unique to this court community, was that the judges had the prosecutors assigned to them manage their dockets, even though the bench had a well-staffed scheduling section in the court administrator's office.[1] The judges felt prosecutors were better able to ration the court's trial time. Mutual trust, personal compatibility, and exchange considerations usually evolved out of this practice to add another complicating dimension to relations between prosecutors and judges.

By efficiently moving cases for judges, assistants could draw on the credits they earned to get out of sticky situations involving policy cases. For example, one assistant who had been extremely effective in reducing the size of a judge's docket felt his performance had engendered a spirit of reciprocity with the judge.

Prosecutor: My judge lets me run the docket. My judge doesn't want to have any part of the docket. . . . When I started out, my judge's docket was always vegetating around ninety to one hundred pending cases. The docket is now about a constant forty. . . . If you've got a judge that wants to go away, they don't want to have a lot of cases.

Interviewer: You mean vacations?

Prosecutor: I think the judge had fourteen weeks of vacation last year.

Interviewer: So, if you're in some trouble or if you need something, the judge is going to be responsive, true? Is that right?

Prosecutor: That's all very true.

Interviewer: Can you tell me how that works?

Prosecutor: Sure. I walk in with a policy case that cannot be plea bargained, such as armed robbery. The judge will look at me in chambers and say, "Can you prove it?" And I'll tell the judge, "No problem." And the judge'll break the guy's arm to plead.

Courtroom Credibility: Trial Competence and Responsiveness

The personal and professional reputations of assistants within the court community mattered greatly to them. Assistants strove to win

1. The assignment office handled the judges' civil dockets, but few of their criminal dockets. If judges did not want their prosecutors to run their dockets, they usually took over the task personally and used their staff as aides. This tradition of individual prosecutorial scheduling, plus the judges' option of shifting docket responsibilities to the assignment office or handling their dockets themselves, made this court different from the others.

reputations for courtroom credibility, a compound of work-related skills and interpersonal relationships. One assistant summed up the feelings of others when he said, "I've got to have credibility with the judge."

> If I go in and tell him everybody's a real bad guy, he'll end up not paying any attention to me. So I try to pull my punches. . . . I look at establishing credibility as the most important part of being an effective prosecutor, besides being able to try a case.

In the following anecdote, a trial prosecutor describes his first appearance before a judge known for his impatience and demanding personality and how he felt he made a lasting impression as an attorney who could not be deceived by glib legal argument.

> This judge always tests people. In one of the first motions I argued, there was this attorney and he was citing all kinds of cases . . . F2Ds this, ALA that. He's arguing for about twenty-five minutes, and the judge had just reamed out two attorneys before this one. So everybody was waiting for the judge to explode.

> He'll say things like, "Didn't you go to law school?" Or he'll say to an attorney, "Counselor, you're obviously not prepared. Don't come into my courtroom unprepared. You're doing your client a misservice. You're taking up people's time. Look around this courtroom. There are a lot of people in here that have to be heard." There are attorneys who are petrified to go into that courtroom. I know of attorneys who will not under any circumstances go into that courtroom.

> Anyway, this guy keeps on arguing. And the judge turns very quickly to me and says, "Mr. ———, what do you have to say about that?" And I stood up and I said, "Well, quite frankly, Your Honor, I didn't understand a word he said."

> At which point everybody went "Ahhh. Is he ever going to get it." Then the judge says, "Neither did I. The motion's denied."

Trial Competence: Legal and Social Credentials

Lawyers entered prosecutors' offices anxious to learn how to try cases, to develop litigation skills, and to gain an insider's knowledge about the courthouse. Many did not expect to stay long. As one assistant said after a year on the job, "It depends on how much trial experience I get. So far, though I've had a lot of pleas, I haven't gotten the trial experience I should get." While deputies learned their craft, however, they were also practicing it. As one pithily reported, "I learned more law bullshitting after work than by actually reading the criminal law manual." This assistant's experience was not unusual; training for most novice assistants was typically a haphazard matter.

For example, in a smaller, conservator office, recently hired assistants were supposed to begin on minor cases before moving on to more serious matters. However, the heavy demands placed on the office during trial terms frequently curtailed this gradual breaking-in process. One new assistant, after a single training session with the first assistant, then spent a week observing a murder trial; this was the extent of the assistant's training period. This assistant was not alone. Two other new appointees found themselves trying felonies six weeks after joining the office; others reported the same experience within two weeks on the job. An assistant summed up the office tradition as follows: "They have a very unique way of breaking people in. They say, 'Here's a file. There's the jury. Go try it.' "

Initiation was also abrupt in larger, hierarchical offices. An assistant in one of these offices recalled, "It can be a little troublesome if you're reading the case file for the first time while you're picking the jury. I had to do that in the first trial I had here. I literally knew nothing except the defendant's name." An assistant's recollection of the first time he selected a jury illustrates the way many others muddled through as they learned their courtroom skills.

I knew the law. I understand the law. But the nuts and bolts of actually going through a trial you pick up along the way. Two days before trial, I said to myself, "Hell, I don't even know how to pick a jury." So I ran around asking everyone, "What the hell happens?" What I did, basically, was make photocopies of *voir dire* questions asked by different assistants on different cases from the transcripts. I made up my own format.

So you sit there the first time with all these people around you. You look through some jury slips and make notations on them to make it look like you know what you're doing, and of course you don't. . . . But once you do it, you know what's gonna happen. . . . The nuts and bolts are important, because they determine how relaxed and forthright you're gonna be in front of the jury, and it's the first time you meet the jury. The impression you create there is gonna last throughout the trial.

Establishing credibility under these circumstances could be difficult, since judges were the prosecutors' most critical and important audience. As one assistant said, "I think the judges know more about our performance than our chief of the criminal division." At the same time, judges often offered advice and tips to assistants. A deputy remarked, "Some judges will say, 'You dumb son of a bitch. For crissakes, what are you doing?'" In the following comments, a second prosecutor explains how judges helped him to improve his court work, while a third describes his forthright approach to tapping the judges' knowledge and opinions.

Some of the judges will call us up to the side bar and say, "That was disgusting the way you did that." After a case is over, they'll say, "I liked this. I didn't like that. You left a lot of hearsay in, so be on the lookout for that. Your cross-examination of that one witness stank. You could have asked it a lot of different ways." Judge ——— did that with me numerous times. . . . He'd say, "Come on over, let's talk about the trial."

When I first started here, I made a point of sitting down with each judge and chatting with them. I would ask them, point blank, "What's your opinion of this? How do you like to run your courtroom? And what could I have done different?" Most judges I've found will be more than helpful as long as you don't take a "the stupid son of a bitch doesn't understand what I'm saying" attitude.

Women prosecutors thought they faced higher hurdles in establishing courtroom credibility. One female assistant complained, "I have the feeling that I have to prove myself, because, one, I am new, and, two, I'm a woman." A second argued: "I think in terms of the judges and your fellow lawyers you must prove yourself if you are a female, but if you are a male, it's almost as if you're cloaked with credibility." The courtroom, she felt, provided a forum in which she could show everyone that she was their equal.

Thinking back to my earlier days, I found a lot of male attorneys didn't take what I was saying seriously. . . . But once you get into a courtroom, and once they see you have self-confidence, that you're prepared, and that you cannot be intimidated, then after a short period of time, all of the sudden they realize this person is here to stay. It didn't take too long, and I saw their attitudes change. . . . You get a reputation and it spreads real fast.

Another female prosecutor with similar experiences also put her faith in the courtroom. "I think the only way you can prove that you're one of the boys is go in there, try a case, try it well, and show them what you're made of." Despite these expressions of faith in courtroom meritocracy, the court communities somewhat grudgingly granted female prosecutors reputations for high trial competence. A negative though not especially robust association (Tau-b = -.16; p < .10) between a prosecutor's gender and his or her reputation among judges and defense counsel for trial competence suggests that female assistants did not entirely overcome court community prejudices.[2]

Responsiveness: Knowing the Players

Assistant prosecutors also learned the importance of personalities and courtroom relationships in their work. For some assistants, this meant that good prosecutors had to at least adjust to, if not know how to use, the idiosyncracies of others to their advantage.

> The thing of it is that you're really an actor, and, like a good actor, a good prosecutor, in my opinion is one who can play a lot of different roles. You're dealing with the same material, but you're presenting it in a different way each time you appear in front of a different judge. You can't be mechanical. You just can't be, because you've got different personalities to contend with.

The importance of knowing personalities in the courthouse was vividly described at some length by the following prosecutor. As this prosecutor discovered, despite his best efforts, it was possible to win a few battles but to lose the war.

> Judge ——— does not like to try cases. His philosophy is that the best result is the parties settling it between themselves. The function of the court is to make it so difficult to get the court to decide something that the parties, in frustration, finally turn to each and say, "Look, we'd better do something about this case."

> He has various methods. He'll call people out for trial in a civil case, for example, every day for a month—insist that they be there. He'll

---

2. The issue of gender bias in courts has drawn attention in a number of states, several of which have prepared reports addressing the problem. See William Eich, "Gender Bias in the Courtroom: Some Participants Are More Equal Than Others," *Judicature* 69(April–May 1986):339.

call their case, and he'll make it look like he's gonna start the trial, and then he'll adjourn it, but make them stay there all day. Eventually, they're gonna say, "Hey, he's not gonna decide the case. If we want some justice, we'd better decide it ourselves." And he'd do that in criminal cases, too.

At first I'd get nervous, because he'd set a trial like three days after the arraignment. But after a while, when he asked, "Are the People ready for trial?" I'd say, "Your Honor, the People are always ready for trial. I'd like this case set for this afternoon." But I never called my witnesses in, because I knew he was never gonna go to trial. When I had to, I'd get them in. But I knew if I did that, the judge would never call the case. If I wasn't ready, he'd call it. That way he would get me in the position of "Boy, I'd better compromise. I'd better sell this case."

It was pressure/counter-pressure. At the time it was a matter of your self-worth whether or not you could get the judge to try a case. If you could get the judge to try a case, you could kind of walk around the office and say, "Well, you guys don't know what you're doing when it comes to Judge ———." Well, I think I had three or four trials in a couple of months, and I thought I was terrific. Then I didn't see another trial for about eight months after that. He brought me down to earth real fast.

Prosecutors constantly talked about judges and defense attorneys. Their styles, quirks, attitudes, personal interests, and much else were all grist for conversation and speculation. Knowledge was a resource that reduced uncertainty and could be used in negotiations. As one assistant, like many others, put it, "I've got to be able to second-guess a judge; I need to know what he is gonna do." This knowledge became even more important for assistants working in offices with few policies, as the following prosecutor suggested when he described how he decided what he wanted in a case.

I know the judges who are sitting and what different judges are gonna do. I know what the case is about and I may know what the [sentencing] value is. Now, one judge may give a guy probation and then another judge may give the person one-to-five on the exact same offense. By knowing those two possibilities exist, I might reach a negotiated plea in between, something like six to twenty-three months, which sort of takes the gamble out of it. I might be lower or higher, depending on which judge I go before. . . . Knowing what I believe is the collective action of the different judges, I arrive at a reasonable figure, given the different judges that represent justice in this county.

The courtroom styles of judges and their trial or legal abilities were also favorite conversation topics among prosecutors, as shown by this assistant's comparison of two judges.

Judge X is not well respected. He knows the law, but his ego is just so incredible that, along with his paranoia on top of it, well, it's very dangerous to deal with him. . . . Judge Y is another problem judge. Very nice man. Everybody in the community was in favor of his appointment, myself included. But I think he just doesn't have the ability to draft complex legal conceptions.

Another assistant in another court contrasted the styles and problems of two judges in whose courtrooms he had worked.

Judge A, as far as I know, has never sentenced-bargained or given any indication of what he'll do in a case. . . . However, he has a reputation for being the fairest or one of the fairest judges in the county. He may be one of the lightest sentencers around. He has that reputation. Plus he is very consistent and strives for consistency. So, number one, attorneys know they're not going to get any assurances. But, number two, they're not afraid of what's gonna happen.

With Judge B it's different. Number one, he does certain things in terms of telling attorneys what their clients might get. Number two, he doesn't remember what he says. Number three, he's extremely inconsistent. From defendant to defendant, from codefendant to codefendant, and from one defendant one week to the same defendant the next week.

Prosecutors compared notes on judges endlessly. The following assistant summed up what prosecutors look for and what they hope to find through these comparisons.

All courts have levers, okay? Maybe there are seven levers in Judge ———'s court or five in Judge ———'s. Sometimes all seven are exercised by the prosecutor. Sometimes four are exercised by the prosecutor and three by the court.

Knowledge of courtroom styles and personalities was itself a lever that allowed prosecutors to know which levers they could pull and which ones they could not. Defense attorneys, of course, did not go unnoticed. The following examples from comments made by assistants in one court community were typical of those made by others elsewhere.

> People in the office have given me hints. Like, a certain attorney likes to be real friendly to you in court. You shouldn't let him do that because it looks bad. He's doing that as a tactic. . . . Or another attorney will always file a motion right when he walks into the courtroom.

> *   *   *

> This one attorney seems to go in cycles. He can be nice, then for a couple of weeks at a time he won't talk to you. . . . Another one is hard to get along with because he takes the position that "I'm gonna screw the commonwealth however I can."

Besides learning the personalities in the courthouse, assistants also had to learn the nature of their own role in the court. They quickly discovered they had to stand firm against the demands of attorneys and judges. They soon realized that their role in court gave them a different perspective of defendants than other members of the courthouse community.

> The most disturbing thing is that of all the crimes you are aware of, very few people are convicted. Then almost nowhere do you see them go to prison. . . . More than likely they'll get chance after chance after chance. . . . Like this one case this morning, the judge told me, "Don't worry about it. Why are you so upset? He'll do it again and then we'll get him." It's just a job to the judge. He wants to clear his docket. I guess I'm getting a little bit more hardened, but you can't really separate yourself off.

Assistants were sometimes surprised to find that they needed to be tough and that they had naive notions about judges and defense counsel. They had not expected they would have to use their authority as prosecutors to override the objections or entreaties made by attorneys and judges. In other words, they had to be sure that in being responsive they were not viewed as being gullible. For example, an assistant who, as a former law clerk in the court, thought he knew the ropes was taken aback when he learned of his image in the court: "Everybody thought

I'd be a soft touch. I sensed pretty quickly what was going on, and I've been tougher than I was." Another former clerk for a circuit court judge made the mistake of believing that "all judges are reasonable and intelligent."

> I'll confess that for the first six or seven months I was real coopera- tive with the judges. They'd give me this song and dance and, out of respect to the office and maybe a touch of fear, I'd go along. . . . Then one day a notorious arm twister said to me, "You've got to do this." And I said, "Like hell I do. If I do this just because you want me to, I might as well clean out my desk and hit the road." I wouldn't have done that when I first started. I would have just offered some chicken-shit plea.

A third prosecutor drew attention to the risks run by inexperienced prosecutors who failed to appreciate the real intent of cooperative defense counsel.

> Defense attorneys only like you personally if you give them what they want. If you do that, they'll love you. But they won't respect you. . . . If you treat them honestly, and hold your line on your case whether they like it or not, they're gonna respect you as an attorney. And the new guys haven't learned that yet. . . . When you're here a long time, you get to the point where you don't give a shit. If some guy tells me, "You're a prick," because I won't give his guy probation, I just say to him, "Fuck you, buddy."

In sum, deputies, faced with the complexities of the mixed-motive situation in which they worked, struggled to find a balance between cooperation and conflict, although the advantages of cooperation over the long haul were often more apparent than its disadvantages. One experienced prosecutor concluded, "I've found in this job that the fewer people you alienate, the better it is. In most situations, you've got to work with the judges and the defense attorneys again and again and again." Two other assistants expressed similar opinions. One said, "I don't believe in burning my bridges behind me," and the second stated, "You're walking a fine line, because you want to maintain a good working relationship with everybody." According to another trial assis- tant, "The pure bottom line is that you're never gonna get to the bottom line without the cooperation of the defense attorney."

Most assistants sought a balance between being firm and being re- sponsive. As one assistant reported, "I really appreciated an attorney

TABLE 2.2. Statistical Assessment of the Relationship of Trial Assistant Backgrounds, Attitudes, and Reputation.

	Assistant's View Regarding:			Reputation for:	
	Punishment	Due Process	Court Efficiency	Trial Competence	Responsiveness
Assistant's Background					
Democrat?	−.27*	.16†			
First job since law school?	−.13**				.14‡
Female?				−.16‡	
Views about:					
Punishment	X	−.30*			
Due process		X	−.11‡	.35*	.26*
Efficiency			X	.12‡	
Reputation for:					
Trial competence				X	.43*

Measure of association is Tau-B.
* = $p < .001$
† = $p < .05$
‡ = $p < .10$

telling me the other day that everybody knows that I'm tough but that they also know that they can talk to me." Others expressed similar views, as the following prosecutor's comments suggest.

> It's in everybody's interest that people remain talking to one another. I'm not talking about giving in. It's not something where for the sake of a nice relationship you give in. I'm not talking about that at all. A good relationship is where they can look at you and say, "You are fair to us." That's all that I want them to be able to say.

Reputations, Attitudes, and Backgrounds

The reputations of prosecutors in the nine court communities were related to certain aspects of their backgrounds and to their attitudes.[3]

3. Information about the construction of the indicators in this table can be found in Nardulli, Eisenstein, and Flemming, *The Tenor of Justice*, Appendix 1, 385–88. Briefly, the measures and indicators were dichotomized for this book. The attitude scores for prosecutors (as well as judges and defense attorneys) were originally derived from factor analyses of multiple-item questionnaires tapping attitudes about the purposes of punishment—e.g., rehabilitation versus retribution, the importance of due process as measured by views about protecting criminal defendant rights, and several items regarding the importance of speeding up the criminal process. The reputational scores of prosecutors and defense attorneys regarding their trial competence and responsiveness were

TABLE 2.3. Prosecutor's Reputations for Trial Competence and Responsiveness within the Courthouse.

Responsiveness	Trial Competence (No.)		
	Less Competent	More Competent	Total
Less responsive	33	8	41
More responsive	17	39	56
Total	50	47	97

Tau-b = .43; $p < .001$

Table 2.2 presents information on these relationships. The assistants' backgrounds—their political party preferences, job experience, and, to a lesser extent, their gender—were significantly related to their attitudes and reputations. Democrats tended to have less stringent attitudes about criminal punishment than Republicans. Democrats also had more favorable attitudes about due process matters than Republicans. Novices whose first job after law school was being a prosecutor were less punitively oriented than experienced assistants. With respect to courthouse reputations, novice assistants were seen by judges and attorneys as more responsive to them than the veterans. And, as noted earlier, female prosecutors were less likely to be seen by judges and attorneys as having as much trial competency as male assistants.

Assistant prosecutors with strong pro-punishment attitudes expressed less supportive views about due process issues. On the other hand, views about punishment were unrelated to the assistants' concern over efficiency in the courts. However, the stronger the due process views of assistants, the weaker their worries about whether the courts ran efficiently. Perhaps because judges and defense attorneys tended to be more due process oriented, assistants with similar views tended to be seen both as competent trial attorneys and as being more responsive. Prosecutorial concern over efficiency did not stand in the way of favorable appraisals of the prosecutors' competence. Finally, there is a positive, fairly strong, and significant relationship between the prosecutors' reputations for competency as trial advocates and their responsiveness. Table 2.3 provides more information about this relationship.

Trial competence and responsiveness were positively related (Tau-b = .43; $p < .001$). Judges and defense attorneys tended to divide assistant prosecutors into two major groupings: those who were both skilled

---

developed through a Q-sort in which members of the courthouse communities ranked each other's competency and responsiveness.

litigators and responsive to others and those who were neither. Two smaller groupings included those who were seen as responsive but not especially skilled in the courtroom and those who were seen as not responsive but competent trial attorneys.

Summary

The courtroom craft of prosecution is not easily disentangled from the characteristics of the prosecutor's office; hence they were treated together in this chapter. The work of assistant prosecutors was shown to be greatly affected by whether they were employed by courthouse insurgents, policy reformers, or conservators. The organizational strategies associated with these courthouse styles affected various aspects of the assistants' jobs in different ways. These aspects included such things as how quickly assistants were promoted to handle circuit court cases, the kinds of cases they were assigned to prosecute, and how to dispose of "dogs" or "garbage cases." Two additional facets were the tone of administration or office climate in which the assistants worked and learning how to get around policy obstacles when the occasion called for it or when assistants felt this was necessary.

The assistants' reputations were important to their courtroom craft. Credibility within the courthouse smoothed the way for assistants. A credible reputation, according to the assistants, made negotiations easier. Being known as a good trial lawyer and having a sense for the personalities in the courthouse were valuable resources for assistants. To some extent, the assistants earned their reputations on their own through their dealings with judges and defense lawyers. At the same time, their political preferences, experience in the courthouse, and personal or professional views and attitudes affected the courthouse community's opinion of them.

Part II
The Craft of Judging

Chapter 3
Bench Politics: The Social Organization of Courts and Their Policies

Introduction

Judging is about deciding. At first glance, it seems reasonable, if not obvious, to think of the craft of judging in criminal courts as making decisions about cases. This initial impression is further enforced by the simple fact that judges can be observed in open court announcing their decisions about motions or passing sentences on convicted felons. And, of course, records of these decisions can be inspected in the clerk's office to see if there are patterns in them. This view of judging is not entirely wrong, but it is too simple, and it draws attention from other significant aspects of the judge's craft. Decisions about cases and how cases are processed occur in settings and through procedures that judges create collectively as part of organizing their work. The various facets of this process are often and erroneously dismissed as merely administrative details. However, conceptions of trial courts should recognize that "judicial decision making cannot be divorced from judicial administration."[1]

Courts, in the main, are collectively administered. The judges decide for themselves how they want to be led and how they want to allocate their time and resources to process cases. The chief judge sits at the center of the court as its head. However, not only do the powers of the chief judge vary with state rules, but the chief judge's effectiveness as a leader depends most greatly on the judge's interpersonal and political

---

1. This comment comes from the editor of a book focusing on a federal court of appeals, but it is equally applicable to trial courts. See Arthur D. Hellman, ed., *Restructuring Justice: The Innovations of the Ninth Circuit and the Future of the Federal Courts* (Ithaca, N.Y.: Cornell University Press, 1990), xiii.

skills, not formal authority.[2] Chief judges are usually "first among equals." Their influence in shaping court policies reflects their ability at creating consensus or at building winning coalitions among their brethren.

Two consequences flow from the collective administration of courts. First, court policies will reflect the internal dynamics and social organization of judges. Judges who are prepared to reconcile their differences and willing to set aside personal ambitions or interests will make different kinds of policy choices than would be made if the bench were broken into competing groups or the judges were deeply divided and at loggerheads. Second, courts as a whole may be weak organizational competitors for status and influence within the court community compared to prosecutors. A strong-minded DA can mold an office into a bureaucracy; trial courts are not so easily shaped. Relations among judges scarcely resemble those that exist among chief prosecutors and their assistants. Egalitarianism permeates judicial relationships.

Both of these consequences stem from the norm of judicial independence. The realities of modern courts may compromise the individual autonomy of judges, as the following comment about American trial courts suggests.

There was a time in America when trial judging was mostly an individual enterprise. . . . In the past twenty years, judging has increasingly come to take place within a more formal organizational context. In particular, judges have more colleagues. . . . Small courthouses that could be managed by a series of autonomous judges have given way to large organizations. . . . Judging now takes place in an administratively rationalized or corporate setting in which the characteristics of collegial and power-dependency relationships are present.[3]

Despite this general tendency, judicial independence sets in motion powerful countervailing centrifugal forces that can fragment relations

2. This is true not only of state trial courts but of appellate courts, including the U.S. Supreme Court. A comparison of trial court leadership in Chicago, Los Angeles, and Philadelphia can be found in John Paul Ryan et al., "Judging in America's Trial Courts," in *American Trial Judges* (New York: The Free Press, 1980), 227–45. J. Woodford Howard, Jr., discusses the social organization and leadership of three circuit courts of appeal in *Courts of Appeals in the Federal Judicial System: A Study of the Second, Fifth, and District of Columbia Circuits* (Princeton, N.J.: Princeton University Press, 1981). A general introduction to the same topics with regard to the Supreme Court can be found in David M. O'Brien, *Storm Center: The Supreme Court in American Politics*, 2nd ed. (New York: W. W. Norton and Company, 1990, 2d ed.).

3. Ryan et al., *American Trial Judges*, 240–41.

among judges. This may be particularly true of smaller courts outside large cities, where the bureaucratizing effects of size are less strong.[4]

The centrifugal and centripetal forces within courts mean that decisions about organizing court work generate political conflicts on the bench. Judges must decide how to divide their time among different tasks, allocate work and cases among themselves, choose whom they want as a leader, and settle on how they want to be led. State rules rarely govern these decisions, and in many instances local customs circumvent them. With few guidelines other than personal preferences and professional norms to follow, the policies judges select for their court's operations reflect local bench politics. Complicated, contentious issues of judicial autonomy versus the collective interests of the court lie at the heart of these decisions. Equally difficult problems centering on equitable distributions of work loads and efficiency in the court also surface. Court policies ultimately reflect the social, professional, and political relationships among judges and how the judges resolve these conflicts.

The court is at the center of courthouse life. How judges organize their work directly affects the interests of everyone in the courthouse community. The stature of the court depends on the courthouse community's response to these policies. This chapter explores the formal and social organizations of the nine felony courts, how the judges allocated time and work in their courts, and the effects of these policies on the courts' relations within their courthouse communities. Bench craft was a two-fold matter centering on the ability of judges to act cohesively and collectively to pursue common goals and on the role of chief judges in fostering these efforts.

The Social Organization of Courts: Collegial, Competitive, and Conflictual

On appellate courts, conflict and dissension among judges is publicly evident through the judges' votes on cases. Split decisions suggest the existence of coalitions, cleavages, and clusters. Trial court judges as a group do not make decisions about individual cases; thus inferences about judicial relationships outside the courtroom cannot be made from their decisions. The behind-the-scenes information needed to describe the internal dynamics of trial courts has been scarce.[5] As a

4. See the discussion on the relationship among size and courts in Eisenstein, Flemming, and Nardulli, *Contours of Justice.*

5. See, however, the descriptions of Baltimore, Chicago, and Detroit in James Eisenstein and Herbert Jacob, *Felony Justice: An Organizational Analysis of Criminal Courts* (Boston: Little, Brown and Company, 1977), and the sketches of Los Angeles and Phila-

consequence, far less is known about the social organizations of trial court judges than of appellate court judges.

The social organizations of the nine courts in this study fell into three distinctive groups: collegial, competitive, and conflictual. In collegial courts, harmonious relationships existed among the judges, and the judges were able to act jointly on common problems. In competitive courts, the judges divided into groups of various sizes and followed courtroom practices that created sets of diverse policies within the courthouse. Conflictual courts were divided over many matters ranging from how guilty pleas should be handled to how cases ought to be scheduled on the courts' calendars. The result was stalemate between contending groups in some instances and disintegration of collective policy making in others.

Collegial Courts: Consensus and Egalitarianism

The Diverse Sources of Collegiality

Collegiality among judges—a sense of comradeship and willingness to compromise—emerged for several reasons. Similar political or professional backgrounds, shared tenures and experiences on the bench, and business or even family ties fostered collegiality, but they did not guarantee it, nor were they the only factors. The following vignettes give a sense of the conditions that gave rise to collegial benches in five of the court communities.

- On the first bench, time, experience, and family ties fostered collegiality. Each of the five circuit-level judges had been a lower court judge for an average of five years before his election or appointment to the higher court. Excluding the most recent member of the bench, the younger brother of one of the incumbent judges, the average circuit court tenure of the four judges was sixteen years.
- Time, similar ages and backgrounds, and politics also forged bonds among judges on the second court. The five judges had worked together for seven years. Excluding the newer judges, three of the judges had spent thirteen years together. Four were in their sixties. Three had been district attorney, one succeeding the other, before becoming judges. Most were members of the county's political "old boy" network. The court's chief judge succeeded in getting a close

delphia in Ryan et al., "The Social, Political and Legal Environments of Courts," in *American Trial Judges*, 196–224.

friend appointed to a bench vacancy. The judges were so close that, as one of them said, "We think alike without even talking."

- Similar factors bound the third bench. With one exception, all six judges came to the bench as Republicans. Three were elected together after campaigning in the same hard-fought primary. They were close in age, had served for roughly a decade on the bench, and had known each other personally and professionally for longer than that. Half of the judges at one time or another had worked in the district attorney's office. Two drove together to the court every day. One judge had practiced law in what he called a "very political" firm whose senior partner once had been on the bench and in which one of his current fellow judges also had been a partner.

- Different factors were at work in the fourth court, where the three judges in the felony division of the court were not like one another. They were not alike in age; one was over sixty-five, another was in his mid-forties, and the third was thirty-three. Nor did they hold very similar attitudes about punishment. The two older judges had opposed each other across the bar as defense attorney and prosecutor. Nevertheless, as one judge put it, "We get along together pretty well because we talk things over all the time." Perhaps as a consequence, they developed common policies regarding bail and probation.

- Just two judges handled the entire felony caseload in the fifth county. Despite differences in their political backgrounds (one was a Democrat, the other a Republican), experience (one had been on the bench for two years, the other for over seventeen years), and attitudes, their courtroom styles and practices were very similar, perhaps because the press of cases discouraged idiosyncratic behavior on the bench. For instance, they remained aloof from guilty plea negotiations and, despite its effect on their courtroom schedules, transferred to each other those trials in cases they refused to accept as guilty pleas.

One of these courts nicely illustrates how a collegial bench can overcome the parochialism that often infects judicial relationships. On various occasions, the judges used the *en banc* procedure, through which the bench as a whole issued an opinion or decision. In one politically charged instance, the court denied a request made by the director of a local citizen's crime commission that a grand jury be formed to investigate crime and corruption in the county. The director publicly hinted, according to the local newspaper, that "numerous present and past public officials from the executive, legislative, and judicial branches of government" might be implicated by the investigation. He demanded an outside prosecutor for the grand jury because, the paper reported, the current DA might "otherwise be put in the situation of having to investigate friends and associates." The judges "banked" their decision, as the following judge explained.

This bird [the crime commission director] comes in, dumps this hot potato in the chief judge's lap, and says, "Here's a petition for a grand jury." The chief's picture is in the paper and all that stuff. We decided the best thing to do was "bank" the darn thing, because, you know, some people would think he was the only one against it. It was just one of those things where it was "damned if you do, damned if you don't." We felt we might just as well tell everyone the whole lot of us were against it by having all of us sign it.

This sense of joint responsibility, fostered by personal ties and friendships and by enough time on the bench together to work out professional differences, produced a bench with little rancor or conflict.

The Role of Chief Judges in Collegial Courts

Collegial benches are egalitarian; relationships among judges are familiar and casual, not formal. The following judge's remarks about his court were typical.

The thing about our court is that we're all pretty good friends. Actually, most of us are of the same vintage. We were practicing lawyers together and we've known each other for twenty-five and thirty years on a very close basis. We respect each other. We feel perfectly free to go to someone if we have something that we want to talk to them about.

Collegiality and egalitarianism defined the chief judges' role in these five courts. Their influence rested on consensus, not formal authority, and on their ability to reshape this consensus. This consensus, however, included a sharp distinction between policy and administration.[6] The judges granted the chief judges prerogatives in matters they felt were managerial. They resisted encroachments on their courtroom autonomy and on what they believed to be the substance of their work—namely, sentencing and legal decisions. Where chief judges were elected by the bench, the other judges had an institutional means

6. Howard found the same distinction in the U.S. Court of Appeals; Howard, *Courts of Appeals in the Federal Judicial System*, 225–32.

of buttressing this distinction. But even in courts where the most senior judges as a matter of state rules automatically became chief judges, judicial norms about courtroom independence trimmed the chiefs' sails.

For example, in one court, the chief judge's authority in scheduling and docketing matters did not violate the expectations of the other judges. One judge described the chief judge's position in this court.

Judge: Judge ———, our [chief] judge, has been more of an administrator. We do, from time to time, meet and discuss cases in a general way as well as specific cases. . . . Judge ——— is just one of us when we do that. . . . He certainly has made no attempt to impose on us what he feels we should do with regard to cases.

Interviewer: What kinds of things might get you in trouble with the [chief] judge?

Judge: Mostly scheduling cases and working on schedule. I've had the experience of having him call up or I meet him and he's said, "Why did you ever do that in that case?" And then we talk about it. I never had the feeling that he was trying to impose his opinions into what I'm doing, but rather to express, perhaps in a very strong way, that he doesn't agree with what I did.

Interviewer: How compelling is that?

Judge: I assure you, when he expresses an opinion about my schedule, I take that as something more than just an expression of opinion. But if he tells me that he disagrees with a sentence that I may have imposed or a particular finding that I made, I don't pay much attention to it. I just think, "So what?" But scheduling and that sort of thing—I do pay attention to that, because I feel he has the right to impose his will there.

Another judge expressed a similar opinion. In passing he referred to an egalitarian norm regarding the assignment of murder cases, the importance of being consulted, and the limits of the presiding judge's authority.

[The chief judge] and I have been close friends for years. Judge Y and he are close friends. He consults with us. He doesn't have to under the law, but he does. The only things he assigns are murder cases. There is no sense in my getting ten and somebody else none. So he passes them around. . . . He's over here every day talking to me. . . . We talk every day. We don't establish uniform sentences, of course. I think every case should be judged on an individual basis.

A third judge quickly summed up relations between the chief judge and the rest of the bench by simply stating, "There's no set pattern of 'You do this' and 'You do that.'" Still, within the confines of the chief judge's relations with his fellow judges, this chief judge exerted decisive and forceful leadership. As he put it: "I like the saying, 'The buck stops here.' Somebody has to make the ultimate decision. That's the way it is."

In other collegial courts, chief judges shared their authority with others, thus diffusing it throughout the bench. For example, a judge on one of these courts, who was not a chief judge, pointed out, "I'm something of an administrative judge."

We don't have an administrative judge as such. Our chief judge happens to be a person who does [family court work] exclusively. He has very little to do with the civil or criminal side of the court. As a result, I'm doing the administrative work for both civil and criminal work.

There's a group of lawyers coming in at eleven o'clock. All they want to talk about are cases that are not really assigned to any judge yet. And I've found myself giving a great deal of time to administrative policy things which take up my time. It's not completely satisfying to me. I find that I'm interrupted in my regular work much more frequently than I would like to be.

In another court community, the chief judge turned over to a younger judge the sensitive task of dealing with county commissioners. This junior judge was from the same generation as many of the commissioners and enjoyed politicking with them over budgetary and policy matters. The chief judge was confident that the bench's interests were well served by this devolution of responsibilities.

Another chief judge claimed, "The other judges are my equals. . . . I have no authority to enforce anything. . . . I have no disciplinary power to punish those that don't comply with what I want to do. . . . They're all my equals." Another judge, referring to the chief judge of the criminal division, pointed out, "He isn't going to tell you how to rule on a case. He's not going to tell you anything like that. Most of it's of an administrative nature."

Collegiality and an elected chief judgeship also encouraged cautious leadership. A chief judge outlined his position and offered an illustration of it in the following way.

We go on a year-to-year basis here. Being chief judge is always really at the pleasure of the other judges. I was elected last year for the second year in a row. It could end abruptly if they disagree with something. So far no chief judge since I've been around here has been terminated in the middle of his term.

I thought a court administrator would be helpful in place of a director of court services when the director retired. . . . I discussed this with the judges. Some of them do not like the idea. So we're going at it very cautiously. This is not a centralized, dictatorial office at all. Things are not done by centralizing everything in the chief judge's office and running everything from there like an octopus.

This chief judge sustained collegiality in his court by following a docket policy that gave judges ample room to satisfy their desire for independence. According to chief judge, "I allow the judges to handle their own dockets to a large extent, but if I see that there's some weakness there. . . . well, remember your capacity to reach your goal depends upon whether you have the wherewithal to do it." Docket and calendaring policies were tailored to the interests of the judges.

Competitive Courts and Policy Diversity: A Case Study

The Social Organization of a Competitive Bench

In this suburban court community, the judges energetically competed over the state of their dockets, their willingness to put in long hours, and their track records in finding new ways to do their work. According to a former court official:

The judges here really compete among themselves. . . . A monthly report that they get shows where they stand in line with the others and what their caseload is and how old it is. And one judge calls the others to let them know that he has finally worked his way up to third place.

Competition, plus the bench's size (there were fourteen judges), produced fragmented relationships among the judges. A close observer noted, "They are too isolated. They are a kingdom unto themselves." A clique of three and sometimes four judges enthusiastically took the lead in urging the others to move their cases. One member of this group said they were like "sheep dogs" who made sure the other judges did not slacken their pace or stray from the fold. This attitude was irksome and annoying to some judges. One pointed out, "I'm not as concerned as some of them are with moving the docket." Another said, "I like to move the docket, but only within reason."

At the center of this clique was a vigorous, controversial judge who took great pride in his administrative talents. He was instrumental in creating the court administrator's office. He pushed his ideas about how the bench should operate on whoever happened to be chief judge, usually to the chief judge's chagrin. Even judges close to this activist drifted away from him as they wearied of standing in his shadow and grew tired of his hectoring. A knowledgeable member of the court outlined the unfortunate experience of a younger judge who had innocently accepted the senior judge's tutelage.

> Judge ——— was [the younger judge's] mentor and he wanted to push him along as quickly as possible. ——— got him elected chief judge just two years after he got on the bench. He pushed him into that grand jury role [a highly controversial grand jury investigation involving a police department and the prosecutor's office] when [the younger judge] wasn't even comfortable as a trial judge yet. So tremendous problems were facing him and he couldn't accept the criticism that the grand jury received. It was very difficult for him. He now sees criticism as a very personal thing. . . . Judge ——— should never have pushed him; he didn't do him any favors.

The group centered around this strong judge was joined by two occasional allies, but the judges lacked unanimity. They were not the invariable core of winning coalitions when the bench voted on issues before it. In addition to this cluster, there were two pairings of judges and several isolates. Two brothers formed one of the pairings, while the other pair rested on an old friendship. The isolates included a senior judge, a junior judge (who raised his colleagues' hackles by discussing internal court matters with a newspaper friend and by publicly criticizing a recently appointed judge), and two other judges who, because of poor health in one instance and family problems in the other, stayed to themselves.

This competitive and diffuse social organization was partly a matter of simple numbers and differing personalities. It was also a reflection of the court's suburban setting. The court was still evolving as an institution and gaining prominence as it grew. The judges looked for opportunities to impress on it a stamp of innovativeness and to establish the court's reputation for efficiency. The judges were relatively young; almost all of them came to the bench while in their early forties. In this affluent county, where social activities, housing, and educational goals for children were geared to upper income levels, wearing a black robe often entailed financial sacrifices. (Two judges, in fact, left the bench to return to private practice for this reason.) The judges were upwardly mobile lawyers in the prime of their working lives who saw the court's reputation as a major propellant for their careers.

Court expansions, retirements, resignations, and deaths added yeast to this judicial organization and kept it in ferment. During one eight-year period, eight new judges took seats on the circuit bench. As these judges put on their robes and settled into courthouse life, new relationships emerged, old ones receded, and different constellations of interactions appeared. Equally important, these judges had to learn how to run their dockets. As they toyed with different techniques, keeping some and discarding others, these experiments, when added to the bench's competition, created diverse courtroom practices and policies.

Paradoxically, egalitarianism and the absence of hierarchy relaxed some of the competitive tension among the judges. Policy disputes were supposed to be settled through majority vote. This could have produced disgruntled minorities, except that a single judge's opposition was traditionally enough to veto a proposal, as happened when one judge held out against a continuous jury calendar that would have eliminated the court's nonjury interludes between trial terms. The bench also relied on ad hoc, temporary committees. The judges created committees when they needed one rather than establishing several standing committees that could have served as centers of power. Finally, the judges followed a tradition of rotating annually the position of chief judge.

Under the state's rules, circuit judges elected a chief judge to serve renewable two-year terms. In this county, the chief judge customarily resigned at the end of the first year so that someone else could be elected. For example, during one five year period, five different judges sat as chief judge. The bench also chose varying numbers of alternate chief judges, with the first alternate normally elected the chief judge the following year. This tradition, the judges explained, arose because the onerous chores the chief judge had to perform made it a struggle to keep up with even a reduced caseload. It also produced a political bonus. With but two exceptions during this period, the chief judges and alternates were up for reelection either during the year they were in office or after it. (One of the reasons the number of alternates varied, in fact, was that the number of judges seeking reelection varied.)

Courtroom Diversity in a Competitive Setting

The judges on this competitive bench refused to wed themselves to any particular procedure for long. In order to keep up with each other, the

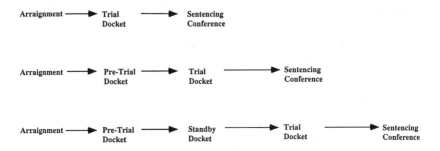

Figure 3.1. Docket management approaches in a competitive court.

judges continually looked for different ways of doing things and were quick to seize those they felt had promise. Consequently, how criminal dockets were managed varied from courtroom to courtroom and within courtrooms from one time to the next. A knowledgeable onlooker remarked with just a bit of exaggeration, "It's kind of mindboggling. Not only do you have fourteen different ways at any one time, you have fourteen different ways every other week. They change because the judges are so aggressive and statistically minded that they're constantly striving. They're never satisfied."

Variegated courtroom policies took root and flourished as the judges nurtured different dispositional hybrids. They continually changed and recombined how they arraigned defendants, scheduled cases, conducted pretrial conferences, and appointed counsel in indigent defendant cases.

Figure 3.1 summarizes the three major docket management approaches used by the judges in terms of stages or "dockets." The judges differed in their use of pretrial conferences and in whether they placed cases on a standby basis pending a trial date. Two judges put their cases directly on their trial dockets after arraignment; the rest of the bench was divided evenly with respect to pretrial conferences. A handful of judges used "mail arraignments" to eliminate the need for counsel and their clients to appear in court. Three also experimented with a "pre-plea" procedure through which they ordered presentence reports at the time defendants were arraigned. If defense counsel thought a guilty plea was likely but wanted to see the probation department's recommendation first, the judges ordered a pre-plea report. Both of these practices, the judges felt, speeded up the process.

Policy diversity had its price. Some judges used what the courthouse disapprovingly termed "cattle calls" because the judges had attorneys and their clients in all of the judges' pending cases appear on the first

TABLE 3.1. Counsel Appointment Practices.

	Concentration of Appointments by Judges		
	Least	Moderate	Most
Mean number of attorneys assigned cases*	50	39	26
Mean number of assigned cases per attorney*	1.7	2.2	3.7
Mean proportion of appointments to "top 45" lawyers†	37.3%	51.7%	71.2%
Number of judges	7	4	3

*For January–March 1980.
†For July 1979 through June 1980.

day of new trial terms. The results were often jammed courtrooms and thick knots of lawyers and worried clients crowding out into the corridors outside the courtrooms. Having every case scheduled for trial during the term called into court on the first day was controversial, sparking criticisms from the bar. The other judges could not stop their colleagues from following this practice, despite the complaints, as the following judge explained.

> The running of the court is left up to the judges as long as their dockets are moving and they're not shocking the conscience of the other members of the bench or the bar. And let me tell you, there's been a lot said about the couple of judges who use the cattle call. . . . The bar association brought it up again at the last annual dinner. It passed a resolution and sent it along to us. It's come up at our monthly meetings, but it hasn't changed those judges.

In the other eight courts, assignment of indigent defendant cases to lawyers was controlled by either lower court judges or administrative officials, not by the trial judges who heard the cases. In this county, however, the circuit court judges appointed private defense counsel to represent indigent defendants who would then appear before the judges who had made the assignments. With over two-thirds of the sampled defendants represented by appointed counsel, the practice of criminal law in this court community was largely "public" for defense attorneys. This policy permitted judges, if they chose, to create stable courtroom workgroups by concentrating their appointments.

Table 3.1 indicates the judges' practices and the degree to which they concentrated their appointments. Roughly half the judges spread their appointments fairly widely across the defense bar. The other half concentrated their appointments to varying degrees. Judges who spread out their assignments naturally appointed fewer cases to more attorneys than those judges who focused their appointments. Moreover, there was little overlap between these sets of attorneys; judges who sent cases to many different lawyers tended not to use the counsel who were regularly appointed by other judges. This shows up most clearly with regard to forty-five attorneys singled out as "regulars." Judges who scattered their appointments assigned a smaller average proportion of their cases to these regulars.

Conflictual Courts and Policy Disputes

Splintered Bench, Fractured Policies: A Case Study

Bickering, backlogs, administrative instability, and external isolation plagued a circuit bench in an autonomous county otherwise known for its tradition of municipal reform, concern for efficiency, and regard for "good government." Shortly after the bench added a fourth judge, the court needed an extra "visiting" judge the following year to help the judges clear up their dockets. Five years later, another backlog crisis struck the bench. During these five years, four court administrators came and went. One of the judges gave a quick rundown of the court's efforts to find a reliable, suitable court administrator.

> Our first court administrator was exactly what we wanted. . . . But he got kicked upstairs to the state's regional court administrator office. . . . The second one . . . well, when we found out about some of the things that were going on at a noon meeting, he was out of the building by 1:30. . . . The third one was a nice, incompetent individual. . . . Everybody wondered, "What's he doing? Why doesn't he do something?" Now we got a guy that's really gung-ho, works real hard.

County officials and the local bar held the court in low regard. Bench relations with the county's commissioners deteriorated badly; they only improved after a recently appointed judge became chief judge and started repairing the damage. As he stated, "Our name was 'mud' for a number of historical reasons." (A previous court administrator alienated important county officials, and one of the judges created hard feelings by using his judicial authority to force the county to hire new personnel for his courtroom.) Bench relations with the bar were little better. Civil attorneys complained that the backlog of criminal cases made it difficult for them to find an open courtroom for their cases. The criminal bar publicly expressed its disgruntlement when the court's four judges, unable to come to an agreement about the legal issues raised by mass arrests of homosexuals in a public restroom, wrote separate, conflicting opinions. The attorneys openly criticized one judge for being slow in releasing his opinion and condemned the opinion as poorly argued and written.

Personal differences and policy discord among the judges caused the court's difficulties. Two judges, elected in the same year, mixed poorly. One felt ill-treated upon his arrival at the bench. He complained about his courtroom and the personnel he inherited from a retiring judge. It rankled him that he was barred from hiring his secretary from his old law firm. He still fumed as he talked about his first years on the bench.

I had no secretarial help for a long time. I inherited an assignment clerk who couldn't type. My court reporter was supposed to do the typing. It's ridiculous when a circuit judge can't get any typing done. I couldn't bring my legal secretary along. She was with me for eight years; she was one of the best. But I was obligated to take the assignment clerk because a senior judge wanted her out of his court-room. And seniority rules. . . . Maybe I shouldn't get into this, but then we had a difference of opinion during my second year here that resulted in the other judges firing my court reporter, although they say she quit.

Rickety relations between the two first term judges collapsed com-pletely when one accused the other of "prostituting" himself for nego-tiating a sentence in a guilty plea case. As their terms neared an end and the two faced reelection, their relationship had not improved. They went their separate ways during the campaign, unlike six incum-bent judges in another county who joined forces against a lone chal-lenger by running as a slate with the slogan, "Keep the Best of the Bench." As one of the feuding judges remarked, "We're so different, we're not sure we want to make it a slate. . . . I would antagonize someone he might not, and vice-versa." Ultimately, one fell to a lower court challenger supported by the county's bar.

A key official lamented, "There is no singleness of purpose on our circuit bench. For a long time now, no judge has said, 'I don't agree with it, but for the good of the whole I will go along with the majority.' Never! That's why we have four different systems of criminal justice in this community." Docket policies reflected the unravelling of the bench's ability to act jointly.

For a time, shortly after the first election of the two incompatible judges, all four judges cooperated among themselves by coordinating

TABLE 3.2. Case-Processing Policies of Judges in a Conflictual Court.

Did Judges Hold Sentencing Conferences?	Did Judges Hold Pretrial Conferences?	
	No	Yes
No	Judge A	Judge B
Yes	Judge C	Judge D

the amount of time during the year that they devoted to their civil and criminal caseloads. The judges synchronized their work schedules to create regular, rotational sequences in which two judges heard criminal cases for three weeks while the other two handled civil matters. At the conclusion of this period, after a week's hiatus, the judges switched their responsibilities for three weeks. This rotation of civil and criminal work occurred five times throughout the year to create an even, predictable allocation of time. Each judge spent fifteen weeks on his felony docket, producing a bench-wide total of sixty working weeks. Within three years, this self-imposed discipline broke down. While collectively the judges gave criminal matters more time by allowing a total of sixty-three weeks for felony cases, each judge now marched to the beat of his own drummer. Each judge gave differing amounts of time to his criminal docket and refused to synchronize the weeks when he heard felony cases with the weeks when the other judges were hearing these cases.

The judges also scrambled their case-processing practices without any apparent concern that each courtroom operated differently. It was typical of the bench that these practices did not overlap. As Table 3.2 indicates, the judges' courtroom policies produced four different ways of handling felony cases. Two judges refused to hold pretrial conferences; they felt they were a waste of time and that they would get the judges involved in plea bargaining. According to one judge, "I won't put myself in that position. Two of our judges will learn eventually that they have no business entering into that." The other judges disagreed, although one admitted, "I have on rare occasions done it, but I have never said, 'Okay, if you'll belly up on this charge, then this will be your sentence.'" Two judges declined to hold sentencing conferences in chambers prior to normal pronouncement in the courtroom, although two others routinely held these conferences.

The Chief Judge: Picking Up the Pieces

The chief judge's challenge, a close observer felt, was whether he could "get the judges to agree to work together." Another member of the court community concluded, "By definition, by nature, a judge believes that the world revolves around his courtroom and the sun rises and sets on him. By definition, they're prima donnas." The bench's chief judge was its least experienced member, a retired bank attorney recently appointed to the bench who had been elected chief judge by default by the other, more senior judges, who could not agree among themselves as to which one of them they would support. (In contrast, recall how the competitive bench rotated this position to help the reelection bids of judges.) The chief judge was fully aware of the court's political problems, and took several steps to correct the situation. One step was drafting a set of objectives. As he explained:

> The judges hadn't done anything like that before. I think, going back to my business experience at the bank, I could say, "Here is a problem. Here are ways of solving it. Why don't we start to do something about it?"

The chief judge identified nine objectives dealing with various matters that he felt would reduce the court's backlog and lead to earlier trial dates in civil and criminal cases. The eighth objective raised the issue of consistent courtroom policies. In his memorandum, "Circuit Court Objectives," the chief judge declared:

> The various judges are advised that the four Courts are inconsistent in some of their policies. This is wasteful both of time and of energy on the part of the attorneys. Also, courts should be consistent to the extent that it is possible. If the Bar can advise where present policies are inconsistent, an attempt will be made to make all policies the same. In order that the nature and type can be determined, input from the Bar will be welcome.

To gain the judges' cooperation, the chief judge involved them in implementing his list of objectives. He assigned at least one objective to each judge and designated the judge as a liaison with the bar regarding that particular objective. The chief judge tried to avoid the appearance of pressing solutions on his fellow judges. As he stated when he described his feelings about being chief judge:

> What I'm doing is making each one of those guys a part of answering the problems as we go along, rather than just saying, "Okay, here's what we're gonna do." They participate in and help make the decisions. So, in a sense, it's a consensus thing. Now, sometimes I've got to say, "This is the way it's gonna be." But that's not very often.

The chief judge also began to patch up relations with the bar. After discussing his objectives with his fellow judges, he went to the bar association.

First, I discussed it with the judges and got their agreement. Then I went to the board of directors of the bar association and got their enthusiastic agreement. They couldn't believe that something like this was happening. Then we had a joint meeting between the bench and the bar and went over all of these objectives.

The judge's concern for the court's tarnished image and his efforts to polish it caught the eye of the courthouse community. According to one well-placed observer:

Heretofore, I think that, with one or two exceptions, most judges didn't have the time, wouldn't take the time, whatever, to keep communication lines open. . . . The individual we have now as chief judge is more in tune I think to the public relations aspect and what ought to be done with the community.

The chief judge quickly showed his sense for the importance of good community relations in righting the court's listing status. He approached the county commissioners to discuss the court's problems. And, as luck would have it, a millage campaign to fund anticrime programs in the county gave him a chance to show the court's concern for the problem.

A week before I became chief judge, I wrote to each one of the county commissioners. I told them that I was the new chief judge, here are some of the problems that I see, and I'm looking forward to working with you. Because I knew if we were gonna get anywhere with our budget or salaries or some of the other things that I had in mind, we were gonna have to get a better footing with them.

Then we got into the millage campaign. I was one of the first ones to plunk down $100 to help defray the cost. And I saw to it that I got on the committee. I did some speeches. I was on the radio on a taped commercial. . . . Here I was, thumping the tub, not for the court, but for somebody else. Well, you can't be wrong when you're doing that.

Sketches of Two Conflictual Courts

In one suburban county, the judges feuded over the role of the presiding judge and the way the court assigned cases. Despite the Republican party's dominance in recruiting judges for the bench, the many professional and political experiences the judges shared in common, and strong feelings within the courthouse community that "we are one family," the judges split more or less along ethnic fault lines. The "ethnics," who prided themselves in moving their dockets quickly, bridled at what they felt was the presiding judge's high-handedness. The "establishment" and generally protestant judges took a less urgent, more relaxed stance about their work and supported the chief judge.

One critic of the chief judge complained, "We've got a bastard in our county who's a dictator, and he does what he wants. You can quote me. He's a first-class bastard. He does what he wants to do. He wants to be the leader." Another opponent cited a personal experience to show how, at least in his eyes, the presiding judge used his case assignment authority to achieve a political end.

[The chief judge] can assign you a tough case that could knock you out of the box if you're running for [reelection] that year. . . . I had a case that is the leading case in labor law. . . . I had 16,000 or 17,000 unionists march on this courthouse. . . . I was a little worried, with all of them yelling, "We want the judge! We want the judge!" I made a very unpopular decision. That was the year I was running, and that case was given to me for one reason—to defeat me.

The establishment judges held more sanguine views of the chief judge's powers and leadership. According to one, "There is not a more efficient administrator in the world than our [presiding] judge." This judge added:

When you really take a look at the position's lawful power, [the chief judge] really does not have that much power. He has power in the sense of the type of individual he is. He sets the pace. We have a [presiding] judge that's in here at seven o'clock every morning. . . . I think the real power of [the chief judge] comes from his personality and leadership.

Another judge described the presiding judge's position in the following way:

[The chief judge] is the captain of the court. But in this court, traditionally, the presiding judge has not adopted that attitude. His role, I suppose, if you'll pardon the analogy, might be closer to the Pope, who is said to be the first among equals.

In courts with "individual calendars," cases are assigned to judges who are solely responsible for hearing all phases of the cases until they are concluded. With individual calendars, judges sink or swim on their own in keeping up with the cases assigned to them. In courts with "master calendars," cases are assigned to various judges at different stages, so that one judge may hear a motion in a case while another will preside over the trial or take the guilty plea. Master calendars place a premium on joint cooperation and a sense of shared responsibility.

This conflictual court used a master calendar. The comments of two ethnic judges summed up their perceptions of the establishment judges regarding the work of the court and illustrated their frustration and anger.

There are judges here who do not work. I'm told there is a judge on our bench who, when he gets a case in the morning, if it turns into a plea, goes back to his chambers until the afternoon. And then in the afternoon, the same thing happens. So he might have two pleas during the course of the day. There are those of us who work. As soon as a case turns into a plea—even before it's finished—we send down for another case, and when the first one finishes, the second one goes right in.

* * *

I spoke to one of these judges. And he said, "I didn't get elected to work hard. I worked hard as a trial lawyer." My reaction was, "You God-damn son of a bitch! You're making it more difficult for me by goofing off." So, when I got home that evening, I said to myself, "What the hell am I doing? Why am I breaking my balls?"

The second suburban court fractured along divisions within the county's Republican party, divisions based on personal cliques and factions. The court's fissures, according to knowledgeable attorneys, were most likely to open over the appointment of associate judges to the court. In this state, unlike the other two, lower court judges were appointed by the circuit-level judges and not elected by the community at large. Not surprisingly, controversy erupted among the judges over these choices, because the positions were patronage jobs and a way of rewarding friends. Equally important, they were the first rung of the ladder to the circuit court. In effect, the circuit judges were picking their future colleagues.

Unlike the conflictual bench just discussed, this court's policies for assigning work mitigated some of the strains among the judges. The judges handled both criminal and civil matters during the course of any particular week. The judges, one enthused, relished the chance to switch gears by moving from civil to criminal and back again. As generalists, the judges often found it necessary to rely on attorneys to "spoon feed" them the law, as one judge admitted.

From a judge's perspective, if you really enjoy the law and want to enjoy your job, there's nothing more enjoyable than covering everything. Like, I have an armed robbery trial today. Monday I've got a breach of contract jury trial, the next Monday a medical malpractice case, and the Monday after that a rape. We find it much more rewarding to be involved in all aspects. And, although we won't be up on everything, if it's something we can't handle very much, then we let the lawyers spoon feed us a little.

This case assignment practice relaxed work-related tensions. Judges could not complain about unfair work loads or favoritism in the kinds of cases assigned to them. Each judge received more or less equal shares of civil and criminal cases. Moreover, the presiding judge's ability to punish judges by assigning them to less attractive court work was diminished by the fact that the bench regularly rotated the position among themselves. Finally, although no informal rules dictated the length of assignments to the general trial division, which had responsibility for criminal and major civil matters, judges expected that their aptitude and personal preferences would be taken into account.[7] The chief judge explained how he thought the bench perceived his role and how he assigned judges to different divisions.

Over the six years I've been here, we've had two chief judges. Based on what I've observed during that period of time, what the chief judge does is a matter of how dominant his personality is and to what extent the other judges will go along with him. Of course, in the administrative end, such as making assignments, someone has to be the last word and he is the last word. That's if he does his job.

He determines who's gonna sit in divorce court and who's gonna sit in juvenile court and who's gonna be in what division and so forth. The chief judge tries to put people where they show an aptitude for a

7. This is to be contrasted with the court in Chicago, where assignments to different divisions reflected partisan allegiances; Eisenstein and Jacob, *Felony Justice*, 112, and Ryan et al., *American Trial Judges*, 217–19.

particular area and also to preferences where that's possible. If somebody wants to sit in divorce court because that's where he spent his life as a practicing attorney, then that type of thing is considered.

Policy Politics in Courts: The Example of Master and Individual Calendars

Court policies allocate time and work among judges. The methods used by the court are a significant issue for judges and the courthouse community. The question of individual versus master calendars illustrates the concerns underlying policy politics in criminal courts.

Individual calendars give judges more authority over their caseloads and afford them opportunities to innovate or at least to vary how they handle their cases. A political benefit of individual calendars is that they do not require consensus among judges as to how cases should be handled. Judges may adopt whatever ways of doing their work they please. Master calendars, in contrast, narrow the judges' options. With cases centrally assigned on a day-to-day basis, judges must pull together to dispose of the court's caseload. Individual styles may vary, but since the judges are not responsible for cases from their inception to their conclusion there is less room for isolated experimentation in managing cases in the courtrooms.

Bench politics and thus the social organization of the courts were greatly involved with the issues raised by the way in which cases were assigned to judges. The question "What works best?" was often ignored by judges, who instead wondered "What's fair?," asked "Who's working?," and worried about "Who will be blamed?" and "Who will be praised?" Equity, efficiency, and accountability lay behind these questions. If sore feelings, bad blood, and personality clashes broke into the debate, these already difficult issues became even harder to resolve.

Comments by two judges reveal the indeterminacy surrounding the choice of court calendars. The first judge argued that since judges could not know with certainty what would happen to cases on their dockets, a master calendar was needed so cases could be shunted into idle courtrooms. Interestingly, this judge worked in a court with an individual calendar.

> The principle is sound. No judge can tell from day to day exactly what his docket is gonna look like. If you schedule two or three cases for trial and they fold, then you're in a position to take a case from another judge. If you do that, you've done an awful lot of good. You've moved the case; you've satisfied the lawyers; you've kept the docket moving.

The second judge, in another court, saw things differently. For him, no one knew better than the judge what would happen in cases. Judges with individual calendars stayed with cases from start to finish. They became thoroughly familiar with them at the same time the participants got to know the judge. Moreover, the performance of each judge was more visible, which seasoned the process with an element of competition. (Another judge who worked in a court with an individual calendar put it this way: "I work ten, twelve hours a day. I'm on my ass behind that bench all day. . . . But you have to have recognition for doing that, because man is a competitive animal.") However, second judge who praised individual calendars sat on a bench with a master calendar, a fact that distressed him.

> The individual calendar is much better from two standpoints. One is that you get cases disposed of, because a man assigned his own cases knows his own time best, knows how he works, and can get rid of them. And then there's the fact that people get to know that the judge can handle cases, and he gets to know the capacity of the other judges. The other judges may feel pressed, but that isn't bad really.

When dissatisfaction with the current way of doing things surfaced, as these two comments suggest, it was common for the perceived virtues of the alternative to be the old way's vices turned inside-out. Thus, the perceived merits of master or individual calendars were the mirror images of the flaws of the current, unsatisfactory policy.

Individual calendars eased judicial worries about equitable work loads. Each judge, randomly assigned an equal share of cases, was responsible for disposing of them. Indeed, one judge referred to the individual calendar as a "fairness docket." However, it did not guarantee fairness. There were times when even its most ardent supporters wanted exceptions to the rule. For example, because of the luck of the draw, a judge could fall behind because he or she had received a string of complex, time-consuming trials. The judge might call for help. Bench collegiality influenced the response to this plea, but as one judge noted:

> I find there is a basic jealousy between judges. If this judge is very efficient and works hard and has a short docket, while another judge is inefficient and doesn't work as hard and has a longer docket, the first one says, "Why should I help?" There's that attitude.

Judges also asked for favors when they went on vacation or needed a brief leave from the bench. They knew the favor had to be returned. A strict accounting, nevertheless, came as a surprise. In one instance, after two judges swapped cases a few times, one was taken aback when he asked for further help and his colleague replied, "Well, you owe me two or three." At first nonplussed by the remark, the judge concluded, "Okay, I'll start counting, too."

Finally, judges with individual calendars did not trust the random draw when it came to high visibility cases. Judges on one suburban bench, for example, made sure that each judge had an equal share of homicides by assigning them on a rotational basis. This meant each judge reaped the publicity of presiding over cases that drew media attention.

Feelings of unfairness vexed judges who sat on courts with master calendars. Because cases were assigned centrally but not randomly, judges often thought they were treated unequally. For example, riffles of displeasure occasionally disturbed the placid relations between judges in a collegial court because the prosecutor's office, which controlled case assignments, steered its newsworthy cases to one particular judge. This habit perturbed the other judges, as the following judge confessed, although they did nothing about it.

> This is somewhat personal. But there is a certain feeling that the district attorney's office gets more exposure by taking a case to one particular judge than if he takes it to one of the rest of us. And that is true. The newspaper reporter rarely sits in my court. . . . We do get along remarkably well, but there's no doubt that there's an undercurrent from time to time about this.

Master calendars, like individual calendars, allowed judges to work as quickly or slowly as they wanted. But because, with master calendars, cases went to courtrooms as they became available, fast-working judges received more cases, which with time could fuel feelings of exploitation, inequity, and frustration. These judges saw themselves as the only ones putting their shoulders to the wheel. Their labors, however, were rewarded only with more work, more cases, and little public praise. For them, the bench's drones, their work was never done. A suburban judge's exasperation was typical of judges who felt that master calendars allowed others to take advantage of their willingness to work.

> We have certain judges who write books, write law review articles, speak at Kiwanis or Rotary, and lecture at Reno at the Judiciary School. They don't carry their share of the load. There are other judges (I'm one of them) who handle one hundred to two hundred

cases a week of criminal court. Some judges are handing ten cases a week. One of them just came back from four weeks in Reno lecturing on evidence. I'd say he is one of the weaker judges on evidence, but he lectured and got paid for it.

Individual calendars allowed judges to go their own ways without "beggaring their brethren." If some judges kept up with their caseloads and still had time for off-the-court activities, the rest of the bench had no cause for complaint. The judges budgeted their own time; they were not captives of a central assignment office. For those with interests and ambitions outside court, an individual calendar gave judges an opportunity to pursue them without shedding part of their caseloads onto other judges and without seeming to be shirkers to the public, as the following judge explained.

Since I've been on the bench I've always had the shortest docket, because I handle it more efficiently, and yet I probably put in the least time of the other judges. That allows me to go to [the state capital] and to other meetings of committees that I serve on. Yet I can always say to the public, if they ask "What are you doing in [the state capital] instead of sitting in court?", that I'm helping the court in another way. Besides, I enjoy it.

Individual calendars solved the problem of equity and defused it as a source of conflict. The court's joint responsibility for its work loads was transformed into an individual one. Equally important, individual calendars weakened the chief or president judge's assignment powers and thus the power to punish and reward. The price for these benefits, at least for these nine courts, was greater inefficiency. Disposition times were longer in courts with individual calendars than in master calendar courts.[8]

Some judges, while disgruntled with their court's master calendar and anxious for a change, recognized this trade-off. As one judge admitted, "The most efficient way is the general [master] docket. But there's a problem of equity. If you're a chief judge, you can't worry about equity. Your job is to get rid of the list. You have to be a sheep dog. So you stick with the general docket system because it's the most efficient system." Satisfaction with master calendars rested on the shifting sands of support or trust in the chief judge and on feelings of fair treatment among judges on the bench.

8. Roy B. Flemming, Peter F. Nardulli, and James Eisenstein, "Timing of Justice in Felony Trial Courts," *Law and Policy* 9(April 1987):179.

Summary

The social organization of courts—whether they are collegial, competitive, or conflictual—affects their status and influence within the courthouse community. The calendaring and docketing practices of courts allocate both time and work. These policies touch the interests of everyone in the courthouse. Yet courts usually have few means at their disposal for overcoming parochial interests on the bench. For example, the chief judge's powers are often undercut by local customs. As a consequence, policy making raises difficult issues for judges. Their self-interests and the norm of judicial autonomy often collide with the court's interests as an institution and with the interests of prosecutors and defense attorneys. Moreover, seemingly mundane matters, such as calendars and dockets, raise difficult questions about equity and efficiency. Decisions about these matters nevertheless must be made. These decisions both reflect and reinforce the court's social organization.

Chapter 4
Bench Craft: Moving Cases, Policing Pleas, Doing Justice

Introduction

The traditional focus on judging concentrates on case decisions and their relationship to the backgrounds, attitudes, or role orientations of judges. Judges, however, do not make these decisions singlehandedly; felony dispositions, like guilty pleas, typically are jointly produced outcomes. The traditional focus gives little attention to how individual judges organize work in their courtrooms, even though this is one area where judicial privileges are most often honored. In the instance of guilty pleas, for example, courts vary widely in the amount of time spent on processing individual cases, in the detail with which defendants are advised of the consequences of pleading guilty, in the role played by attorneys in the plea ceremony, or in the role judges take in guilty plea negotiations.[1] Most of the time, these differences reflect not state laws or rules of procedures but judicial preferences in the local courts.

The recollection of a U.S. Supreme Court justice nicely describes the realities not only of the Supreme Court but of trial courts throughout most of the country. The justice recalled that when he first came to the Court he expected to find "one law firm with nine partners," only to be corrected by a more senior justice who told him that the Court was more like "nine firms, sometimes practicing law against one another."[2]

1. For a comparison of six jurisdictions, see William F. McDonald, "Judicial Supervision of the Guilty Plea Process: A Study of Six Jurisdictions," *Judicature* 70(December–January 1987):203. For information drawn from a national survey of trial judges, see John Paul Ryan and James Alfini, "Trial Judges' Participation in Plea Bargaining: An Empirical Assessment," *Law and Society Review* 13(Winter 1979):479.

2. The anecdote from Justice Potter Stewart is quoted by David M. O'Brien in *Storm Center: The Supreme Court in American Politics,* 2nd ed. (New York: W. W. Norton and Company, 1990), 156.

Trial courts are often congeries of single-member law firms located in the judges' chambers and courtrooms with the judges working as solo practitioners. And, like attorneys running law firms, the craft of courtroom judges involves matters large and small, ranging from the administration of their "firms" to organizing their work and presiding over trials.[3] This chapter looks at three aspects of the judges' bench craft in some detail. The first aspect of their craft was organizing their time and scheduling cases in order to dispose of their caseloads. The second facet deals with how the judges monitored the guilty pleas that passed through their courtrooms. The final aspect involves the organization of sentencing work and "doing justice." Throughout this chapter the central concern is with how the judges shaped the courtroom process and structured interactions, because of the importance of these actions in the work of defense attorneys.[4]

Moving Cases: Making Time and Scheduling Cases

Regardless of whether their courts used individual or master calendars, the judges decided themselves how much time they wanted to spend in their courtrooms. Some judges relished their time in the courtroom and saw the courtroom as the place where they wanted to do their work; others felt they could use their time more judiciously elsewhere. In courts with individual calendars, where judges usually controlled case scheduling, judges could decide which cases on their dockets they wanted to hear and when they wanted to hear them. Judges on benches with master calendars did not have this luxury.

Judge Time Is Court Time

Prosecutors and defense attorneys need a judge and a courtroom to dispose of their cases. This simple fact led some judges to believe that the simplest, most effective way of moving cases was to spend as much time on the bench as possible. These judges, in effect, held themselves hostage in their own courtrooms. They believed that cases moved only when they were behind the bench. In the eyes of these judges, elab-

3. Information on how trial judges allocate their time among their various responsibilities can be found in John Paul Ryan et al., *American Trial Judges: Their Work Styles and Performance* (New York: The Free Press, 1980).

4. The more traditional concerns of the literature over the relation between the characteristics of courtroom personnel and sentencing decisions in guilty pleas are addressed in considerable detail in Peter F. Nardulli, James Eisenstein, and Roy B. Flemming, *The Tenor of Justice: Criminal Courts and the Guilty Plea Process* (Urbana: University of Illinois Press, 1988), see especially Part 4, 305–63.

orate docket management methods were unnecessary. Their motto could have been, as one judge proclaimed, "I do my work in the courtroom." In various ways, the following sampling of comments by other judges with similar feelings reflected this sentiment.

I come in at 8:00 in the morning. I work until 4:30 in the afternoon. Then I leave. I'm not docket-conscious. I just tell them, "Keep me busy." That's the way I work it. My docket takes care of itself.

* * *

It's up to the judges to move the cases. The judge gets that degree of cooperation that he insists on. . . . You let people know this is your docket, you intend to control it, and you intend to keep the cases moving.

* * *

I don't view myself as one who takes an active role in plea negotiations. In fact, it's my policy not to get involved in them. . . . However, I do view myself as being very active in attempting to move the docket. . . . To do that, first of all, you have to be prompt when it comes time to get on the bench. You demand that of the attorneys who appear before you. You control the time you work. . . . You can't be real arbitrary, but by the same token, I don't have anything else to do during the day except to be here. So you keep everyone's feet to the fire.

For these judges, the key to a current docket was time in the courtroom. Some simple principles about moving cases emerged from the judges' discussions. These principles amounted to a folk theory of docket management, a theory that applied equally to civil and criminal cases and could be used by judges working with either master or individual calendars.

- First, establish your authority in the courtroom. Sitting behind the bench does not mean the judge has to accept the disposition pace of the attorneys.
- Second, set an example. Be punctual. Start early. Keep lunch breaks short. Leave late. If the judge is in the courtroom, the attorneys will be there, too.
- Third, if you show attorneys and court personnel that you want to hear cases, it puts the burden on them. Many attorneys actually

like judicial "workhorses," while others will curry favor by keeping judges busy if that is what they want. If you tell attorneys you want to try cases, they will get them into the courtroom for you.

- Fourth, deep involvement in plea negotiations is not necessary. A judge known in the courthouse as someone "who loves to try cases" gives both sides a chance to call the other's bluff. Attorneys will settle cases if the threat of a trial is real.
- Finally, watch your continuances and postponements. Lax practices regarding these decisions are self-defeating, since they undermine the other principles.

All judges could follow these principles; the type of calendar did not constrain their choice. However, tinkering with case scheduling could only be done in courts with individual calendars. Judges with master calendars had to wait for the assignment office to send them cases. One of the judges in a master calendar court claimed with some exaggeration that he was at the mercy of his court's assignment clerk.

Interviewer: You don't know what cases are your cases until . . .
Judge: Not 'til I walk down that road.
Interviewer: If you finish a case and you're ready for another case, do you let [the docket administrator] know?
Judge: You don't even let [the administrator] know anymore. She knows! And that next case is in here.

Individual calendars let judges experiment with different ways of scheduling the court appearances of cases assigned to them. How judges chose to schedule their cases was only partly a problem of deciding how to manage their court time. It was also a question of how they felt about case scheduling as a means of influencing the work habits of attorneys. The one problem inevitably involved the other.

How to Schedule Cases: Dates Certain, Cattle Calls, or Standbys?

If a judge has "x" number of cases and "y" number of days to dispose of them, when should the judge call the cases for trial? In courts with individual calendars, judges solved this problem in three different ways.[5] One option was to give attorneys a "date certain"—that is,

---

5. As pointed out in Chapter 2, prosecutors in some of the courts often managed the judges' dockets and scheduled the appearance of cases. While this strengthened the prosecutor's hand in some instances, the judges still set the basic policy rules on how cases would be called. The issue of who actually called the docket will be discussed later. Instead this section focuses on the issue of *how* felony matters were scheduled.

lawyers were notified of the specific dates on which each of their cases would be called. The attorneys, assured of when their cases would be tried, presumably prepared accordingly. Alternatively, judges could call their entire docket or list of pending cases on the very first day of the trial term through a "cattle call." Attorneys knew they and their clients had to appear in court, but they did not know when their cases actually would be heard. Judges using the third option, the "standby" approach, set specific trial dates for particular cases. They then created a second queue of cases that did not have trial dates. Instead the judges assigned priorities to the cases and used them as backups to their scheduled cases. Attorneys were notified accordingly.

Most judges adopted the date certain policy and spread their cases over a trial term. This policy, however, created a problem with no easy solution. Either too few cases or too many could be scheduled for a particular day or week. Too few cases wasted the judges' time. Too many cases meant some would be postponed or continued. Only with hindsight would the "correct" number of cases be known with certainty. From one day to the next, there was no foolproof way of knowing that the number of cases scheduled for that day would be the "right" number. As the following judge discovered, conflicting schedules were one reason for this uncertainty and thus mistakes; another was that attorneys sometimes concealed their intentions.

There's a feel to scheduling. You've got several courts and so many trial attorneys. The cross-scheduling gets real bad. And the attorneys play games. They'll use one trial notice against another. . . . But if you buy into that, then you'll end up in trouble.

"Cattle calls" eliminated this guesswork. The few judges who used cattle calls kept attorneys guessing; they were not susceptible to the attorneys' "games." Lawyers knew their cases were on the trial docket for the current trial term. What they did not know was *when* their cases would be called. One judge argued that cattle calls forced attorneys to prepare their cases.

I set maybe six to fifteen felony cases for jury trial every Monday. Now, obviously, I can't try them all at once. So I have the lawyers all come in at one time. The problem is to get them talking so I can assess priorities without giving an indication that "well, you're fifth on the list so you don't have to worry about preparing." You don't *ever* want to give them that impression. You want to have them all prepared. That's my style.

Another judge extended the logic behind this reasoning. Instead of bringing in six or fifteen cases at a time, why not call every case on the docket? This judge felt he would be busiest if he required *every* pending or open case on his docket to appear in his courtroom on the first day of the trial term. The solution to setting too few cases was simple—schedule all pending cases for the same day. As he explained, "If you set six cases a day and they all settle, you do nothing the rest of the day." While some judges in other courts used different, modified forms of the cattle call, only a couple of judges used the cattle call in its complete form. A knowledgeable attorney described the dynamics of these cattle calls.

> Every case on the docket will be set—I guess maybe fifty or sixty cases. The judge takes the bench by 8:30. . . . What happens is that the judge's clerk takes the computer printout and starts with case number one and goes right down the list. He'll call every case and the prosecutor might say, "Judge, you disposed of that case on a motion a month ago." And then the clerk'll call the next case. That might be a plea and the judge'll say, "We'll pass that matter."

> Let's say the next case the defense attorney says, "We're ready for trial." The judge will then tell the attorneys to approach the bench. The judge says to the prosecutor, "Have you offered anything in this case?" And he'll say, "I offered him an attempt." Then the judge looks at the defense attorney, "Why don't you take it?" The attorney might say, "Well, judge, my guy thinks he can beat it because there's an identification issue here." The judge looks back at the prosecutor, who says, "I'm ready for trial. I've got three eyewitnesses. Let him try to beat that."

> At which point the judge turns to the attorney and asks, "What's his record like?" The attorney says, "Well, he's got three prior felony convictions." Then the judge tells the attorney, "With that kind of record, he better take that plea, because if he goes to trial and gets convicted, with his prior record, I'm gonna have to give him the maximum." It's not very subtle.

By the end of the call, the judges had winnowed out the cases that were most likely to go to trial. These cases were called on a case-by-case basis over the course of the trial term. The judges prepared no master list. As one case was completed, the judges decided which case to call next. Attorneys were left on tenterhooks as to when their cases might begin. Cattle calls, the judges thought, cut down on bluffing and stalling. A prosecutor confirmed this hunch: "The first day of trial term we play a kind of game with the defense attorneys: 'We're ready. Are you?' It's the only time I get a lot of pleas to be perfectly honest, because it's time to put up or shut up."

Cattle calls turned the tables on lawyers. Instead of being at the mercy of attorneys, judges put the lawyers at their mercy. In contrast, date certain policies accommodated lawyers by establishing presumably predictable trial queues, although the price of accommodation was often lost court time and disrupted dockets. If a case "folded" and went as a guilty plea after an attorney had assured a judge that it would be a two-day trial, the judge's courtroom went empty until the next scheduled trial or until another case could be found to plug the gap in the judge's schedule. On the other hand, if a case took longer than expected, cases next in line would be "bumped" to another day. With cattle calls, judges controlled the sequence of cases in their trial queues, but at the expense of inconveniencing attorneys, who were uncertain as to when their cases would be called.

Standby was a compromise between these two options. When cases folded instead of going to trial or had to be postponed, standby cases were inserted, according to their priority, into these unexpected openings. One judge described how he used standbys in his courtroom.

I have what I call a day-to-day [standby]. I have a yellow pad with all my cases. I say, "Okay. You're on a day-to-day basis. That means that you stay in touch because if I call in the afternoon, you'll be in trial the next morning. And if I call in the morning, you're gonna be in trial in the afternoon.

Standbys had the advantage of seeming to reduce postponement rates. Since judges did not set trial dates for cases they put on standby, they did not have to adjourn, postpone, or continue them. Assessments of courtroom performance based on continuance or postponement rates could be ambiguous under these circumstances. Cases could remain on standby for lengthy periods without ever being postponed. In courtrooms without standby lists, cases went directly onto the judges' trial dockets. Inevitably, many of these cases would be postponed or continued one or more times for various reasons.[6]

6. A suburban court provides an example. According to tabulations kept by the prosecutor's office, 40 percent of 3,538 felony cases were adjourned during a six month period. When compared to this bench-wide proportion, adjournment rates were considerably lower in courtrooms where the judges placed cases in standby queues than in those where the judges did not. For example, one judge who placed every criminal case directly on the trial docket granted adjournments 67 percent of the time. In contrast,

Policing Guilty Pleas: Four Styles of Interventions

The judge's role in the guilty plea process is much like a police officer's on the beat. Most of the time, patrol officers adjust their policing styles to local standards of social order. They generally respond to trouble rather than initiating contacts with citizens or ferreting out crimes. Their handling of violations of local rules and disruptions within the community reinforce these standards. Still, on occasion, through proactive or independent interventions, the police can create expectations within the community of future police action and thus redefine community norms and rules. Judges play a similarly mixed but mostly reactive role in criminal courtrooms.[7]

Most of the time the judges served as "watchmen," reactively guarding local norms, protecting judicial prerogatives, and intruding only when they felt it was necessary. In one state, the court rules, copied after the American Bar Association's standards, discouraged many judges from entering into guilty plea discussions. Local customs curbed overt participation in other courts. And finally, judges sometimes learned to their regret the costs attached to getting involved in the plea process. The comments by three judges in three different courts illustrate these reasons for taking cautious, reactive postures in guilty plea negotiations.

> We are not allowed to participate, under [state] rules. Our supreme
> court has been a great exponent of the American Bar Association
> guidelines. . . . I understand some jurisdictions really took advantage

---

judges who placed cases on standby had much lower rates; the average was 25 percent, and one judge granted no adjournments at all! The reason for these differences is not hard to find. In each standby courtroom the average number of cases set for trial was about 180. For the other courtrooms the number set for trial was 50 percent higher, at roughly 270 cases. With a larger number of cases but equal amounts of trial time, adjournments, not surprisingly, were more frequent in courtrooms where cases were not detoured to standby status.

7. Slightly more than two-thirds of roughly 2,200 judges assigned to criminal cases reported in one survey that they did not attend plea negotiations and that they simply ratified the terms of pleas. The reported likelihood of more active participation rose with the size of the court. The major breaking point was at sixteen to twenty-five judges. In courts with more than this number of judges, the degree of reported involvement climbed steeply. Since all nine courts in this study fell below or within this band, the reluctance of judges to immerse themselves in plea negotiations described in this chapter may reflect the size of the courts. State rules prohibiting judicial participation in these negotiations also dampened reported involvement by judges. For an analysis of the factors affecting judges' self-reported involvement in guilty plea negotiations, see Ryan et al., *American Trial Judges*, 175, 181–83.

of the situation. . . . Frankly, participation wasn't participation at all, but direction. And that's a shame.

* * *

Judge ——— accused me of prostituting my position as a judge when I gave an indication of my sentence in a guilty plea.

* * *

I have a rule: prosecutors and defense can't come into chambers at all. . . . I got an appellate court decision back on a guy who pled guilty who kept saying his attorney assured him that he talked to me and I was going to give him a particular sentence. This attorney was a friend of mine . . . that son of a bitch. We live in a fishbowl; you can't do anything. And you can't bum around with lawyers anymore.

For some judges the lesson was clear: stay away from direct guilty plea supervision, much less involvement. Indeed, a handful of judges did no policing at all. They simply made sure that the guilty pleas were properly entered and that legal niceties were followed. In effect, judges turned over to the prosecutors and attorneys the authority to check guilty pleas and their content. By accepting every plea, it could be said, the judges became little more than clerks in their own courtrooms. Two suburban judges who reported they never or almost never refused a plea disagreed with this view.

I do not reject any pleas. I don't agree with many I approve. Unless something really shocks my conscience, I will normally accept it. . . . I'd say that I've sat in criminal court a year and half, maybe two years. In that time there's been maybe fifteen or eighteen pleas that I've rejected. . . . I realize the public thinks it's a sell-out. But pleas rarely are, at least from what I've seen.

* * *

I am one of the judges who gets most of the plea agreements, for the simple reason that I will never turn down a plea agreement. . . . I will accept any plea agreement that the DA agrees to. I will never change one. . . . I will never change a plea agreement, because I figure this is an adversary proceeding between the defense attorney and the Commonwealth. They know the cases better than I.

TABLE 4.1. Policing the Guilty Plea Process.

Reactive or Proactive Intervention?	Formal or Informal Intervention?	
	Formal	Informal
Reactive	Reject pleas	Ball park pleas
	Refuse to be bound by sentencing recommendations	Impose trial penalties
	Maintain consistent sentencing; allow withdrawal of pleas	
Proactive	Institute pretrial conferences	Ad hoc, day-of-trial
	Allow "pre-plea" reports	Discourage reappointment of indigent counsel
	Require presentence investigation reports	Lobby prosecutor for changes in policies

Most judges refused to play such passive roles in the guilty plea process. They avoided active, direct involvement but still tried to influence the timing, form, or content of guilty pleas in less direct ways. Table 4.1 classifies these techniques by whether they were reactive or proactive and by whether they were formal or informal methods. Judges intervened in a reactive manner when they rejected pleas, refused to be bound by recommendations attached to pleas, or penalized defendants who demanded jury trials. Such actions usually reaffirmed local standards governing the form and content of guilty pleas while discouraging jury trials. Judges acted proactively when they required reviews of cases prior to trial or when they took less formal steps to shape the guilty plea process. They also acted proactively if they altered the incentives influencing the behavior of defense attorneys.

Formal actions differed from informal ones, although the distinction was sometimes blurred. Formal actions, in general, required judges to exercise their authority in the courtroom. Pretrial conferences had to be scheduled, presentence reports ordered, or pleas rejected. Informal interventions were a matter of lobbying the participants in the plea process or of providing information and assurances that cleared the way for pleas.

Judges did not use one method to the exclusion of others. They picked and chose those with which they were most comfortable and, to some extent, those that fit local courthouse customs. The mix of means varied among judges and across courts. The following discussion begins with the reactive forms of policing guilty pleas and then moves on to the proactive methods.

Reactive, Formal Interventions

When a judge turned down a guilty plea, the grapevine quickly spread the news. If the judge refused another plea in a similar case and then a third, the attorneys' "book" on judges soon included a new entry on that judge's plea preferences. Declarations from the bench that sentencing recommendations would not be heeded had the same effects. In a more positive vein, some judges assiduously strove for consistency in their sentencing and allowed attorneys to withdraw pleas if the judges' sentences exceeded expectations. These methods were reactive, because judges did not initiate negotiations over pleas. The judges responded to what attorneys put before them. At the same time, as these actions accumulated over time, they became part of the courthouse culture and shaped the court's guilty plea process. They were formal acts, because judges exercised their authority in open court with respect to specific cases.

To *reject guilty pleas* as a matter of routine was not feasible, and few judges did so regularly. As long as pleas followed the court community's going rates or did not offend the judges' sense of justice, the pleas were accepted. To reject a plea, then, was a signal that the prosecutors and attorneys had exceeded the bounds of court community norms. As a sampling of the judges' comments indicates, judges refused pleas when they objected to a sentence recommendation or felt a reduction in the primary charge was not appropriate.

> Criminal cases begin to fit within a pattern. Sentences begin to fit within a pattern. . . . Everyone knows what the ranges are. . . . They [prosecutors and defense lawyers] have been around long enough to know that if a plea bargain comes in and it's not within the range, we won't accept it.

> * * *

> I'm a pragmatist. . . . If a plea fits within a scale of what I would say is reasonable, I will accept it. I do reject pleas. And I reject them both ways, both from the standpoint that the prosecutor wants too much and the defense wants too little.

*   *   *

I'd say that 65 percent of the time, I'll go along with their plea bargaining if it's within reason. . . . I'm getting more and more concerned about charging a fellow with armed robbery and then letting him plead to robbery. Now, he had a weapon or they wouldn't have charged him that way. Why are they closing their eyes to the weapon now? I've asked them about it, and they say, "Well, he'll take a plea to that." I told them, "If you can't make a case, don't indict him."

*   *   *

If you've got a man charged with five burglaries and he wants to plead to two, I don't see any harm in it. If he's charged with burglary and he wants to plead to unlawful entry, I don't approve of that. . . . I don't want real burglaries knocked down. I can see throwing a couple of charges out and pleading to the balance. But they don't even try anything else with me because I've told them I don't want it.

*   *   *

Very often I'll say, for example, "I'm rejecting this [sentence recommendation] because it isn't enough. I want this individual to go to the outpatient center for treatment of his problem." I've rejected many pleas on that basis. And they'll immediately walk back in and say, "Judge, we agree with you. We're amending our plea."

Many judges felt that sentencing recommendations as part of guilty pleas infringed on their prerogatives and sought to *retain their sentencing authority* by refusing to follow these recommendations.[8] They declined to be bound by the recommendations and said so in court when guilty pleas were entered. As one judge stated, "I don't want the district attorney to recommend a sentence. . . . Occasionally one will move in that direction, and I usually tell him that I'm not interested." A judge in another court said, "I won't agree to a sentence in advance. . . . I put on the record, 'I'm not bound by this.'" Judges who objected to sentence recommendations generally wanted to see a presentence report before they pronounced sentence.

8. The nine courts were nearly evenly divided on this issue. The judges in four courts refused to accept sentencing recommendations, while in four others, and occasionally a fifth, the judges usually followed recommendations in guilty pleas.

Here's how I run a plea bargain. . . . I want them to understand that what they recommend to me is only that, it's a recommendation. The ultimate sentencing prerogative and duty are mine. That's what I get paid for. I'm here as a judge and I'm supposed to be the person who makes that ultimate determination.

*   *   *

I'm trying a case this morning, apparently, because I would not accept the plea where they recommended a sentence. Now that's my fault. But it just isn't in me to turn over to them my responsibility to the community. . . . They don't have the information at the time of the plea that I do from our presentence reports. They're plea bargaining in the dark.

Attorney uncertainty about sentences, not necessarily their stringency, often blocked guilty plea negotiations. *Consistent sentencing patterns* by judges made the attorneys' work easier. As one judge claimed, "All they want is consistency out of a judge. Attorneys hate judges who have no idea of what they're gonna do. With me, they know what I'm gonna do. That's what they're after." One major ingredient of this tactic was enough time on the bench to establish a sentencing reputation. Another was giving attorneys the option of withdrawing pleas if the sentences fell outside their expectations. The following judge explained how he was able to avoid direct participation in plea negotiations without impeding the flow of guilty pleas through his courtroom.

I don't get into plea bargaining at all. I will not make any deals. I know what I did in 1964 when I first got on the bench. I didn't make any plea bargains then and I don't now because I never have. . . . I just tell them, "Plead him guilty first. . . . Talk to the prosecuting attorneys. They'll tell you what I've done in the past on these kinds of cases. I pretty well do the same thing. I don't make deals with criminals." Now, if later on my sentence is beyond what the prosecutor told him he thought it would be, then, if the prosecutor has no objection, I'll let him withdraw the plea. That's as far as I'll go. I'll tell you this much, it doesn't slow things down at all.

Reactive, Informal Interventions

Judges who wanted to avoid a reputation for or the appearance of plea bargaining were not without other means of facilitating negotiations. They could display a hands-off attitude by *ballparking* sentences or, as one judge put it, by talking about "generalities and how I think." This gave judges a way of meeting attorney interests without committing themselves to specific terms.

> I don't deal. No deals. No bargains. "I ain't got no contract with the defendant." That's what I tell defense counsel. Yeah, we'll talk about generalities and how I think. Besides, if you've been around for a while, you already know what I think. But for the guy who hasn't been around for a while, I'll tell him generally how I feel. No deals, though. "Don't tell that client of yours that he's got a lock on it." No deals. That's my style.

*   *   *

> I will not give a number out. If the defense attorney looks at me, like, "What do you think?", I'll say, "If your guy is as clean as you say he is, then I can tell you this, I will not send him to prison. You can take that back with you." Now I put that on the record. I've pulled prison as an option. I don't know if it's quite cricket, but I only go that far.

*   *   *

> To me, sentence bargaining is where the defense counsel wants to be sure what his client is gonna get. . . . But I just do not do that. I will talk in parameters. I might say, "If that's all he's got, I'm not gonna send him to prison. I don't know what I'm gonna do." I say, "It's clearly understood there's been no agreement between the prosecutor and the defense counsel that this court has agreed on any sentence whatsoever. Period." And that's the way I do it.

A second reactive, informal method of governing the guilty plea process was to impose *trial penalties* on defendants who insisted on a trial. Judges admitted they might sentence defendants more severely after a trial under certain circumstances.[9] Many admitted they might impose a heavier sentence if they thought a defendant committed perjury. Others felt they were sometimes swayed by what they learned about a defendant and the case after a trial. Trial penalties, by discouraging "unnecessary" or "illegitimate" trials, encouraged a steady stream of pleas.

9. Statistical evidence regarding trial penalties in the nine courts was mixed. See Nardulli, Eisenstein, and Flemming, *Tenor of Justice*, 244–45, 257–59.

A responsible defense attorney should tell his client that there will be a time when the People will rest in the trial. "What are we gonna do? Are you gonna get up there and cross wits with them? If you do, you may be digging yourself a grave, because if the jury says, 'You're a lyin' son of a bitch,' and the judge says, 'That jury is so right,' then you're probably gonna get yourself some more sentence." Fair enough? You've got a right to a trial. You don't have a right to lie under oath.

* * *

If it's a legitimate trial, it doesn't make any difference to me. But I had one just recently where this fellow got on the stand and lied. . . . The result is he got himself more than he would have gotten away with on an ordinary plea.

* * *

Judges get to see a lot more facts in a trial that are never reflected adequately in the presentence report. The blood . . . the gore . . . the sadism . . . the dishonesty. . . . The judge's nose gets rubbed in all this, and it shows up in the sentence. Almost invariably, a trial doesn't work to the defendant's advantage, because most criminals are not nice people.

Proactive, Formal Interventions

Pretrial conferences are supposed to help judges manage their dockets more efficiently. They are controversial because they seem to undermine traditional precepts regarding the judge's role. Some critics argue the blindfold slips from Justice's eyes when judges conduct settlement conferences in civil cases, since their involvement jeopardizes judicial impartiality.[10] The issue becomes more contentious in criminal cases where the presumption of innocence is at stake. Many judges cited this as a reason for not holding pretrial conferences in felony matters, while others argued that pretrial conferences did not live up to their promise.

The frequency and style of "pretrialing" varied considerably within and across courts with individual calendars. (None of the master calen-

10. Judith Resnick provides a critical view of what she calls "managerial judges" in "Managerial Judges," *Harvard Law Review* 96(December 1982):374–448. For a thorough review of the issues surrounding pretrial settlement strategies in civil cases in federal courts, see D. Marie Provine, *Settlement Strategies for Federal District Courts* (Washington, D.C.: Federal Judicial Center, 1986).

dar courts had formal pretrial conferences.) Some judges used them to clear away the legal underbrush of cases destined for trial. A few took advantage of the opportunity to hammer out the terms of guilty pleas. While the pattern was far from perfect, judges who were comfortable with pretrial conferences in civil cases also held them in criminal cases. Less experienced judges favored them because they could use the conferences as a quick way of becoming familiar with their caseloads. The comments made by the following judges offer a few illustrations of what they hoped to achieve through the conferences.

> My conferences are not on the record. They're for me to get acquainted with the case to see what it's like—how long it is going to take to try it, if there are any difficulties that I should handle before the trial date, and so on. . . . Say, you've got a jury sitting there, cooling its heels, while attorneys bring up motions that should have been brought up beforehand. Well, my conference is to try and eliminate that, so when I call the jury in we can begin the case. . . . If you don't keep on them, they'll just float away.

*   *   *

> I figured if I spent a couple of hours on a pretrial conference and saved two weeks of court time, it was a good investment. . . . Many times the attorneys need a third party, some catalytic agent to get them off dead center. . . . On felony matters, what happens more often than not is the first thing you hear is, "Judge, we're gonna plead. Can we have a few minutes to put the plea on the record?" It works fabulously well.

*   *   *

> Now the judge should not, ethically, get into plea bargaining. But, on the other hand, I think the judge can ask about it. And every once in a while, maybe one out of a dozen cases or one out of twenty, I find one where somebody dropped the ball. . . . So I'll say right there at the pretrial conference, "Get out in the hall and talk to your client." You nail it down if you know it's not gonna go.

Whether pretrial conferences led to discussions about the terms of guilty pleas depended on more than judges' involvement in these conferences. Prosecutor policies could tie the assistants' hands. For instance, in one court community, assistant prosecutors lost their jobs if they violated office policies prohibiting sentence negotiations. Nevertheless, pretrial conferences often turned to the subject of sentencing in this court. Most of the judges shied away from explicit sentencing bargaining; many voiced the same objection, "I don't deal with criminals." Still, one judge candidly admitted that the prosecutor's policies left with him no other choice if he wanted to conduct his own pretrial conferences.[11]

Interviewer: What about the prosecutor's policies of no charge bargaining for certain crimes?

Judge: They certainly narrow down quite a bit the effectiveness of pretrials, because, if it's an automatic policy case, there's nothing for us to discuss other than "Do you want to plead as charged?" We end up discussing possible sentences.

Pretrial conferences were not a foolproof means of culling out guilty pleas and clearing the way for trials. Judges expected too much, lacked the needed skills, or simply bumped up against ethical or legal barriers. The following judge complained of the problems he had with his conferences.

I try to have very in-depth pretrials in criminal as well as civil cases. But I get frustrated. In criminal cases, if they're triable, I'm faced with something that doesn't come up in civil cases, and that is not being able to force the defendant to disclose his defense. He doesn't have to disclose his defense. If I start getting into that, I have to disqualify myself.

So the only way my pretrials will work is if I kind of lean on the prosecutor. I tell them that I want what they've got [with respect to evidence in the case] and then I say to the defense, "How are you gonna refute that?" But they're never prepared!

They call it "banging heads," and I suppose I do in pretrials, maybe more than others do. . . . But I spend all my time working on them. And then when I'm convinced and they're convinced that they've done a good job, and now we say, "Okay, let's go to trial," they cave in! It's a blow to your ego.

11. Sentence bargaining became more prevalent after the chief prosecutor cracked down on plea bargaining. It continued after several years for the same reasons Church outlined in a study of the effects of a similar policy in what he called "Hampton County." See Thomas W. Church, Jr., "Plea Bargains, Concessions and the Courts: Analysis of a Quasi-Experiment," *Law and Society Review* 10(Spring 1976), 377.

The time spent on pretrial conferences was supposed to pay dividends by eliminating cases from the trial docket that would fold and go as guilty pleas or, worse yet, lead to unnecessary trials. The rewards of pretrial conferences depended greatly on how well judges managed their time. Pretrial conferences were no panacea for judges who used their time poorly. A knowledgeable attorney described one such judge.

This one judge had criminal pretrials set at 8:30 in the morning every single day of the week except Monday. That was done regardless of whether it was a criminal term or civil term or a nonjury term or jury term or vacation term or anything else. He had the computer spitting out notices [to appear] constantly.

At 8:30 there would be five defense attorneys and their clients there plus the prosecutors. But it might be a civil day. This meant there might be twenty-five civil cases out in the courtroom. And the judge would want to speak with all those civil attorneys to see if any of them wanted mediation, whether any were going to trial, whether any were going to settle, whether any of them needed more time to get ready.

And he'd leave the five criminal defense attorneys and prosecutors sitting there for two or three or four or five or six hours. Maybe during the course of the entire day he'd never get to them because he was in chambers doing all this talking.

A judge can't use his time in that manner and be efficient. What happened is that he picked up a reputation of not being able to get things done. A reputation of where, if you got to that court, he wouldn't release you and you'd spend your whole day there.

So then what happened is that the attorneys wouldn't show up. They'd all go to their other court assignments first and come to his court last. Which meant it might be 4:30 in the afternoon. And he might have an evidentiary hearing going on on a divorce case. Even though the attorneys at that point could work something out, you couldn't put it on the record because the judge was doing something else. . . . The judge was a workhorse, but if he was anywhere near being efficient, he could work half as much and get twice as much done.

Judges generally knew little about the defendants or cases that attorneys brought before them. By *allowing "pre-plea reports"* and presentence reports, judges could draw their own conclusions about cases. Pre-plea reports were ordered by a small number of judges in two suburban courts at the request of attorneys when the judges arraigned their clients. These reports were like presentence reports. Consequently, they reduced uncertainties that blocked guilty plea negotiations, as one judge explained.

> All of us in isolated instances had the defense lawyer and prosecutor say: "Look, Judge, if you get a pre-plea, the guy can see what's gonna happen, and he'll probably plead. But he's got a prior record, and he doesn't know whether he's gonna get life or five to twenty." So you call the probation department and get a report. You give the defendant the report, he relaxes, and he pleads. Or he doesn't. In either case, it clears the air.

Pre-plea reports in one of these courts openly acknowledged what had been a judicially blessed practice followed by defense attorneys who took advantage of the state's "Youthful Trainee Act" (YTA). These motions led to the preparation of a report that included the probation department's recommendation regarding probation. YTA motions became popular after the DA banned charge reductions in drug cases.[12] Although the motions were filed some time after arraignment in circuit court, their purpose was the same as asking for a pre-plea report—to clear the air about probable sentences.

Two of the three states did not require *presentence reports* after a conviction or guilty plea, which meant that attorneys could ask to waive their preparation. Judges in three of the six courts generally went along with whatever attorneys wanted. But judges in the other three courts refused to pronounce sentence without a report from the probation department. By holding back their sentences in this way, the judges removed sentencing from negotiations over guilty pleas and thus influenced the content of guilty pleas in their courts. Sentencing recommendations were rarely part of the plea packages in these three courts. Comments by two judges illustrate how this proactive approach shaped the guilty plea process.

> We always say the same thing: "We're not bound by this plea bargain. We'll take a look at the presentence investigation. If it supports what has been represented to the court, we'll consider it. If not, we will

12. Church reports that the proportion of similar dispositions rose from 3 percent to 16 percent after the "Hampton County" prosecutor instituted a similar policy. Church, "Plea Bargains, Concessions and the Courts," 389.

not." Otherwise I think it's the judge projecting himself into an area where he doesn't belong.

* * *

Now, that's a policy of mine. I won't permit the attorneys to waive a sentencing hearing. Whenever their client is getting probation or the agreed sentence is probation, I want to see the report. I want to know who I'm putting on probation, because in the final analysis the judge is gonna be held to account.

Proactive, Informal Interventions

Trial dates often led attorneys to rethink their positions. A judicial nudge might be all that was needed to switch a plea of not guilty to guilty. With the prospect of a trial close on the horizon, the judge's "bargaining" position improved and the likelihood of *ad hoc, day-of-the trial* interventions increased.

On the day of trial, we might call both the prosecutor and defense attorney and ask them, "Is this gonna be a plea?" If they say no, then the next question is, "Do you have any special *voir dire* questions you want to ask the jurors?"

* * *

That's it. I don't go beyond this to say, "Can't you get together?" because I don't know the facts. But we still get into discussions on the day of trial, though. Sometimes the defense attorney says, "Judge, if he's convicted, is there a chance that he might get probation?" That's kind of the thing I mean. But I don't put pressure on them.

* * *

Judges here don't participate in plea bargaining until it's brought into court. . . . It's not a regular practice, but during a court term, somebody might come in and say, "If this fellow were gonna get [a regional minimal security prison] rather than prison, he might plead." During the trial term, when you are waiting for trial, that might happen.

Judges reluctant to participate in plea discussions but anxious to keep their trial dockets clear of cases that could be resolved through pleas found ways of tipping off attorneys about their views. They tried to cue attorneys that they were prepared to make sentencing adjustments.

These adjustments rested on trust and mutual understanding, not explicit agreements. Attorneys familiar with the judges knew the signals; less knowledgeable ones had to learn them, which could be hard in courts with stiff prosecutor policies. According to one judge, "A lot of our new lawyers still feel that you've got to knock down the original all the time. I try to infer in particular cases that they'd be better off just pleading their clients, and I'll take that into account." He then elaborated on the problem of teaching attorneys when to pay attention to his hints when the prosecutor was being obstinate.

I've got a guy that will plead to armed robbery right now. It carries a life maximum. And he's got three of them. . . . The prosecutor's offering a plea to two and dropping one, which isn't a hell of a deal. I think he would take it if I would say that I will not give him life. I might give him any number of years, but I'm not gonna give him life. I hinted a couple of times, but the lawyer isn't picking up on it. So I asked the prosecutor, "Well, why don't you recommend to me that I not give the guy life?" But the prosecutor says, "I'm not gonna do that." So there you are. . . .

On another occasion, this judge succeeded in going around a balky prosecutor by getting a defense attorney to respond to the judge's cues about filing a Youthful Trainee motion.

The prosecutor refused to plea bargain in an armed robbery case even though the individual in this case was just a tagalong. With mandatory prison sentences for armed robbery, you could stick a seventeen year old in that state prison meat grinder for a first offense without even a juvenile record. I just couldn't picture a first offender there. So I talked to the prosecutor to see if he could give some kind of reduced charge so I wouldn't have to send this kid to prison. He wouldn't do it. So the defense attorney finally got the idea and applied for YTA and I accepted it to avoid the mandatory prison sentence.

Judges significantly *influenced defense attorney incentives* for those who represented indigent defendants. In one court community, judges appointed attorneys from individual lists of lawyers on a case-by-case basis. According to one prosecutor, "There are favorite attorneys around here who get appointments because they move cases. I'm not saying that they sell their clients down the river, but they don't waste time, and the judges appreciate that." Another deputy discussed what these judges looked for when deciding to give defense lawyers further appointments.

> If you're a young attorney and you come in and want an appointment, chances are you'll get it. You'll get appointed to something. And the judge'll ask me, "Well, how 'bout this guy? Does he seem prepared? Make appropriate arguments? Is he reasonable?" If he's got a guy who's charged with breaking and entering and they caught him with the goods in a bag, crawling out the window, and he wants to go to trial, the judge will ask, "Why do you want to go to trial? What issue is there to try in this case?" If the attorney says, "My man says he didn't do it," well, you know, that guy probably will not get any more appointments.

When judges were unhappy with attorneys, they stopped sending cases their way. As one judge frankly declared, "I know their work. I know whether they're honest or dishonest. If they're dishonest, they're long gone. If they waste my time, they're long gone."

In another county, the bench's opinion of attorneys carried weight with the county commissioners when the county awarded the contract to several attorneys to serve as counsel for indigent defendants. The judges were very displeased with an earlier set of contract attorneys. The attorneys who won the new contract were well aware of what the judges expected of them. According to one of the judges:

> The previous group had no conception of what they were doing to the system. I don't think they were representing their clients any better because they wouldn't plea bargain. It was contrary to their philosophy. To them, it was "Every person is entitled to his day in court." The present ones plea bargain and get their client off on a better deal. . . . They've got a different philosophy, a philosophy of doing the best they can for a client—on a plea bargain, if possible.

Elsewhere the judges also had ways of influencing defense attorneys. In one of the states, the judges appointed the chief public defenders. Chief public defenders who ran afoul of the bench quickly learned the error of their ways. One bench forced the chief public defender to give up his post after he offended one of the judges. Another public defender bowed to the demands of the judges that his assistant public defenders be assigned to the judges' courtrooms. "[The PD] hated that when it happened," one of his assistants reported, "because then he lost control over us."

Rigid guilty plea policies created problems for judges. If pretrial conferences, pre-pleas, or requiring presentence reports failed to solve the problems, the judges at times *lobbied the chief prosecutor* to relax the policies. A judge recalled how he finally convinced an insurgent DA that his ban on plea bargaining in concealed weapon cases needed to be lifted in some instances. (This judge was politically well connected and supported the chief prosecutor. He was the only judge whose court-room prosecutor remained with him for several years, a stark exception to the chief prosecutor's policy of periodic rotation.) This judge recalled:

> We showed him a couple of cases that would just shock your con-science that this person was gonna have a felony conviction. I mean, it could be a business guy with a permit to use the gun only for work purposes, but he's out socially and he's got the gun in the car or something like that. Now, we're gonna give this guy a felony? Well, he took a look at it and said, "I'm gonna think about it." Well, next thing you know, he has a new policy where if there're no priors for CCW [carrying a concealed weapon], he will leave it to the discretion of the assistant to make a deal or not. This has helped tremendously.

Judges in another court community with an insurgent DA faced a slightly different obstacle. Under state law, attorneys had to agree to a conference with judges when they felt they needed a judge to review the terms of tentative pleas. The prosecutor's office prohibited assistants from taking part in these conferences because the chief prosecutor feared the judges would twist his assistants' arms. In order to get around this prohibition, the judges encouraged defense attorneys to enter "blind pleas." Such pleas did not include sentence recommendations. As one judge remarked, "I just say to defense attorneys, 'Plead blind. Plead 'em blind. You know where I stand, right? Plead 'em blind.'" This judge discussed a case in more detail to illustrate how he applied pressure on the state's attorney for a policy exception.

> I had a kid in here for selling coke, enough for a [mandatory prison offense]. No record. Finished high school. Lived with his father and mother. His father was an ex-policeman, in fact. Pretty good home life. They got him for selling coke to an FBI agent. They had him dead; he was cold. Now, I didn't want to send this kid to the peniten-tiary for six years or even with good behavior for three. It was a

horrible thing. The kid was scared stiff. I think he really learned his lesson.

We tried to have a conference. I tried like mad. I kept saying, "You got a tentative plea agreement?" But the prosecutor kept saying, "My bottom line is six years in the penitentiary. What else can I do? You know it's six years because it's a [mandatory prison offense]. Besides, that's what the Indictment Committee says." Well, we jockey around a while. So I tell him what kind of probation I would give the kid. "Go back to the Indictment Committee and tell them what kind of probation I would give if they reduce it. . . ."

Everyone knew that as long as it stayed a [mandatory prison offense] that the lowest thing I could give was six years. . . . Finally, the prosecutor comes back and says, "The committee will go for it." So they reduced it. Now, that's a case where you negotiate up front.

In a county where the DA's office did not have rigid policies, the office's lenient warrant standards created problems for the circuit court. The judges complained about the quality of the cases and grumbled about the mounting number of cases awaiting trial. A younger judge lobbied the prosecutor directly and indirectly through his assistants and through the courthouse grapevine, but without success.

We have a super chief judge. He has the respect of everyone. But he doesn't feel he should put pressure on [the DA]. What I do is that I know the feelings of the other judges, and when they complain about the garbage they're doing, I pass that along to [the DA]. I try to convince him that he's not getting the results anybody wants. He just doesn't see that. The judges view him poorly because of that.

Most of his assistants are carrying my message back to him. I know he's got a lot of my messages back because I intend it that way. I guess I'm trying to get the assistants to revolt. I want them to say to [the DA], "Hey, you aren't the guy up there getting all this crap. We are. We think you ought to reconsider that." Apparently it's not getting through to him, though. I don't know why. He's not a strong person. I would think that if enough assistants got together, then he would change. But he hasn't. I don't understand why he doesn't.

Judges in another court community had greater success. They worried that the defense bar took advantage of the prosecutor's inexperienced staff. The judges urged him to review all guilty pleas. Soon after their request, as the following judge explained, the DA started personally approving all guilty pleas before they were presented in court.

> As a matter of court policy, we require that the district attorney, not a subordinate, certify in the file that he concurs in that plea bargain. . . . We don't ask for the reasons on the record; for a number of reasons, that is not always possible, from their point of view. And that's probably the principle reason why we want the district attorney to certify he's satisfied with the plea. . . . We know that he is subject to the public's scrutiny and criticism, and so he will not lightly recommend plea bargains.

Doing Justice: Aspects of Organizing Sentencing Work

The actual sentencing process took various forms in the courts. In some courts it occurred as part of the guilty plea ceremony. The judge accepted the plea and followed the sentencing recommendation after ratifying the plea in open court. In others, sentencing was postponed until after a presentence report was completed. The court communities in one of the states were distinctive in that after the presentence reports were completed most of the judges held "sentencing conferences" in chambers prior to going into open court. The comments of the following judges sketched a description of these conferences.

> I take the presentence reports home, look them over, and make up my mind as to what the sentence ought to be. Then, when I get here in chambers, I've got the sentencing panel's recommendation and I talk to the probation officer and the prosecutor ahead of time. If they have some different ideas and there's some reason I ought to adjust my thoughts a little bit before defense counsel comes in, I adjust it a little bit there. Then I get the defense counsel and we sit down and talk. Sometimes I'll make adjustments because of what he says. He'll steer me back. I'll give in to him sometimes.

* * *

> The prosecutor sits there, the probation man sits there, and the defense sits there. Then I read to them what the sentencing panel said. I say, "What do you think? Agree or disagree? What's your reasons?" Not any long thing, though, because my mind is probably

95 percent made up beforehand. . . . Some decisions are automatic. A lot of them I have questions about. Too hard. Too soft. Too something. And when I'm talking to them, they might tell me something that will enlighten me or change my mind.

Sentencing conferences satisfied several judicial needs. The presentence reports could be checked for errors or omissions. The judges could see how the attorneys reacted to the information or recommendations in the reports. Most important was the opportunity the conferences gave attorneys to express their true feelings about cases and to say things that would prove embarrassing if said in open court. As one of judges said, "You know, in chambers, they're gonna say a heck of a lot more and tell me a lot more than if they have to put it all on the record." Another judge explained this advantage in more detail.

If the defense attorney has to get up in open court, he's gonna have to say this man should be on probation, when you damn well know the guy should be in prison. In chambers, you can sit down and he can say, "Yeah, judge, I know he's got to go. But how about giving him four and a half instead of the recommended five? So I know that I've done something for the poor slob? I charged him $500. How about a couple of months?"

Or they come in here and say, "That son of a gun has done this, this, and this." But here's where the human factor enters into it. You can't put it on the record because the defense lawyer would be subject to a bar grievance if he didn't say every time that his client ought to have probation. . . . He won't be able to tell me things like, "He's a no good son of a gun and he deserves to be zinged, but not that bad, judge." Putting the whole thing on record is gonna destroy what is really the human part of this whole thing.

A few judges refused to hold these conferences, for various reasons. As one judge recalled, "I used to until the state appellate defenders made an issue of something that was said about a defendant at one of my conferences." Another complained, "I got fouled up once. I made a horrible mistake of letting in an attorney who was related to the defendant." He went on to explain:

He wasn't representing him or anything at the presentence. What does he do, but file a motion on something I said. Boy, I can tell you that guy hasn't been in this office since. He had no business being in here; I was just being kind. And they you get kicked in the teeth.

These judges worried about the appearance of such conferences in the eyes of defendants, victims, and their families or friends, in addition to the court of appeals and state appellate defenders. Closed-door sessions, they felt, jeopardized the legitimacy of the process by making it vulnerable to accusations of special pleadings and favoritism. Other judges did not disagree, but thought the benefits of informal candor outweighed these disadvantages.

Most sentencing ceremonies were cut-and-dried rituals, but they did not have to be, if the judge chose to use sentencing as an opportunity to talk directly to defendants. If there was a point the judges wanted to make, a lecture they wished to give, or a lesson they hoped to impart, the time when they pronounced sentence was their chance. One judge noticed that the sequence in which he took his cases could be used to send messages to defendants waiting their turn.

You can play with the crowd. It's just amazing. When I was a lower court judge, I used to do it on some days. If I wanted to get done quickly that morning, I'd sentence the first guy to jail, and I'd get all not guilty pleas right afterwards. I'd set them all for trial and get off the bench. But if I went the other way, I would spend the whole morning there. . . .

I do that now with my sentences. Like, maybe, I'll sentence two or three at a time. I'll put them in order of probation or prison, and if I see one that I might give probation to, I'll put the guy who's gonna go to prison in front of him. Now, that guy is holding his breath. He can hardly talk. I know if I sentenced him first that he'd never get the jolt that he had come just that close to going to prison.

If you plan on giving him a speech—"One more time and you're gone!"—he knows that since he just saw a guy go in front of him, this isn't bullshit. He just saw you send a guy out the door. So, if you want him to understand that totally, that's the way to do it. Mix up your probation with your prisons. It's effective.

In one court in another state, plea conferences were used occasionally in the same way, although their formal purpose under the state's rules of procedure was to see if the judge would accept a guilty plea. The conferences were held most often in one suburban county because of the prosecutor office's obdurate bottom lines. They were off the record, giving the judge the freedom to say things that would be impossible in open court. One judge graphically described one such conference.

Usually there's no record. I'm just sitting there talking to them and in this one case we're kicking around what this kid should get. A lot of times I'll scare the hell out of a kid by starting off by saying, "Well, I want penitentiary time on this kid. He's got a couple misdemeanors. He's never gonna make it on probation." And the kid starts to sweat.

Then I say, "You know what happens to you down there? First of all, you're gonna be put in a cell and they'll gang-rape you. You'll have a hell of time in there. You'll be sucking cocks for three days straight." But a lot of kids you can tell them all you want. A lot of them don't really understand. That's the trouble. You're not talking to people like us. That's the problem. What does get to them? I can't tell because I'm not like them. But I try.

I probably shouldn't talk quite as tough as I do. But when I do it, I do it off the record. I'll say, "Listen, you little son of a bitch. You're a leech. You're a drag on society. You're running your mother ragged. You're driving your father nuts. You're a leech, a bum." Maybe it affects him, maybe it doesn't. I don't know.

Summary

Judges designed their own work routines and exercised considerable latitude in how they wanted to handle their work. They set their own work rhythms. Their decisions on how to budget their time and schedule the appearances of cases created courtrooms with very different work tempos. Judges similarly policed the guilty plea process and conducted their sentencing ceremonies in varied ways. They picked and chose those methods with which they were personally, professionally, and politically comfortable. But again the result was sometimes a courthouse in which there were as many ways of processing a guilty plea and sentencing a convicted felony defendant as there were judges. For prosecutors and defense attorneys, diversity in the judges' bench craft put a premium on knowing how judges organized their work if they hoped to practice their own crafts effectively.

Part III
The Craft of Defense

Chapter 5
Defensive Craft: Why Getting Along Is (Mostly) Going Along

Introduction

Defense attorneys lack the stature and authority of judges. They rarely, if ever, have the political clout of prosecutors. In effect, defense attorneys stand in the shadow of their clients' criminal stigma. Few prosecutors are regularly asked the kinds of questions the public asks defense lawyers, such as, "How can you defend those people?" and "How can you sleep nights?"[1] Attorneys in public defenders' offices or lawyers who are assigned to represent indigent clients must even overcome the doubts of their own clients, as typified by the question, "Did you have a lawyer when you went to court?" and its now classic reply, "No, I had a public defender."[2]

In addition, the career prospects of defense attorneys are financially dependent on the court community in ways that those of judges and prosecutors are not. Judges do not receive their salaries from prosecutors, and prosecutors do not depend on judges for cases. The court community, however, through its policies on the representation of indigent defendants, shapes the market for criminal defense lawyers, distributing cases and paying attorneys for representing poor defen-

1. See James S. Kunen, "*How Can You Defend Those People?*" *The Making of a Criminal Lawyer* (New York: Random House, 1983), and Lisa McIntyre, "But How Can You Sleep Nights?" in *The Public Defender: The Practice of Law in the Shadows of Repute* (Chicago: University of Chicago Press, 1987), 139–70.

2. The client's view was first described in Jonathan D. Casper, "Did You Have a Lawyer When You Went to Court? No, I Had a Public Defender," *Yale Review of Law and Social Action* 4(Spring 1971):4. Casper's article spawned a rather substantial body of research probing the experiences and views of criminal defendants. For a review of this research plus one of the few explorations of the attorney's perspective, see Roy B. Flemming, "Client Games: Defense Attorney Perspectives on Their Relations with Criminal Clients," *American Bar Foundation Research Journal* 1986(Spring 1986):253.

dants. These policies determine the extent to which criminal defense work is public or private in character and influence the size of the criminal defense bar. For the nine court communities as a whole, over half (57 percent) of all the felony cases were handled by either public defenders or attorneys who were paid by the county or court. The lowest proportion was 34 percent and the highest was 80 percent. For seven of the courts, an average of ten attorneys represented the defendants in these cases. In the other two counties, where the average proportion of public cases was over 75 percent for felonies, roughly seventy-five attorneys were involved. The demand for criminal defense work, then, was largely publicly determined, and the pool or supply of attorneys was also relatively small in these court communities.

As a consequence of these and other incentives, the work and political crafts of defense attorneys emphasized traditional, client-oriented, professional concerns. Careers and courtroom work centered on representing individual clients, not challenging the status quo. Most defense lawyers doubted whether it made economic sense or whether they would be politically successful if they approached their work with the zeal, fervor, and goals of legal reformers. The few who did soon became object lessons for the more cautious. Attorneys thus took a case-by-case approach to their work. The views of a chief public defender (PD) about the role of the PD in court were also typical of those held by assigned and contract attorneys.

When I look at the public defender's office, there are two ways you can do it. One is that we can take an overall approach and say, "We're gonna reform the criminal justice system. We're gonna make sure that the jail is corrected. We're gonna make sure that every case in which a judge does something wrong or makes a mistake is appealed." We can look at it that way.

Or we can say, "If this were my private practice, what would I do in handling a criminal case? Should I be looking out for the best interest of my client? Or should I, like the first way, be looking out for the best interests of some future client who might get arrested?"

I take the position (and fortunately it's the position that the judges and county commissioners like, and which I honestly think is the right position) that we should handle each case and each client on their own. We look at this place as a private law practice.

This case-by-case, putatively client-oriented approach muted challenges to the institutional status quo within the court community.

Instead it focused on what was "best" for individual clients, which comported with customary notions of professionalism and of doing justice.[3] This approach did not violate courthouse norms. It did not threaten the status of judges and prosecutors. Attorneys generally stood on firm ground if they could explain a particular course of action in terms of the needs or interests of specific clients. Ironically, this professional perspective weakened the institutional position of defense attorneys, whether public or private, within the courthouse community.

Webs of Relationships in Court Communities

Court communities are occupationally, politically, and geographically circumscribed. Lawyers continually run into other attorneys, prosecutors, and judges who have common work interests and experiences, similar educational backgrounds, the same stakes in local politics, and sometimes even family traditions in the practice of law. For example, in one industrial county, several firms were composed of fathers and their sons, several more were partnerships between brothers, and a couple were family firms with three generations of lawyers. Indeed, five families, each with two or more attorneys, had at least one family member sitting as a judge in either the lower or the upper court. Courthouse communities can be intensely parochial, especially if they are not large. Thickets of informal relations between attorneys, judges, and prosecutors took root easily, grew quickly, and thrived throughout the courthouse.

Defense attorneys often knew prosecutors from their high school days or from college or law school. For instance, a head public defender had shared a room in law school with the county's chief prosecutor. Even in large counties, the odds of running into someone from high school or law school were surprisingly high because of suburban segregation and because of the middle-class backgrounds of most attorneys. To cite just one example from one of the suburban counties, a defense attorney was the former high school civics teacher of a prosecutor who in turn had played Little League baseball with another defense attorney.

Politics also brought attorneys and prosecutors together. In an industrial county, an assistant public defender managed the chief prosecutor's election campaign. In one of the autonomous counties, a private attorney assumed a major role in the prosecutor's bid for office.

3. McIntyre uses the term "myth of competency" to describe this set of ideas among public defenders which leads, she argues, to the highly decentralized, loosely structured offices that are typical of public defenders. See McIntyre, *Public Defender*, 121–36.

Another lawyer in this community first met the prosecutor at a fundraising kaffeeklatsch organized by the attorney's politically involved mother. A suburban chief public defender raised campaign money for the DA because they both had gone to Notre Dame University. As he explained:

> Notre Dame guys just hang together. It's like going through the Marines. . . . So when ———— ran, it was a natural thing for me to do. . . . Just because a guy is a defense counsel doesn't mean he can't help out his friend. . . . It looks bad, but it really isn't.

Various links existed between attorneys and judges. In one county, a private attorney served in the navy with a judge and later on handled matters involving the estate of the judge's father. This lawyer also hired an attorney for his firm who subsequently went on to become a judge. In another county, a lawyer went through law school with one of the judges. A public defender clerked for another judge, an apprenticeship served by many lawyers in other counties. A suburban lawyer referring pseudonymously to his firm said, "This firm originally was Smith, Jones, and Dale. Smith went on the bench. Jones went off on his own. I merged with Dale, and now he's on the bench." In another county, two judges were former law partners of a practicing private attorney.

As these examples suggest, relations among attorneys and judges criss-crossed the court communities. Several more examples further illustrate this point.

- An attorney active in Republican politics dropped by the chambers of several judges to tell them about the Reagan inaugural festivities she had attended.
- The clerk for a judge who had been treasurer of the county Republican party dated an attorney who had once been married to a nationally prominent financial backer of the GOP. This judge got together with another attorney for drinks so they could plan a weekend skiing trip.
- In a suburban court, judges doled out masters and guardianships to public defenders and attorneys whose families were celebrating the birth of a baby.
- A law firm leased its offices in a building owned by a judge.
- A judge golfed with attorneys but scrupulously paid his own tab at the "nineteenth hole."
- Because a judge officiated at the marriage of an attorney and his spouse, the attorney felt he could "talk to him about things outside

the law." The attorney added that he represented the former clients of another judge on the bench.

- A public defender and a judge were involved in a poorly concealed romantic liaison.
- Another public defender's father was a judge on the bench, his mother was a state legislator, and his uncle had barely lost a bid for a higher court seat.
- In one of the industrial counties, roughly one-fifth of the attorneys were related to one another in some fashion through a handful of families.

Many of these relationships simply reflected coincidence or happenstance. Others did not. Attorneys looked for things they had in common with the people with whom they worked. The following attorney highlighted the value of this strategy.

I found out in a hurry you've got to have more than just a work relationship with people. I ran into [a new lower court judge] who's a total jackass. A political hack. Conscientious, but a moron. But I made certain I took the time to bullshit with him about his family, his health, about sports. It turns out we had a common acquaintance. I do that all the time. I try my best to find some common ground so the two of us can talk before we start to fight with one another.

By searching for grounds other than court work for relationships, attorneys mitigated the potential for hard feelings, grudges, and conflict lying just below the surface of formal courtroom protocol and procedures. "After a trial we go out and have dinner," a public defender said. "People ask, How can you go in and scream at each other and. . . ?' But that's just the way we are. It makes for a healthy practice and a good trial."

Reputations in the Court Community

The Importance of a Reputation

Lawyers' careers are tightly intertwined with their reputations. "You get a reputation real fast," one attorney explained, "because everybody is around the judges all the time. And it's 'Oh, this guy doesn't know what he's doing' or 'This guy is good in trial.'" Another attorney pointed out, "There's not that many people around, and after you've been here for a while you sort of know the reputations of others." A third reported, "Every active trial attorney has a reputation. . . . This guy will fold, avoid a jury. Another will go to trial. They'll have a reputation. . . . The word just spreads. It's commonly known."

It is hardly surprising that lawyers wanted to make a name for themselves. A good name attracted referrals from civil lawyers or, in some jurisdictions, appointments from judges. It meant market visibility and new clients coming in from the street. A good reputation prepared the foundation for public defenders thinking of entering private practice. Beyond these career implications, a lawyer's reputation for credibility and trustworthiness bore directly on his or her day-to-day court work.

"If you don't have credibility," one lawyer bluntly stated, "you don't have nothing." He then warned, "Trickery and deceit only get you there a few times, and then what goes around comes around, and you're through." Another lawyer advised, "To operate well around here, you have to establish a certain integrity or you're in trouble." A third attorney and former prosecutor claimed, "I have a lot of friends in the prosecutor's office. And more often than not I can count on them. But you develop that through a lot of years of fair dealing and no sleight of hand." A public defender elaborated on the kind of relationship he thought he needed in court.

> I think the basis of a good relationship is two things. Never bullshit. Never say you have a defense when you don't. And secondly, when you give your word, live up to it.

Two other attorneys explained why, as the first one emphasized, "It's critically important that you have trust in a man."

> You gotta remember the judge is up there and he's thinking, "Should I take this plea?" He looks down and sees a tricky son of a bitch, or he sees a guy like me who's been straight with him. You know what? Nine times out of ten he'll go my way.

> *   *   *

> I have seen guys get a reputation for being a liar, and it affects them with the judge. The judge is less likely to accept something they tell him. It affects them with the other side. The district attorney won't make deals. Nobody trusts them. That's gonna hurt the client.

Attorneys had to earn their credibility; it did not come with their law degrees. One attorney claimed, "You have to be able to go in the back

room and say, 'Look, you know and I know my client is a fucking jerk,' "
but he then quickly cautioned, "You can't do that on the first day on the
job." A public defender sensitive to how first impressions can affect
reputations said, "A lot of judges find young district attorneys and
public defenders are disrespectful and unreliable, so I try to avoid
that." The need for credibility sometimes clashed with professional
obligations. Opportunities that could be used to the advantage of
clients might be set aside in order to establish or maintain credible
relations within the courthouse.

> There are times when you gotta go in and tell the judge, "Don't give
> my guy probation. He's gonna screw up. Give him thirty days in jail
> or sixty days." You say that in private. If you say that on the record,
> you're an asshole.

*   *   *

> I don't take advantage of a young assistant, at least I don't try to.
> There have been many cases where the DA made a deal with me and
> I look at him and say, "Hey, that's not enough. You're too low."
> Because it's fair.

*   *   *

> When I have a good defense or there's a gaping hole or something,
> the first time I talk to the DA on discovery, I'll say, "Look at this. You
> got a real problem here." . . . I use it as leverage to get a better deal up
> front instead of trying to sandbag the DA at trial.

*   *   *

> You can't go around crying "nol pros" all the time. What I do is I save
> the nol proses for the cases I think really deserve it. And the proba-
> tions for the cases I think deserve it. On the other cases, it's "Don't do
> the crime if you can't do the time."

Most lawyers felt a process of reciprocity with prosecutors and judges
was in their mutual interests both in the short run and over the long
haul. One attorney, echoing the words of a lawyer in another court,
underscored this expectation of reciprocity to make his point.

> Prosecutors know through daily give-and-take that it's not gonna be
> too long before they're gonna come to the defense attorney and ask

for a favor. . . . They know that eventually what goes around comes around. . . . It's sort of like the Golden Rule.

Most lawyers recognized the importance of reciprocity and rationing resources (as one lawyer pointed out, "You just can't do justice for everybody"), although a few did not. One public defender, for example, said, "I don't believe in the notion that the public defender's office must sometimes compromise an individual client's interests for the good of the system as a whole. I don't believe in that. . . . To hell with whatever might befall you." Another defender in the same office described his colleague as a legal "Univac" who backed prosecutors and judges into corners so often with technical motions that "even when he's wrong, they think he's right." Nevertheless, he disagreed with this approach and pointed out, "Everybody dislikes him." He then explained, "You learn real quick you're not winning any friends. . . . You can do more for your client if you have a relationship where you can talk to these people." A defender in another court made a similar argument. "If I totally antagonize them," he pointed out, "they might say, 'Hey, why deal with this guy? He's an asshole. Shaft him.' "

Elements of Attorney Reputations

Credibility, as defense attorneys saw it, was a mix of qualities. Trustworthiness was considered very important; so was cooperativeness, although some attorneys felt it was not as critical. Trial capabilities are another important component.

Lawyers naturally prized a reputation for being skilled in the courtroom and for being unafraid of trials. They felt this not only bolstered their chances for success in the marketplace, it enhanced their bargaining position in the courthouse. One lawyer declared, "Winning in court makes a difference in how a prosecutor deals with you. He knows if you're bluffing or not." A private practitioner basked in his self-reported glory. "I've got this tremendous relationship with the prosecutors," he claimed. "I've tried so many cases, they know when I've got a good defense and if I can win the case or they can't. They know I'll try my cases." According to a public defender, "They have to know you're not afraid of going to trial. . . . They have to understand you're not just gonna let them get away with crap." A fourth attorney stated succinctly the value of having a reputation for being willing to go to trial and winning, "If they know you're gonna fold every time, it takes away some of your bargaining power."

"Being nice" by being cooperative or responsive and "being good" by going to trial and winning were two facets of the attorneys' reputations.

TABLE 5.1. Elements of Defense Attorneys' Reputations: Trial Competence and Responsiveness within the Courthouse.

Responsiveness	Trial Competence (Number)		Total
	Less Competent	More Competent	
Less responsive	59	23	73
More responsive	31	69	100
Total	81	92	173

Tau-b = .37; $p < .001$.

They were not mutually exclusive; some attorneys sought reputations for both, as a lawyer in a suburban court tried to explain:

In my opinion, the way to get along and to do well as an attorney in criminal law is to be fair, be polite, be courteous, and also be a good lawyer. . . . An awful lot of success depends on how you handle yourself. I mean, it's great to win. But if you can win and still be liked . . .

Even the attorney quoted below, who developed a reputation for aggressiveness by filing motions, acknowledged the strategic importance of not bruising egos or hurting feelings in the courthouse, especially those in the prosecutor's office.

We have to go over there on each case and sit down and ask about discovery, discuss plea bargains. . . . You have to keep open channels. You can't cut yourself off. You have to have businesslike relationships. And it should be grounded in trust and respect. It should be. Unfortunately, you've got to be wary, because it's human nature that they'll take what they can get.

From the perspectives of judges and prosecutors, the responsiveness and trial competence of defense attorneys varied, as indicated in Table 5.1. As with assistant prosecutors, the responsiveness and trial competence of criminal defense attorneys were moderately and positively related (Tau-b = .37; $p < .001$).

Judges and prosecutors saw less than a third (29 percent) of the attorneys as unresponsive and less competent at trial than other lawyers. Nearly 40 percent of the attorneys were viewed as both nice and good. Smaller proportions of attorneys were classified either as nice but not good trial lawyers or as competent but relatively unresponsive attorneys.

An important difference existed in the evaluations of public defenders and private attorneys. No relationship existed between type of attorney and reputations for responsiveness (Tau-b = -.04; p = n.s.). However, there was a relationship with respect to perceived trial competency (Tau-b = .24; $p < .01$).[4] The tendency for the court communities to rank public defenders as less skilled trial attorneys may have reflected the relative youth and lack of experience of defenders. Private attorneys were older and had more years of trial experience under their belts.

Defense Careers: Economic and Political Aspects

Market Considerations in Private Cases

Attorneys starting private practice face a chicken-and-egg problem.[5] Trials offer attorneys the advertising benefits of courtroom exposure. Yet trials are time-consuming, carry opportunity costs, and may not be profitable if attorneys do not charge enough. Trials become "loss leaders" for attorneys who lack name recognition in the marketplace.[6] An established attorney suggested that a neophyte's low overhead makes this stratagem easier, although another lawyer in private practice pointed to the gamble fledging attorneys are taking when they accept low-paying cases.

> Lawyers trying to establish themselves will take cases without an honorarium up front just to get the client. They can sit there and look at the walls all day long, but they need the practice and they need the experience. Also they don't need the kind of money we need to run an office like this.

4. One state relied exclusively on assigned counsel or contract attorneys to represent indigent defendants. These attorneys were treated as private attorneys. The similarity and difference in evaluations was not affected by whether they were excluded from the comparisons.

5. Most of the discussion in this section, and indeed, in this chapter and the following one, center on the problems of "street lawyers" who practice criminal law. Their problems differ markedly from those facing attorneys who handle white-collar crimes for high fees that can be used to finance the costs of adversarialness. This becomes very clear from the analysis in Kenneth Mann, *Defending White-Collar Crime: A Portrait of Attorneys at Work* (New Haven, Conn.: Yale University Press, 1985).

6. Lochner's research of no fee and low fee legal work, while not focusing on criminal work, is rare and provides useful insights into this aspect of the legal profession. See Philip R. Lochner, "The No Fee and Low Fee Legal Practice of Private Attorneys," *Law and Society Review* 9(Spring 1975):431.

*   *   *

We had an influx of new attorneys in town who were willing to take felonies for $500, $600, $700. Which for negotiations isn't all that bad. But try getting stuck sometime for four or five days in a trial. Even if you get $2,500, if you start adding in preparation time and everything else, it will take you two or three weeks to get back to where you were before you left your desk. It can be a losing proposition.

Attorneys suffered damaging blows to their reputations if their decisions backfired and the courts saw the trials as unnecessary and as a reflection of the attorneys' inability to control their clients. An attorney recalled the misfortune of a former law clerk who shortly after leaving the court and starting practice "tried a case that never should have been tried. . . .His name was on the front page of the paper, the judge being quoted that he was the worst attorney he'd ever seen." Such horror stories quickly passed into courthouse folklore. Novice defense attorneys could not dodge this gamble, however. The decision to go to trial posed an acute dilemma involving economics, client interests, and the attorneys' reputations.

Deciding what to charge is another difficult puzzle.[7] As one attorney recalled, "When I first started practicing, ——— came in and sat down with me. He said, 'The most important, most difficult problem you'll encounter as your own boss is setting fees.' And I'll be damned if he wasn't right." The issue of fees was a complex of questions centering on what should be charged, what the client could afford, how much time the case would take, and other matters, not the least of which were the attorney's sense of self-esteem and the equal treatment of clients. The attorney just quoted further explained the difficulties he faced when he first started his practice.

You're in a quandary because one person comes in and you charge him $1,000. The next person comes in. . . . You find out where he works and how much he makes and when you tell him what your standard fees are, you see his eyebrows go up. Should you make an adjustment and only charge him $750? If you don't, can you stand to see $750 walk out the door? Things like that are hard to resolve. It's a major consideration in private practice.

7. Some useful information regarding the economics of private criminal defense work can be found in Wice, "Making a Living," in *Criminal Lawyers,* 95–128. An early study of criminal lawyers whose private practices had not yet been shaped by the "due process revolution" is reported in Arthur Lewis Wood, *Criminal Lawyer* (New Haven, Conn.: Yale College and University Press, 1967).

There are other considerations. I've got burned by having, let's say, $2,000 as a standard, just a rule of thumb, for a felony and someone walks in the door and for some reason I only charge him $1,200. . . . Then other people come in and I quote them $2,000 and they've said, "Well, you only charged so-and-so such-and-such." And then my face turns red. . . .

Setting a fee is one thing, collecting it is another. Private attorneys, regardless of their experience, knew their retainer could be the last money they would see from a client. And even retainers were often hard to pry out of prospective clients.

It's a definite problem. My suggestion is to get the money up front. Now that's easier said than done. I can't say there's a hard and fast rule for it. I try to get a retainer. On some cases where it appears it might be settled prior to trial, I'll bill the client accordingly. In other words, if it's just gonna be a preliminary hearing, I'll say, "Just pay me for the preliminary hearing and we'll talk about the rest further down the line." That way at least I get my foot in the door with them. They can see what I do and I can see if we have a case or not. . . . So I try to get my money up front as best I can. If I can't, then I try to take it on a piecemeal basis.

A law came to the attorneys' aid in one state. State rules allowed for "bail assignments" through which refunds from the security deposits posted by defendants to secure their pretrial freedom were turned over to their attorneys to pay their fees. The comments by two attorneys illustrate the dependency of attorneys on judges in collecting these monies.

The general rule is I want to get a good chunk of the fee out front. Then I look to bond assignments, which completely depend on the judge. Last week I had a case where I had three-quarters of the fee out front, $1,500 out of a $2,000-fee. Now $500 was still tied up in a $1,000-bond, but there was a sizeable restitution involved, something like $1,200. The judge, after first checking the file to see if there was a bond assignment, decided not to take the restitution out of the bond money.

*   *   *

The judges will cooperate, with very few exceptions. They understand that the chances are that the only money you are going to see is the money that's been posted on the bond. I mean, clients have a choice, they can either pay their attorney or be set free.

The Financial Squeeze of Assigned Work

Attorneys who worked on court-assigned cases in two courts also faced money problems. Collection was not an issue (although attorneys grumbled about bureaucratic delays in getting their checks), but the amounts were. In the attorneys' eyes, the courts were stingy and far from generous, as one attorney complained:

> The courts are tight with their money. . . . If you represent a criminal client the way he should be represented, it's a lot of your time. They couldn't compensate you for what you really deserve. Any felony is worth $2,500-minimum . . . but you can't get that kind of money from the courts. . . . I tried a heroin case that took three days of trial plus the prelim and a lot of investigation on my part. I was paid $750. I've been paid more than that for traffic cases!

Attorneys in the court where this lawyer practiced earned an average of $401 for assigned cases compared to an average of $335 in the other court. (By comparison, the payment per case for contract attorneys in an autonomous county averaged a substantial $545 per case.) Although these relatively low fees could be parlayed into good incomes if attorneys received more than their fair share of cases, appointments or assigned cases, with a few notable exceptions, were distributed widely in both counties. However, even lawyers with more than their fair share of assigned work found it difficult if they had to rely solely on these criminal cases for their livelihoods. A popular, experienced lawyer lamented, "They're paying some of the overhead and some of the bills. . . . I don't know how other guys make it, to tell you the truth." He then griped that being popular with judges put his partner and him in a financial bind.

> We'll tell the judges sometimes, "Hey, you're not doing us any big favor by just giving us all the murder cases or where you know there's gonna be a trial. . . . Give us some larceny in building cases, some of the easy cases that we can get rid of in [the lower] court in one trip. You're not gonna dispose of an armed robbery in one trip. We'll end up going to court any number of times and make only $450."

A prominent attorney in another county also grumbled about the reduction in fees he suffered when the court assigned serious felonies to him. In this instance, because he preferred not to handle minor cases on an assigned basis, the reduction was that much more severe.

> I usually end up with more serious cases when I do appointments. I don't particularly like to do appointments. The reason I don't like to do appointments is because the pay is so bad.

> As an example of that, I tried a nine day murder case last year for $1,600, including preliminary examination, pretrial motions, sentencing, the whole shot. . . . I lost money!

> It was ridiculous, and I told the judge about it. His attitude was, "Don't worry about it, you'll make it up on your larceny and B-and-E [breaking and entering] cases." I said, "Judge, you know I don't do those cases. I give them to the other guys." I think he felt kinda bad about it.

While complaints about low fees were common in both counties, attorneys in one of them confronted an additional problem. The court's fee schedule baffled attorneys. No schedule as such existed, and the criteria used by judges in approving fee requests were only vaguely known, as the following attorney protested.

> It's almost impossible to figure out. There are some cases, you get a check for $500 and you've got five actual working hours in the case. Or you get a check for $500 and you've put fifty-five hours into it. Who the hell knows what they base it on!

These practitioners had no firm idea of how the court translated their efforts into dollars. Attempts at explaining what affected their fees in assigned cases came up short and frustrated attorneys.[8] Uncertainty among attorneys about their fees reflected the struggle by the circuit court to find ways of paying lawyers that reduced inflated fee requests and minimized the economic incentives affecting how they handled cases, as well as avoiding the appearance of favoritism. A judge explained at some length the bench's difficulties.

8. Variance in the fees was better explained in the second court than in the first with respect to the primary charge against the attorneys' clients, the prior record of their clients, work activities such as holding preliminary hearings or filing motions, and whether attorneys disposed of a case through a guilty plea. Regression analyses using these factors as independent variables explained .22 percent of the variance in fees paid in one court but only .04 percent in the other.

The lawyers used to put down what they did and then the time after it. They would total the hours and say, "Here's what I want." Well, the county controller took a look at it and it seemed to him some were getting paid at a higher rate than others. And being the lamb that he is, he asks, "How do you justify that?" Well, we hadn't thought of it that way. . . . So we said to attorneys, "No more hours. Just put down what you did. . . ."

That worked for a while, and then a lot of motions were filed. You might look at a motion and say, "Why the hell did you file this motion? It's a bullshit motion." So you didn't pay the attorney, or you might pay him. It became inconsistent. Or a ticklish legal point needed a lot of research, and you wondered, "How much do I pay him?" So we got into that.

Finally, we decided that we'd pay them by court appearances only. Which isn't really fair, necessarily, but it's consistent. Then we found the lawyers increased their court appearances. Well, we thought since we weren't compensating for any hours, drive time, phone calls, paperwork, etc., we'd accept that. An additional court appearance will help make up for that.

The lawyers are complaining that they don't make diddly off criminal work. I don't blame them. . . . But you go down to the county budget committee and they ask, "Why all this money for guys that commit crimes in our community?" It's not a popular subject. . . . So I say to the bar, "We would like to help you out. I know you're worth more than that. But if these costs keep pushing up, the county will say, 'For economic reasons we're gonna go with a public defender system.'" So it's a pain.

Ties That Bind: Politics and Indigent Defense Work

Appointed Counsel in a Suburban Court

Appointments to represent indigent defendants dominated the marketplace for criminal defense work in one of the suburban court communities. These appointments were often the first criminal cases handled by trial attorneys after entering private practice. Getting on the list of attorneys eligible for appointments involved little more than contacting the court or judges, making the necessary introductions, leaving a business card, and waiting. Two attorneys described their experiences in this court.

> I got a criminal appointment the day I was sworn in. Judge ———— had a clerk who was a friend of mine from college. He called me and said, "How would you like to be sworn in a little early?" This was like a week ahead of time. . . . So the judge swore me in, my parents were there, and it was a proud day for everybody. Then [the judge] handed me my first assignment. . . .

> *   *   *

> When I started practice, it was a policy of most of the judges to give an appointed case to a new attorney. So at that time, with nine judges, you got nine right off the bat and two from the probate judges. That's eleven. So your card got in the Rolodex. . . . The cases came around every two or three months.

An attorney's Rolodex card might show up more quickly in the beginning if the lawyer was a familiar courthouse face whom everybody was anxious to help. However, all attorneys had to attain the judges' approval if they hoped to receive the judges' assignments regularly. The following comments by an attorney and by a judge make this point quite clear.

> If you go to trial on every single case, you're not gonna get the appointments. . . . They don't want us pleading people that should not be pled either. Now, there are some judges that could care less. . . . But if they have some confidence in your ability, they may question you occasionally, but generally they're gonna know that you're pleading because you feel you should. But at the same time, their primary concern is their docket. They're very competitive among themselves.

> *   *   *

> I tell lawyers asking for appointments that I expect something more than just lip service. Number one, I don't want any letters from their clients. I get horrendous fan mail here. . . . But when I get letters from clients telling me that their lawyers don't see them, or that they aren't doing this or doing that, it tells me that you don't have the right control of them. And I don't want that. So you got to have client control. And secondly, I want lawyers that will resolve these cases.

I'm not saying dispose of them at the expense of the defendant, but don't just run this thing to death.

Defense attorneys knew that moving cases was an important consideration in whether they continued to receive appointed cases. As one acknowledged, "The reason I have such a caseload is that I am known to move cases, and I'm known to dispose of them fairly. And, knock on wood, I've never had any grievances from the state bar." Client control was a pivotal skill for the lawyers.[9] According to another attorney, "If you can't resolve cases because of no client control, then certainly you're not gonna get many appointments, because the judge is gonna say, 'Well, you can't do the job.'"

Contract Politics in an Autonomous County

In many subtle and not so subtle ways, defense attorneys cannot ignore the interests of those who pay their fees.[10] In one county, a group of lawyers lost the contract to represent indigent defendants because the circuit court judges pinned the blame for their backlog problems on the attorneys. According to one judge, "The first group we had took a day and half to draw a jury, and we never recovered from it." Another judge recalled, "They went beyond what I felt a defense attorney owes his client. . . . They were turning over rocks, filing every possible legal motion, and that to some extent contributed to our backlog."

This lesson was not lost on the current group. One of the principal contract attorneys reflected on the differences between his group's approach and that of the previous attorneys.

They spent too much time chasing rabbits, and they went belly-up financially. . . . So they had financial problems, number one. Number two, that translated into a terrible backlog. Largely, I think, because they had a propensity to file motions, and they ran into a personality conflict with the prosecutor, who said, "You ain't getting nothing from me."

The judges, of course, were sick and tired of listening to these flakey, crappy motions. A lot of paper, a lot of time, nothing ever got

9. For more on this aspect of the defense attorney's craft, see Flemming, "Client Games."

10. For a review of research on defense attorneys in criminal courts, see Roy B. Flemming, "If You Pay the Piper, Do You Call the Tune? Public Defenders in America's Criminal Courts," *Law and Social Inquiry* 14(Spring 1989):393.

done—a terrible backlog. So the impetus came from the judges that they couldn't live with this anymore.

We had a reputation for getting the job done—not too much fucking around—and we would handle the contract professionally. They took the gamble, and I think it's worked out for them.

Another contract attorney explained, "It used to be that the previous group, if they had an exam (they almost always had preliminary examinations), would order a transcript and then file one or two boilerplate motions. We don't do that very often." A third contract attorney summed up the matter by saying, "We've found that the secret to properly administering a contract like this is client control."

Public Defenders in Two Suburban Courts

A chief public defender, an eleven-year veteran in the post and a Republican committeeman of long standing, cleared new defenders with the Republican-dominated county commissioners. One assistant insisted that every PD had a political sponsor or connection. "You know," he pointed out, "we've got the governor's nephew, a judge's son, a judge's girlfriend, and all kinds of other people with contacts." Several assistants were themselves GOP committeemen. These political contacts smoothed relations with the county government for the chief public defender but tied his hands when it came to running the office. According to a senior assistant public defender, the office's payroll was padded with what in a large metropolitan area were called "ghosts."[11]

They reward those that are not very competent. They keep them and move them into the background. They move them out of the courtroom into the office, and they do no work. Then they get paid whether they do any work or not. . . . It's sort of funny. . . . Now, X doesn't go to juvenile court, Y doesn't come in, and Z works about one day a week. That's how it goes. The worse you are, the better off you are.

The office's administrative structure was also weakened, as the following assistant complained: "We have a head of felonies that has no function whatsoever. I'm not kidding. You can ask any of the other

11. See "Feds Probing Ghost Payroll," *Chicago Sun-Times,* 22 Nov., 1987, and the description of the personnel policies of the Cook County public defender in McIntyre, *Public Defender,* 92, 107–11.

attorneys." The felony chief candidly confessed, "Most of the judges, I'm sure, don't even know that I am head of the criminal division, even though I've been head for three years." The felony chief then added, "I keep a low profile; there's no reason to let them know."

In the second suburban court, the veteran head of the public defender's office (who at one time ran for the position of DA) succeeded in getting elected to the county's circuit court. He urged the county commissioners to appoint his first assistant as his successor. Experienced members of the office, including an aspirant for the first assistant post, informed the commissioners they would quit if the commissioners selected another candidate. During the ensuing swirl of politics, a different choice was made. The new public defender, like his predecessor, originally had pursued the DA slot but had dropped his bid to preserve party harmony. The party, in gratitude, rewarded him with the public defender post. No mass resignations came on the heels of the new PD's appointment, although the first assistant and the attorney who had hoped to become first assistant left the office.

Many assistant public defenders had political ties in this county. One was an officer in the Young Republicans. Another assistant explained what he felt was his edge in getting a job in the office:

> Our family's been in politics a hell of a long time. I knew [the previous PD], but I also had the advantage of having five years in private practice. . . . So I applied and went through the usual rigamarole, hitting the various political leaders, the proper letters, and everything like that.

The office contained other attorneys without strong party connections, but they still needed party approval to qualify for a job. One attorney recalled:

> I was never very politically involved, and I'm still not. And I remember that I had to go around and have this paper [a letter of introduction] signed by the committeemen from my area and by the area chairman—about nine different people. But that is what it took.

The upshot, as one office member involved in the hiring process put it, was that "great weight" was placed on hiring recommendations from county commissioners or party officials. Another administrative officer revealed the role of partisan politics in the following exchange:

Interviewer: Have you had any of those tough choices where you get someone who has political sponsorship but

	he's not great like someone else who doesn't have it?
Public Defender:	Yeah.
Interviewer:	What do you do?
Public Defender:	Hire him. It's happened once. What we did was put him in an office with two experienced lawyers and we said, "Make a lawyer out of this guy." We just had to grin and bear it.

Part-time work in this office served as a launching pad for the attorneys' careers (as in another county, where the public defenders were permitted to have a private practice besides their job in the office). With their income as public defenders, lawyers could build their private practices with a measure of financial security. Rocking the boat would not further these interests. The office leadership did not stand in the way of this careerist perspective. The previous public defender, who ascended to the bench, was described as "to the right of Attila the Hun" on criminal justice matters. The new chief clearly preferred prosecution to defense; the position of chief public defender was a consolation prize for having given up his quest to become DA. These various factors, as one experienced member concluded, dampened strong pro-defense sentiments. No fire-breathing advocates of defendant rights prowled the office's corridors.

> Let's face it. We're all Republicans. We're all from basically middle-class, upper-middle-class, white families. We have certain morals and ethics. It seems to me that Democratic, Jewish defense attorneys who'd be really pro-defense wouldn't be the kind of guys who'd come into this office.

Public Defenders in Other Court Communities

In five of the six courts, politics involving the PD office was overt. The heads of these offices, appointed by either the county or the court, found themselves in inherently political posts. For example, one of the chief PDs was appointed by the county commissioners after his predecessor had resigned to run for the Republican nomination for district attorney. Being a Republican himself, the chief admitted, played a role in his appointment. He also believed the judges, whom the commissioners had contacted, had recommended his selection. In another office, the Republican county executive paid off a political debt to his campaign manager by appointing him to replace the long-time chief public defender. The new chief, who narrowly lost his own race for DA five years earlier, had been a lobbyist for the oil and coal industries in Washington and had almost no experience in criminal law.

The effects of such ties on specific cases were neither obvious nor easy to detect. But, as a defender said, "You have to realize the pressure is on the chief public defender. There's at least a moment's hesitation and fear about antagonizing the commissioners and jeopardizing the chief public defender's job or making them less sympathetic to us the next fiscal year." Such fears were realized in another court community, where the chief defender lost his job after antagonizing the chief criminal court judge.

A private attorney described the chief judge as "an old war-horse trial attorney" who "controls who is the public defender" and made the office take "an awful lot of shit." According to one PD, the office's troubles started when the assistants, fed up with what they felt was the judge's shabby treatment of them, agreed with the chief's suggestion to use a state rule allowing attorneys to substitute trial judges without cause in order to show the judge their displeasure. Another defender recalled the incident, which he termed a "real mess":

> We had a meeting one day and everybody was bitching and moaning about Judge ———. So [the head PD] said, "What the hell, let's shut him down. Just substitute for him every time we have him on a case." Well, that got around real quick. Judge ——— found out and, well, ——— was public defender for about another month.

Public defenders often received little respect within the courthouse community. One defender went so far as to say that judges "treat us like dirt." Public defenders in a different court had similar feelings. They thought the judges held their office in low esteem. Most of the judges had been prosecutors at some time during their careers, and their views of public defenders seemed to be tainted accordingly. Indeed, with respect to their attitudes regarding due process matters and the value of punishment, the judges stood out because of the similarity between their views and those of the prosecutors. In sharp contrast, the public defenders were at the opposite end of the spectrum even when compared to other PD offices. The bench's views were made quite clear to public defenders, as three assistants discovered:

> You know, they call me by my first name. I feel good about that. I enjoy being part of that community. Unfortunately, my role in that community is, like, "professional asshole."

*   *   *

You learn very quickly that the judges in this county, for the most part, consider all clients represented by the public defender's office as guilty. As a consequence, they feel that we have absolutely no bargaining power, or very little.

*   *   *

I never shot the breeze with Judge ——— because, as a public defender, I was tainted. Now, if I had been a prosecutor, he would have embraced me. Anyway, after I resigned, in the middle of open court, he calls me up, sticks out his hand, and says, "Congratulations. I understand you've left the public defender's office. I want to wish you well. It was a dead-end job."

Another defender discussed how these attitudes, personified by an influential judge's habit of referring to the PD office as "The Office for the Obstruction of Justice," affected the public defenders.

The DA's office is cloaked with respect and it immediately has the *ex parte* ear of the court. . . . Some of our people kind of let their emotional responses come out. Once you know you're deemed to be inferior, it's necessary to be very assertive. On the other hand, I think a lot of people just got ticked off and lost sight of the basic rule: you can't win an argument with a judge.

For one defender who violated this rule, the bitterness of the outcome was hard to suppress.

When I first came here, I had large battles with judges. A typical example: I found out, and this happens all the time, that the judge before whom the case was gonna be tried was having, as he always does, discussion with the prosecution about the case. In this murder case, I filed a motion for disqualification of the judge because of this.

This caused all kinds of flack around here. My boss forced me, under the threat of firing me, to send an apology to the judge because I had acted, according to him, in an unprofessional manner. Jesus Christ! What's more unprofessional than a judge predetermining the outcome of a case?

Professionals or Bureaucrats? Organizing Public Defender Offices

Public defender offices had a bureaucratic potential that contract and appointed counsel systems lacked. This potential was rarely developed. Public defender offices typically are loosely structured, are non-hierarchically administered, and develop few policies.[12] Chief public defenders shun bureaucracy. Unlike their peers in the prosecutor's office, they feel that defense work is a matter of professionalism that cannot and should not be reduced to following policy guidelines.

A chief PD in an autonomous county contrasted his approach to administering the work of his assistants with the prosecutor's style.

> The present prosecutor is a great one for making policies and setting down guidelines. . . . I would no more insult the intelligence of my assistants and do that than I would jump off this building. I think he misses the boat in taking that direction. . . . I'm not a policymaker in that respect. As long as I'm satisfied with what I see, in work effort and in terms of results and conscientiousness, I'm very laissez-faire. I'm not going to rock the boat.

In an industrial county, the head PD held a part-time position. Accordingly, he ran a very decentralized office. Assistants were hard-pressed to name any general office policies. A third, full-time PD in another court, however, also administered his office in a loose fashion. According to one of his assistants:

> We're not subjected to any overview here. You know, these cases are my cases. I don't get yelled at unless something really goes wrong. Over there [in the DA's office], they're tracked.

The management style of a PD in another industrial court was more complex and somewhat contradictory. The chief believed in strong leadership, assumed a formal relationship with his staff, and instituted an evaluation procedure to assess the performance of assistants. However, he spent little time in the office. Consequently, responsibility for the day-to-day administration of the office fell on the shoulders of his first assistant who preferred the traditional laissez-faire approach. As he put it:

12. McIntyre refers to this absence of effective bureaucratic organization as an "anti-structure" or "communitas" which, she argues, is consistent with the public defenders' need to prove their professionalism. See McIntyre, "Myth and Antistructure in Public Defending," in *Public Defender*, 121–36.

I am dealing with professionals, and if they are good public defenders or good lawyers, they have big egos. So that, to some extent, to get the best out of them, I have to take an equal or even subordinate role in an individual case.

The assistants expressed views consistent with this comment. According to one assistant, "It's just like that person is a private client. I have complete latitude on cases to do what I feel is in the defendant's best interests." An administrator mentioned that he often attached a note to a file if he wanted to suggest a particular action to an assistant. "But," he hastened to add, "I don't ever follow up to see if they do it or not. It's none of my business."

A suburban office, despite its larger size, was not bureaucratized. Staff members reported virtually no supervision over how they handled specific cases. Two experienced assistants declared:

It's a good office from the point of view that nobody looks over your shoulder. They give you a file and it's yours.

*   *   *

We've never had rules. They never did have a strict policy on anything. To a degree, maybe that's a strong point of the office. We've got attorneys who are given the chance to grow, become effective trial attorneys, learn from other people in the office through experience, and to be their own people.

The chief summarized his philosophy regarding how to administer the office in the following way:

We treat the public defender's office like a large law office. I don't tell an assistant how to handle a case. . . . I stay out of it. The assistant is given the file. It's his file, and he carries it from the day that he's assigned to the day the case is over.

A Summary and Some Qualifications

Defense attorneys faced numerous pressures to go along with the courthouse community. Social and professional ties with prosecutors and judges muted adversarial urges. Credible reputations involved a balance between trial competence and responsiveness. Public defenders were disadvantaged in this regard, in part because of their relative lack of experience compared to private practitioners and partly because they received little respect from the bench. Both economics and politics militated against vigorous pro-defense actions by attorneys. As a chief public defender put it, "I feel we are under somewhat of a duty not to deliberately disrupt the court, even though we could do it and then, if we had to, justify it because it's a legal right later on." The craft of defense work, then, was shaped in ways that reinforced a model of professionalism that emphasized a case-by-case, client-oriented practice rather than legal reform.

However, tension, strain, and discord occasionally broke through the appearance of cooperation, camaraderie, and comity. Because criminal courts are rife with mixed-motive situations, conflict can supersede civility at either the individual or the institutional level. This conflict can help shape the contours of the courthouse community and give it a particular shape. In many instances, the reasons are political or related to policy disagreements. Sometimes they are related to the perspectives and attitudes of key participants. Examples of these conflicts will conclude this chapter.

In the county with contract attorneys, the lawyers, despite their dependency on the circuit bench, joined with roughly twenty other lawyers in publicly criticizing a circuit judge. The attorneys were disturbed by the poor quality and extreme tardiness of the judge's opinion in a highly publicized case. This open criticism undoubtedly encouraged a lower court judge to challenge the judge's re-election bid for another term on the circuit bench. The judge's poor showing in the bar poll, which the local newspaper published, also embarrassed the judge, who was defeated, a rare event in judicial elections. As it happened, the judge also developed a reputation as a poor docket manager and for being rude to lawyers.

Personality, policy, and institutional factors also came together to produce a simmering feud between these attorneys and the trial chief in the prosecutor's office. The trial chief, one contract attorney said, took "a bullheaded, unreasonable approach" in making sure assistants followed office policy. These feelings about the trial chief boiled over after a hearing described by the presiding judge as "very tense" and "very heated." The trial chief demanded that a contract attorney apologize to a state police officer. The attorney, who had moved to dismiss the case because of police entrapment, had attacked the officer's veracity. A pushing and shoving match between the officer and the attorney led the judge to conclude that the officer had committed an assault and battery on the lawyer. The judge also accused the trial chief of prosecutorial misconduct for his role in the fracas.

Conflict cropped up in an industrial county where a public defender's former law partner had been a judge whom the prosecutor had indicted for possessing guns used as evidence in court. The defender deeply distrusted the prosecutor, because he had reneged on an understanding that if the judge passed a lie detector test the case would not be presented to the grand jury. According to the defender:

> The prosecutor said, "My policy is I never present a case to the grand jury where the defendant passes a polygraph." So we went back and told the judge, "You're off the hook. Let's go back to practicing law." Nine o'clock the next morning I get a phone call that the judge has to testify at ten before the grand jury.

This public defender office had other disputes with the court community. As mentioned earlier, the chief lost his job after he urged his assistants to "shut down" a judge. In another situation, a judge in chambers made a racist comment about a defender's client. When the judge refused to disqualify himself from the case, the attorney, with the support of the office, appealed the case and won. Finally, the office became irked over the prosecutor's practice of "standing mute" in probation cases. Instead of openly agreeing with the defenders in court and recommending to judges that probation was appropriate in guilty plea cases, the deputy DAs remained silent. The PDs forced the prosecutors into five continuous weeks of trials instead of the normal two weeks, pushing many cases close to the state's speedy trial limit. The tactic succeeded in forcing the office to agree to recommendations for probation in guilty plea cases.

In a suburban county, the defense bar, especially the private attorneys, and the prosecutor's office were, as one lawyer described it, "at total odds" with one another. A second lawyer claimed the DA taught assistant prosecutors to believe that "all defense attorneys wear black hats" and "could not be trusted." A public defender thought the district attorney's office punished certain attorneys while favoring others, an accusation echoed by other members of the defense bar. According to this defender:

> Call it a blacklist, shit list, whatever. When the indictment committee meets, one of the things it considers is who is going to defend the case. I think I've not only made the list, I've made it to the top of it.

Anger over the prosecutor's policies led to the formation of a criminal defense lawyer's association. The question of joining the association divided both private attorneys and public defenders. A nonmember explained his decision in the following way:

I have to work with prosecutors. . . . I know most of them personally. A lot of them are good friends of mine. And I guess my feeling is that I don't want to be in a position of polarizing my relationship with them.

Lawyers who joined the association were ambivalent about their decision. On the one hand, the target of the defense bar's anger— the Indictment Committee—promised to reduce sentencing inequities among clients. On the other hand, rumors flew that some attorneys received preferential treatment. According to a private lawyer who backed the prosecutor, the association's roots reached back to the bitterly fought election when the insurgent DA successfully challenged the Republican establishment. As he recalled:

Never before in the history of this county was a campaign run as vigorously as that one. I believe in hitting a guy in the head, but it got a little too personal. . . . I had a very good relationship with the party chairman and the other powers that be until I backed him. And then someone cut my car's tires. I'm not shitting you. . . . I was also almost indicted. This is God's honest truth, so help me.

All of the people that backed the loser turned out to be the defense bar. And so they're upset with the prosecutor because he's too tough. . . . Their objection though, is that they can't go in and talk to him and make deals, because a lot of them want one hundred dollars for fifty dollars' worth of work. . . . Let me tell you something. No deals are made for me, but they tried to show that I'm getting deals.

According to this lawyer, the criminal defense association used its political contacts with the county clerk's office to check court files to see if he or others had benefited from supporting the prosecutor. Another attorney and partner of the candidate backed by the Republican establishment election was involved in this hunt. "We all assisted each other in doing some digging to get something on them," he said, but admitted, "We couldn't find anything." This did not end the rumors carried by the grapevine. According to another lawyer:

Isolated instances float around. But I've had this happen to me at least three times, where you're at an impasse in your negotiations. The state wants one thing and you want another. And invariably it's a high-profile case. And your client says to you, "Look, I've heard about this lawyer that's really in with them. Do you think if I went and saw him . . ." I had one occasion where a client behind my back just went over and saw him, thinking that that's what he was supposed to do. I don't know where it comes from, but I've heard it from clients who could not possibly know each other.

These instances of personal and political conflict were exceptions to the general rule of "getting along by going along." Defense attorneys lacked the organizational potential needed to challenge prosecutors. Attorneys in private practice had little to gain and perhaps much to lose by attacking the status quo. Public defender posts were often largely part-time posts and sometimes headed by part-time administrators. Whether full-time or part-time, chief PDs ran their offices with light hands. This was both a matter of professional preference and a reflection of the political circumstances surrounding their appointments and as the selection of their staffs. Neither bureaucracy nor politics gave the defense bar the institutional strength of prosecutors or judges within the courthouse communities.

Chapter 6
Defending in Courtrooms: Making the "Right" Moves

Introduction

Defense attorneys rarely challenge the disposition routines of court communities. In fact, most of the time lawyers find these routines helpful as they fill in the content of the attorney's courtroom craft. Routines lend certainty to their work, define approximate standards of doing justice, expedite the movement of the caseload, and reduce the time and energy spent on cases. Because not all cases are routine, however, another part of the attorneys' craft is knowing how to handle felonies that fall outside the customary patterns.

Some felonies do not fit the court community's "normal crime" profile.[1] For clients accused of infrequent crimes or who have unusual backgrounds, standard operating procedures may be inadequate and inappropriate. In addition, when defendants are accused of very serious offenses, the courts generally have broad sentencing latitude and the normal routines are less clear-cut and less constraining. As a result, courthouse relationships, professional skills, and personalities take on more importance in these kinds of cases.[2] Uncertainty bedevils courtroom work, but it poses a special problem for defense attorneys under these circumstances. Uncertainty aggravates relations with clients who want to know what will happen to them. As the following lawyer suggests, the defense attorney's first rule of thumb is "know what to expect."[3]

1. David Sudnow, "Normal Crimes: Sociological Features of the Penal Code in a Public Defender Office," *Social Problems* 12(Winter 1965):255.

2. Peter F. Nardulli, Roy B. Flemming, and James Eisenstein, "Unraveling the Complexities of Decision Making in Face-to-Face Groups: A Contextual Analysis of Plea-Bargaining Sentences," *American Political Science Review* 78(December 1984):912.

3. The same injunction applies to lawyers doing civil work. Flood argues that "manag-

The thing that makes one attorney better than another is not necessarily his ability on his feet or his ability in the library. What makes a good lawyer is his ability to forecast the future for his client. That's what it all boils down to.

Courthouse routines diminish uncertainty's vexations. However, routine dispositions and standard sentences or going rates can clash with what attorneys feel their clients deserve and especially with what their clients will accept, which may lead to postconviction problems and professional difficulties for lawyers. Minimizing uncertainty is not always synonymous with doing justice, nor is it always consistent with minimizing regrets. Bending courthouse routines and stretching courthouse customs, however, could expose attorneys to sanctions for breaking or seeming to break the rules of the game.[4] The attorneys' reputations are at risk and their credibility is on the line when they try to slip around these restraints. Attorneys must ultimately learn the craft of knowing when, how, and with whom to elude local norms while minimizing the risks of sanctions.

Opening Gambits: Preliminary Hearings and Motions

The adversarial theory of criminal justice provides attorneys with potentially potent tactical and strategic options that, if successful, can decide the outcome of a case.[5] A preliminary hearing forces the prosecutor to present sufficient evidence before a judge for the judge to establish whether probable cause exists. Failure to meet this criterion may yield substantial benefits to the defense. Due process motions challenge the admissability of statements made by the attorney's client or the physical evidence relating to the alleged crime. Successful motions also could determine the outcomes of cases. In reality, the courtroom craft of attorneys rationed the use of these resources.

---

ing uncertainty" is central to the practice of business law. See John Flood, "Doing Business: The Management of Uncertainty in Lawyers' Work," *Law and Society Review* 25(1991):41.

4. For an analysis of how lawyers are taught how to behave by other members of the courthouse community, see Milton Heumann, *Plea Bargaining: The Experiences of Prosecutors, Judges, and Defense Attorneys* (Chicago: University of Chicago Press, 1977).

5. Indeed, Feeley has argued that these moves may be contemporary adversarial substitutes for costly criminal trials. See Malcolm M. Feeley, "Plea Bargaining and the Structure of the Criminal Process," *Justice System Journal* 7(1982):338.

The "Cardinal Rule": Never Waive Preliminary Hearings?

Waiving preliminary hearings is not a trivial decision.[6] These hearings, which assess the evidence in cases to determine whether there is probable cause and sufficient proof to warrant prosecution of the charges levied against defendants, can lead to dismissals or reductions in initial charges, reveal major weaknesses in the prosecution's cases, or prepare the groundwork for motions or for trials. In waiving the hearings, attorneys lose these possible benefits.

The frequency with which attorneys waived preliminary hearings varied widely across the nine courthouses. Attorneys in the three courts in one state seldom passed up the chance to have these hearings.[7] The hearings also were rarely waived in a fourth courthouse. Waivers were much more common in the other five courts, where the proportion of waived preliminary hearings ranged from a low of 27 percent to a high of 61 percent.

Local policies explained why preliminary hearings were seldom waived in four of the courts. The most important policy was whether the public defender's offices assigned staff members to handle these hearings. For example, in one court the chief defender assumed responsibility for holding the hearings and used what he learned to assign cases to his assistants. As an another example, the public defender's office in a suburban court paid a special cadre of private attorneys on a case-by-case basis to conduct the hearings. The office made sure the attorneys did not pocket the money without holding them. Specialization, in a word, discouraged waiver decisions in these courts.

Why did attorneys in the other five courts waive these hearings? Why did they honor mostly in the breach what one attorney called the cardinal rule: "Never waive the preliminary hearing"? As another lawyer argued, "It's only to your client's benefit, because you've got everything to gain and nothing to lose." The attorneys' decisions rested on calculations that took into account four basic considerations: a concern for efficiency, professional norms, minimizing the regrets or the undesirable consequences of their actions, and the odds of success.

6. This section draws on the analysis of preliminary hearing decisions in Roy B. Flemming, "Elements of the Defense Attorney's Craft: An Adaptive Expectations Model of the Preliminary Hearing Decision," *Law and Policy* 8(January 1986):33.

7. In one of these courts, the grand jury was used to indict nearly 55 percent of the sampled defendants. In another, one-quarter of the sampled defendants pled guilty at the preliminary hearing stage. If these indicted and disposed cases in the two courts are set to the side, the proportion of hearings in each of the three courts exceeded 90 percent.

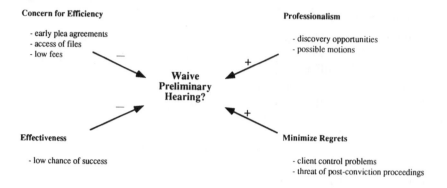

Figure 6.1. Waiving preliminary hearings: Concerns and factors.

Figure 6.1 portrays these competing considerations and their related factors. The most important factor was whether the attorneys could secure an early guilty plea agreement or other nontrial disposition that would make the hearing superfluous.

Experience taught one lawyer that the cardinal rule on preliminary hearings should take into account the possibility of a guilty plea. "The basic rule," he stressed, "is 'Never waive *unless* you're gonna get a plea.'" A lawyer in another court agreed, saying, "Basically, it's my practice never to waive a preliminary hearing unless the entire plea bargain has been completely worked out." For example, one attorney estimated that "the majority of cases where there is a waiver are based on the belief that it's gonna be disposed of by a guilty plea in circuit court." The conclusion, he felt, was obvious: "Why bother to hold an exam?"

In each of the courts where attorneys frequently waived hearings, particular policies or customs reduced attorney uncertainties about the disposal of cases. For example, in one autonomous county, the prosecuting office set the terms of pleas when it issued arrest warrants. Defense counsel thus had a baseline from which to work. In an industrial county, assistant prosecutors were assigned to cases on a vertical basis. Defense counsel could talk about cases with assistant prosecutors at the preliminary hearing knowing the assistants would probably also be the trial prosecutors. Suburban attorneys in another court who were appointed to represent indigent defendants knew who the trial judge and prosecutor would be in circuit court because of the court community's assignment practices. This was a "tremendous advantage" when deciding whether to hold or waive the preliminary hearing, according to the following attorney.

Obviously, the bottom line is sentencing, if you're looking at it from the standpoint of the defendant. For most of the judges that I gather appointments from, I can tell my clients right off what to expect. It's a tool for me to choose whether or not to go to exam or not.

A countervailing consideration centered on the discovery opportunities created by the hearings. One attorney professed he liked preliminary hearings because:

You get to hear what a witness has to say. Otherwise the best you're gonna get is the police report, which normally doesn't go into enough depth to really help you. So a preliminary hearing . . . is a good discovery tool. Basically, that's what we use it for.

However, attorneys could save time by waiving examinations and still not lose these discovery opportunities, if the prosecutor's office opened its files to them. According to a lawyer in a court community where the DA followed this policy:

Part of waiving, I think, is the ability of the attorney to assess the case itself. He develops a pretty good feeling as to whether he can waive the prelim and still go to trial. Because of access to the prosecutor's file, you know 90 percent of the testimony that's gonna go down at the prelim anyway. So why worry about it?

Access to the prosecutor's files pushed attorneys in one direction, but a third concern, client control, pushed them in the other direction. Attorneys felt that balky clients sometimes had to see the prosecution's case presented in a courtroom to get them to appreciate the wisdom of a guilty plea. Lawyers also thought that requesting a preliminary examination countered the mistrust of those clients who questioned their judgment. A public defender recounted that a colleague "wanted his client at some point in some formal proceeding to hear the evidence against him so that when he pled him, the guy knew what cards the other side was holding." As a way of gaining control of clients, holding the preliminary hearing could also reduce the possibility of postconviction proceedings against attorneys.

A fourth consideration in the backs of attorneys' minds lent further support for holding examinations. The hearings often were necessary in order to file motions challenging statements made by clients, identifications by witnesses or victims, or the search and seizure of physical evidence. The final factor pivoted on the financial interests of attorneys and the press of cases on their time and energy. Low fees in some courts and flat rates in another for indigent defendant cases did not encourage unnecessary work or the expenditure of time that could be used in other cases.

In terms of tangible outcomes, the expenditure of time and energy required for preliminary hearings may not be worth it, from the attorneys' perspective. Overall, in all nine communities, no changes in initial charges were made in roughly 87 percent of the sampled cases that were disposed of in circuit court. Thus, regardless of whether preliminary hearings were the rule in a courthouse, the odds generally favored the status quo. Preliminary hearings, then, afforded defense attorneys few benefits.

Going Through the Motions?

Motions based on the Fourth Amendment and the exclusionary rule provided attorneys with another powerful adversarial weapon. The nine counties offered ample opportunities for using it. For example, roughly 60 percent of the defendants prosecuted for committing burglary made damaging statements to the police while being interrogated.[8] Yet due process motions were relatively infrequent.

Across all nine courts, attorneys filed one or more motions in nearly 11 percent of the sampled cases. This is an inflated proportion, because one public defender routinely filed motions to suppress identifications and to exclude confessions in nearly one-third of all cases, whether the motions were relevant or not. With this office's cases dropped from the tally, the overall proportion falls to about 7.5 percent.

Attorneys rationed their resources. They thought motions were more effective when they carefully picked the cases in which motions would do the most good. However, this rationing perspective tipped the scales against motions, because the costs of motions were given more weight than their benefits. As with preliminary hearings, efficiency, professionalism, and client control were considered in deciding whether to file a motion, but an added, perhaps overriding consideration was the attorneys' concern over protecting their credibility in the courtrooms. According to a public defender, "I only file motions when I think there's something there. You piss off the court with a lousy motion that has no merit." Attorneys elsewhere shared the view that motions worked best when used sparingly. A private lawyer declared

8. This section draws on the data and analysis in Peter F. Nardulli, "The Societal Cost of the Exclusionary Rule: An Empirical Assessment," *American Bar Foundation Research Journal* 1983(Summer 1983):585.

that judges and prosecutors perked up and took notice when he filed a motion, because he didn't "paper" the court with unnecessary motions. "When I do file a motion," he said, "they sit back and say, 'Hey, maybe there's something here.'" His view was typical of most defense lawyers, public or private, but not all.

For example, a chief public defender disagreed that motions should be rationed, and he tried to persuade his staff to file more of them. His lack of success proved the strength of the feeling that credibility must be preserved. "You gotta over-motion," he argued, because "there's no reason not to." His assistants disagreed. One assistant PD stated simply, "I don't believe in just papering the court with motions." A superior in the office supported the staff's position. "I tell the boss," he reported, "that filing a motion in every case is the lazy man's approach. You have to develop some modicum of judgment; that's what you're paid for." The public defenders ignored their chief's injunction.

Another public defender's habit of routinely filing motions, plus the experience of another county's contract attorneys, offer further evidence for the folk wisdom behind the rationing perspective of the attorneys' craft. The PD's success rate was virtually nil. Not one of the office's motions to suppress an identification succeeded. Only a handful of its motions to quash confessions were granted. These repeated failures prompted a change of heart. According to one staff member, "Our secretary filed a motion to suppress a confession on everything. . . . But we don't do that anymore because . . . well . . . the judges gave us grief." In the other county, the courthouse community felt the motions filed by an earlier group of attorneys were unnecessary or niggling. This cost the attorneys their credibility with the judges and prosecutors and, ultimately, the contract to represent indigent defendants. As a former prosecutor recalled, "What happened after a while was that the judges got so calloused by their constant bogus challenges that the valid ones got lost in the shuffle."

Economic considerations colored a suburban attorney's perspective of motions. He figured motions did not pay. His firm's overhead at the time was thirty dollars an hour. He estimated that preparing, filing, and arguing a motion would consume five to ten hours. With reimbursements for two-thirds of all assigned cases under three hundred dollars, motions in this county were not financially worth the effort. Another lawyer pointed to changes in court policies that further discouraged motions.

When I was first coming up, a lot of attorneys would bring a motion on the half-ass chance of getting it granted; you got a lot of paper motions. . . . Then the court did away with how many motions you did. You weren't gonna get paid for them. That curtailed a lot of motions.

These financial considerations might have been put aside if the prospects of success had been high, but they were not. For the nine counties, motions to exclude physical evidence succeeded roughly 17 percent of the time. But confessions were quashed in only 2.5 percent of the cases with these motions, and identifications were suppressed 1.7 percent of the time. Most important, motions did not often lead to acquittals or dismissals; the odds of achieving both a successful motion and a nonconviction were poor.

For motions excluding physical evidence, the chance that the motion would be granted and that the defendant would not be convicted was roughly 13 percent, or one out of every eight motions, perhaps a respectable chance but far from certain. The gamble worsened with the other motions. The probability of a dismissal or acquittal after a successful motion to exclude confessions or statements was only .01, or one in a hundred. The probability of motions that successfully suppressed identifications leading to a nonconviction sank to .003, or three in one thousand motions. When faced with such unfavorable odds, the costs of motions loomed even larger in the attorneys' considerations.

Despite these long odds and financial disincentives, the risk of post-conviction proceedings or grievances helped tip the scales slightly in favor of motions. A private attorney claimed, "Many motions to suppress—not all of them—are something that lawyers do just to protect themselves." According to a public defender in this court, "You have to file or else it's ineffectiveness of counsel." This concern seemed particularly strong in another court where motion activity was high and where public defenders were most likely to file motions. Several defenders mentioned this concern, but the candid remarks of one lawyer summed up the attorneys' worries about motions—in particular, about how to maintain credibility with the court while solving client control problems.

I've made a reputation for myself that I don't put in pretrial motions frivolously. . . . But just to cover my ass, I'll put in a pretrial motion so that if there is an issue there that should be litigated, I'm covered. Lots of times (it depends on the judge) I'll go into chambers and the judge asks, "Well, what do you have on your motion?" And I'll say, "Nothing, Judge. I did it in an abundance of caution." Then he'll say,

"Okay, fine. So you're not gonna pursue it?" "Right." That way they know that if I'm pursuing something that I've really got something. I think they respect me for that.

The Middle Game: Trials and Guilty Pleas

The Perceived Risks of Trials

Most attorneys go to trial only a few times a year. These experiences are poor samples for estimating the consequences of choosing trials over guilty pleas.[9] They are unlikely to be representative of what happens throughout the courthouse. The grapevine, of course, spreads the news about trials and about the successes and misadventures of the attorneys. Yet the accuracy and completeness of this information remains an open, unanswered question.[10] Thus, even seasoned attorneys with roughly similar experiences might disagree about the risks of trials, as the following attorneys did.

Interviewer: In some jurisdictions, if you go to trial, your client will serve more time than he normally would.

Attorney 1: I think that's probably universally true.

Attorney 2: I was just going to say, I can't pick an instance in this county where I think that would be true.

Attorney 1: You never know. You absolutely never know.

Interviewer: Has it happened to you?

Attorney 1: I don't know. You never know in advance of the trial what the sentence is gonna be.

Interviewer: Yeah, except you've handled enough cases to know what the sentence is gonna be.

9. Defense counsel may be no better statisticians than ordinary people. They necessarily draw inferences from small and biased samples, make broad conclusions on the basis of vivid, unusual experiences, and in general fall victim to other shortcomings of social judgment. The foibles and limitations of social judgment are investigated in Richard Nisbett and Lee Ross, *Human Inference: Strategies and Limitations of Social Judgment* (Englewood Cliffs, N.J.: Prentice-Hall, 1980), and Daniel Kahneman, Paul Slovic, and Amos Tversky, eds., *Judgment Under Uncertainty: Heuristics and Biases* (Cambridge, England: Cambridge University Press, 1982).

10. The failures and problems of conformity in collective decision-making are explored in Irving L. Janis, *Groupthink: Psychological Studies of Policy Decisions and Fiascoes* (Boston: Houghton Mifflin Company, 1982). The role of information in organizational decision making and how knowledge is translated into policy is explored in Harold L. Wilensky, *Organizational Intelligence: Knowledge and Policy in Government and Industry* (New York: Basic Books, 1967).

Attorney 1:   I'd say, given my understanding of human nature, it happens.

Attorney 2:   See? That's sheer speculation. I don't think they penalize you for exercising your right to a trial. I have never felt that, as a prosecutor or a defense attorney. . . . I agree that when you plead, the judge doesn't hear all the facts. The judge doesn't get to see the pictures of the complainant with his face all swelled up, bones protruding out. I think in that respect it could influence a sentence . . . but it's not because you exercise your right to trial.

As the second, doubting lawyer stated, other factors might account for sentence differences, but these factors, rather than simplifying prediction of the outcome, complicated it further. Complexity increased the perceived uncertainty of trials. In fact, for these nine courts, trial penalties were statistically evident only in one court; elsewhere either the consequences were minimal or jury trials affected the length of sentences only in cases involving repeat offenders.[11]

Defense lawyers did not know with certainty what would happen to their clients if they refused to plead guilty. They could not dismiss lightly the possibility of trial penalties. Consequently, when they counseled clients about their options, caution colored their advice, with perhaps depressing results on their clients' urge to test the prosecution. In one of the suburban courts (where no statistically significant evidence of a trial penalty was found), attorneys heeded the courthouse grapevine and drew their own conclusions.

There's an unwritten rule around here that you're gonna get more at the trial than you would have had you pleaded.

*   *   *

The court will never state that there are penalties for going to trial. . . . They're unstated, but they exist.

11. Nardulli, Eisenstein, and Flemming, *Tenor of Justice*, 243–46, 257–59. For other findings regarding trial penalties, see Thomas M. Uhlman and N. Darlene Walker, " 'He Takes Some of My Time; I Take Some of His': An Analysis of Judicial Sentencing Patterns in Jury Cases," *Law and Society Review* 14(Winter 1980):324 and David Brereton and Jonathan D. Casper, "Does It Pay to Plead Guilty? Differential Sentencing and the Functioning of Criminal Courts," *Law and Society Review*, 16, no. 1(1981–82):45.

*   *   *

Some judges would like you to think that your guy is gonna get clobbered if he goes to trial. . . . They don't object to your feeling that there is a considerable risk of going to trial in terms of sentence.

Simply being in doubt was enough to discount the value of trials. As an attorney in another court said about the odds of the trial penalty, "That's one of the things we tell our clients all the time." This perceived risk added to the strong inertial pull of courthouse routines. Horror stories of sentences egregiously out of line with expectations fueled these apprehensions. Anecdotes about codefendants prosecuted for the same offense who chose different routes and ended up with mark-edly different sentences were staples of corridor chats, office gossip, and tavern banter. The grapevine was loaded with such stories, and although these stories provided shaky foundations for rules of thumb with such important consequences, attorneys found them hard to ig-nore. When combined with the economic costs and disincentives at-tached to going trial, the moral was clear—trials were gambles.

The Policy Contexts of Guilty Plea Work

Defense attorneys work within complex, varied courtroom settings that reflect both prosecutor and court policies. Table 6.1 presents the mix of policies that created the context for guilty plea work for defense attorneys. Three policies interacted to establish these contexts: first, the prosecutor's policies regarding concessions in guilty pleas; second, bench policies allowing for judge shopping; and, third, the judges' willingness to accept sentence recommendations.

Guilty pleas were either "open" or "closed." The distinction de-pended on whether judges routinely accepted sentence recommenda-tions as part of guilty pleas. Pleas were "closed" when judges followed these recommendations, while they were "open" when judges refused to accept guilty pleas with sentencing conditions attached to them. Open pleas bothered defense attorneys, because uncertainty about sen-tences complicated their work. With closed pleas, lawyers knew what to expect; the question of sentencing was settled prior to presenting the plea to the judge. Closed pleas thus facilitated client control. Open pleas did not. A lawyer in an open-plea court talked about this problem.

You know, in a lot of cases, you're really just kind of bobbing and weaving, because you don't know what your client's gonna get. And

TABLE 6.1. Contexts of Defense Attorney Work in the Nine Counties.

Is Judge Shopping Possible?	Typical Guilty Pleas	
	"Open"	"Closed"
No	Industrial[4]	Suburban[1]
	Suburban[3]	Autonomous[2]
		Autonomous[3]
Yes	Industrial[1]	Suburban[1]
	Autonomous[2]	Industrial[3]

Prosecutor's Plea Policies
1. Symbolic: Guilty plea concessions involve only count drops.
2. Minimal: Guilty plea concessions involve few original charge reductions or count drops.
3. Middling: Guilty plea concessions frequently involve both charge reductions and count drops.
4. Maximal: Guilty plea concessions usually involve both original charge reductions and count drops.

you just gotta tell him, "This is what the judge is gonna say. He's gonna tell you that if he feels so inclined he can give you so many years in the penitentiary. Now, in my opinion, you're gonna get probation. But the judge is gonna tell you he doesn't *have* to give you probation."

Familiarity with the judges and local sentencing habits helped, of course. According to an attorney in another open plea court, "Once you've got a feeling for the system, you're gonna know what the judges are gonna do." In a third court, a lawyer agreed that "you want to be able to predict what the judge is gonna do when you've got an open plea." Yet attorneys were reluctant to offer more than highly qualified, general predictions, even though these predictions might not satisfy client expectations. As one public defender put it, "I don't really feel comfortable promising my clients anything, and I never do. But at the same time, I feel apologetic that I cannot reassure them more." Attorneys thus were generally unhappy with open pleas. As one complained, "I personally am philosophically opposed to open pleas for the reason that it's very difficult for me to go to a client and say, 'We're gonna take our chances.'"

Closed pleas reduced uncertainties by resolving the question of sentence prior to entering the plea in court. Of course, this benefit depended on whether the judge found the sentencing recommendation acceptable. Expectations of the judge's reactions influenced negotiations between prosecutors and defense attorneys, if they knew ahead of time which judge would be assigned to their case. This depended on the court's calendar and whether it allowed for judge shopping.

Judge shopping could be used to get around judges who refused guilty pleas or declined to follow sentence recommendations. These opportunities existed only in courts with master calendars. The ability to move cases away from unsympathetic judges was generally a considerable advantage to defense counsel, but much depended on prosecutor-attorney relations and the explicit or implicit cooperation of trial assistants.

A third factor affecting defense work centered on whether guilty plea negotiations focused on charge reductions, count drops, or both. Prosecutor policies clearly governed here. More important, the value of these "concessions" varied. Reductions in original charges carried more substance than dropping supplementary or related charges. Charge reductions often reduced the maximum penalty and thus a client's exposure to more severe punishment. Pleas involving only count drops tended to be symbolic; the number of counts in a guilty plea minimally affected sentencing outcomes.

In general, attorneys in open-plea courts tried to "close" pleas when the stakes facing their clients were high and the attorneys were unsure what the judge would do. The frequency and precise form through which they "closed" pleas varied with the court. Defense counsel in closed-plea courts, conversely, sought to "open" pleas when the attorneys could not accept the prosecutor's terms or their clients balked at them. In this instance, the certainty of closed pleas was sacrificed in order to do justice.

Open Pleas: Two Case Studies

Two very different courts nevertheless shared two things in common: guilty pleas were open, and the courts' individual dockets prohibited judge shopping. The first court community offers an example of a relatively uncomplicated plea process in which judges, defense attorneys, and prosecutors generally cooperated with one another. Unlike the other courts, substantive plea concessions were common in this court. By comparison, in the second court the prosecutor made life more difficult for defense attorneys; concessions were more limited, and assistant prosecutors had less discretion. As a result, judges created ways for defense attorneys to work around the DA's restrictive policies.

Open Plea Uncertainties in a Concessions-Oriented Court

Plea negotiations were unfettered in this court, where the DA's office implemented its general guilty plea guidelines in a laissez-faire manner. In the chief prosecutor's words:

There's a golden rule that you "never say never." A case can go to crap. The only way you can enforce "There'll be no pleas less than such-and-such" is if you have guys fly suicide missions or you just dismiss cases. . . . I don't like to have people fly suicide missions and I think losing cases discourages people. . . . Besides, what do you get if you dismiss before trial because the case went to pot? We could have gotten something out of the guy.

Ironically, defense counsel, at times, were uncomfortable with the prosecutor's flexible standards. Negotiations were easier, but they also were less predictable. Attorneys complained about the office's inconsistency. The courthouse grapevine amplified these complaints. A senior prosecutor bemoaned the fact that defense attorneys quickly learned who got what. "The bar here is small enough," he explained, "that there's a lot of mumbo jumbo around about what people get out of things." One defense veteran commented on how the prosecutor's lack of policies affected his work.

Some of the problems, I guess, are created by whatever policies they may have, because they are made on a case-by-case basis. Because we're a small town, there are certain individuals, certain defendants who are known by everyone, y'know? And if you represent one of those defendants, you don't get a deal. . . . But other than that, everything depends on your defendant, his record. It depends on a situation where one of the cops says, "This dude's an asshole. No deals." That kind of thing. So I don't think we have policy here.

The attorneys sought assurances from a cooperative bench. Lawyers who worried whether judges would find certain pleas objectionable had ready access to the bench. An attorney pointed out, "There's not a judge on the bench that you can't go to in chambers and say, 'Judge, this is my problem. Can you give me some advice?'" Another offered a snapshot of the judges' sympathetic role in clearing away last-minute obstacles to negotiations.

Most of the judges know by looking at you whether you want to go to trial. You come in sweating, look at the judge, and say, "Y'know, Judge, you're looking at a lost week here with a criminal trial, but I might be willing to plead my man to a lesser charge." It's obvious to him that you're begging, "Give me something to get me out of this!" He looks at the prosecutor and says, "Is there any chance . . . ?" And, if the prosecutor says, "Well, maybe we can do such-and-such," then . . . Boom! That's the time, I suppose, when a lot of cases cave in.

Defense work is never free of uncertainty. These defense attorneys toiled in a relatively cooperative environment. Few policies stood in their way, although the absence of prosecutor policies raised anxieties about the consistency of nontrial dispositions. Attorneys in the court community discussed next faced greater difficulties.

"Closing" Open Pleas in a More Restrictive Setting

Attorneys in this court knew from the start what the trial prosecutors could and could not do in policy cases. Moreover, with the assistant prosecutors assigned to judges and courtrooms, defense attorneys knew early on what mix of personalities and relationships would be involved in each of their cases. As one lawyer put it:

> From the defense attorney's point of view, you know where you stand on a case because of the prosecutor's policies. Also, in knowing the prosecutor assigned to a particular judge in circuit court, with those cases that are not controlled by office policy, you have some idea of whether that assistant is more likely to give you something.

The judges denied they participated in plea negotiations. Veteran defense counsel, however, agreed with the following attorney's sketch of how things worked.

> What I do in cases where I'm not really sure is I go in to the judge ahead of time, before the plea is taken (if the judge will see me, and some of them will), and explain to him my feelings for my client. "What are your feelings about the penalty, Your Honor, realizing that you actually can't tell me." The judges will usually give you some idea. "We're looking at some county jail time." "Fine, okay, good." Now I know that's gonna be a year or less. And you ask the prosecutor, too. "What do you think the judge will do on this case if my client pleads guilty?"

Most but not all judges "ballparked" sentences for defense counsel. Consequently, attorneys had to know which judges to approach and which to avoid. While dealing with the cooperative judges, attorneys followed some rules of bench etiquette that evolved from the convention that the judges did not get involved in plea negotiations. This etiquette preserved the image of judicial neutrality and of a bench untainted by "plea bargaining." (As one ballparking judge stated, "I don't deal with criminals.") Decorum and propriety decreed that the lawyers not ask the judges directly what the sentences would be. They carefully avoided giving the judges the impression that they thought their responses were firm commitments.[12] Moreover, they made it clear that they were asking for a favor, that they knew they were indebted to the judges, and would not abuse the privilege the judges granted them. Getting a sense of what judges might do, as the following lawyer said, meant knowing how to read between the lines.

> Some judges will give absolutely no indication of what they will do. Others will not make you a promise but, if you read between the lines, you might be able to arrive at a conclusion as to what the sentence might be.

> For example, say you've got a case that you're gonna plead, and the defendant is obviously gonna get some time, but you want to know how much. The judge will start out, "Well, I don't get involved in sentence bargains." "But we're not asking you to bargain. Just give me a ballpark figure of what you've got in mind." "Well, I don't know."

> It is not something they want to talk about. You can't expect to tie the judge's hands by a specific figure. But if you have someone you're gonna plead on a life maximum offense, you do say, "Hey, wait a minute, Judge. You can't expect me to plead this man blindly. I have some thought of probably what you have in mind based on seeing you and the other judges. But don't ask me to do it blind."

Judges who ballparked sentences also generally told attorneys they could withdraw their pleas if the probation department, which made specific sentencing recommendations, recommended a higher sentence than the ballpark figure.[13] Withdrawing pleas opened an escape hatch for lawyers. The following attorney's experience was typical.

12. In one observed instance in which a defense attorney broke this rule of etiquette, an angry judge was confronted with a guilty plea remanded to his court by the court of appeals. The defendant had successfully argued that his attorney claimed the judge promised a more lenient sentence than the one he received. The judge denied he had ever made such promises. He made his displeasure with the attorney quite clear; the attorney would not receive further appointments from this judge to represent indigent defendants.

13. In this state, courts were required to have presentence reports from the probation department in all convictions. Local customs varied, however, in accordance with bench wishes regarding the specificity of the department's sentencing conclusions. In contrast to this court, the presentence reports included no sentencing recommendations in one county, while in another the report simply indicated whether probation or imprisonment was warranted. Under state rules, presentence reports were discretionary in the other six courts.

I had a guy who was charged with felonious assault plus possession of a firearm in commission of a felony which carries a mandatory two-year sentence.

In that case I went to the judge and I said, "Judge, I know you're not inclined to tell anybody what they're gonna get prior to sentencing, but here's what my guy tells me he's got to have to plead. He's on parole and will go back to serve eighteen months from the rest of his earlier sentence. His parole officer says he won't violate him. So I'd like to have my guy serve the felony concurrent with that since he doesn't want to do any more than two and a half years."

The judge said, "Well, you know I can't promise you what I'm going to do. . . ." Then he suggests, "I'll allow him to withdraw his plea if he doesn't like his sentence." You can't ask for any more than that.

Withdrawing a plea, however, meant potentially more work. As one attorney remarked, at this point, courtroom craft entailed knowing how to develop personal relationships and understandings with judges that would make them willing to listen to what an attorney had to say to them.

I would say that there is always room to sentence bargain with the judges, as opposed to withdrawing the plea—if it's done diplomatically. The art of sentencing is not such an exact science that any two, reasonable people cannot discuss why it should be three years as opposed to two, or two as opposed to five. So there's always room for discussion. And, once again, I say that any defense attorney who doesn't handle himself in a way so that judges want to sit down and talk with him is a fool.

Part of the diplomacy of the attorneys' craft was limiting the number of occasions when they drew on their credibility with judges to ask them to ballpark or to withdraw a plea. They knew they could not afford to abuse the judges' goodwill. As one long-standing defense lawyer estimated, "I can't recall doing it maybe four or five times out of fifty cases."

The state's "Youthful Trainee Act" (YTA) gave defense attorneys a way of reducing uncertainties about sentences that did not contravene the convention of nonjudicial involvement in plea negotiations. Attorneys petitioned the court to have the probation department evaluate their clients for eligibility for YTA, which expunged convictions after a period of probation.[14] The popularity of YTA reflected the judges' and defense attorneys' adjustments to the prosecutor's stringent policies as well as the bench's preference for open pleas. Two attorneys assessed the value of these motions from their perspective.

> The best result you can ever reach is a dismissal. Now YTA is something that will give me that dismissal after a period of time, so the case never appears on my client's record. A pretty good result, and predictable in all manner.

> *   *   *

> It's a tool for saving time and for quickly disposing of cases. . . . You get the probation department's report, and the bottom line is, "denied" or "granted." . . . But if they deny YTA, usually they'll indicate if the guy's a good candidate for probation. So, if he's denied, then you move right into a plea. You tell your client, "Hey, listen. There's no jail time. They've recommended no incarceration, even though YTA is denied." I then talk to the judge and ask him, "If we plead, will you follow the report's recommendation?" And he'll say, "Yeah, I won't give him any time."

"Opening" Closed Pleas: A Case Study

Attorneys generally prefer closed pleas or pleas for which they are confident the judges will accept sentencing recommendations. The advantage of closed pleas is that they eliminate uncertainty about sentences, but closed pleas have a related disadvantage that can create problems for defense attorneys. Compliant judges may put defense attorneys at the mercy of aggressive prosecutors. Stiff sentencing demands by prosecutors, if they can depend on the judges to accept the demands, force defense counsel into something of an "all or nothing" position. They either acquiesce or go to trial. In the following case study, lawyers found they could avoid this dilemma by pleading "blind" before judges who were willing to form an implicit coalition against the prosecutor.

Two Against One: "Blind Pleas" in a Suburban Court

The DA in a suburban court offered little to defense attorneys. He imposed rigid bottom lines on all plea offers. He allowed only symbolic

---

14. Pre-plea reports also helped answer questions about possible sentencing, but only two or three judges adopted this option.

charge concessions, involving just count drops. Defense attorneys, particularly the private bar, accused the office of failing to do justice when circumstances called for flexibility. Some lawyers also said that a few prosecutors tried to bluff them into agreeing to pleas above the bottom line. According to a defense veteran, "They don't necessarily make that bottom line offer to you the first time. Sometimes they do; sometimes they don't. It really depends on the individual prosecutor. You really have to know which one you're dealing with."

Closed pleas could trap unwary attorneys. Consequently, when it was necessary, defense counsel turned to open pleas, or what lawyers called "blind pleas." Open pleas, attorneys estimated, occurred in about one-third of all guilty pleas. They described open pleas as "flying blind," because the judge could pick a worse sentence than the prosecutor's bottom line or even one outside the norm. Familiarity with the judges was crucial when deciding whether an open plea was a safe bet.

Public defenders had an edge over private practitioners. They were assigned to specific judges, not cases, which kept them in the same courtroom and in front of the same judge most of the time. An open or blind plea, public defenders reasoned, served as a cue to judges that the prosecutor's offer was "off the wall." The defenders expected their judges to respond accordingly. A public defender described how the process worked:

I appear almost always in front of one judge. I've come to know him very well and what he will do in a particular situation. If the [prosecutor] comes to me with an offer that I feel is just totally off the wall, I quite often say, "If we enter a blind plea, how many charges do you want him to plead to?" Sometimes they'll knock off a few and we'll plead to a couple. Sometimes they won't do anything.

I have a situation right now where a gentleman has five burglaries. The state wants "X" number of years. I don't think that's warranted. And I don't think that the judge is going to give it to him regardless of whether I plead him to one burglary or five burglaries. . . . It's just a matter of how his record looks.

He can come out ahead by entering a blind plea and the state's attorney has no control over it. It's one of those things that, if they come to me with an offer that's too high, they know that I can do that and that my judge will give a lower sentence, because, again, my judge knows that if I enter a blind plea it's because the state's offer is too high.

Private attorneys did not have this advantage, and the bench's individual calendar did not offer any judge shopping opportunities. Accordingly, they drew on past experiences with judges to decide whether to file an open plea. As one lawyer claimed, "I've practiced before the judges quite a lot, and sometimes I may have to ask other people, but I've been around long enough that I think I can pretty much guess what they'll do." Nevertheless, most private attorneys preferred to talk to judges personally about open pleas. Experience, informed guesses, and advice only went so far in reducing the uncertainties of these pleas. Without an informal chat with judges beforehand, blind pleas, as one regular moaned, "make your palms sweat."

> I mean, you lay awake at nights worrying about blind pleas. I have one pending and I don't even want to think about it. There are judges you would never enter a blind plea in front of. There are others you would. A lot of it depends on the judge and the individual [assistant prosecutor] you have.

> Some judges will bring you into chambers and let you sit down and talk about the case along with the assistant. That varies with individual assistants, though, see? Now, in my opinion, a blind plea is a tentative plea. So you should be able to get a feel for what the judge is likely to do.

The insurgent DA did not assign his assistants to judges in order to keep them at arm's length from the bench. In addition, he opposed participation by his assistants in conferences in which he feared the judges and defense attorneys would pressure the assistants into violating his policies. This complicated the work of defense attorneys, who felt these conferences could resolve differences and thus produce closed pleas. Still, the cue-giving value of blind pleas remained intact, although private attorneys had to live with the uncertainties of these pleas.

Judge Shopping: Mechanics and Rules

When attorneys feared the sentencing consequences of putting an open plea before a certain judge or worried that a judge might refuse a closed plea, they "judge shopped," if they could. In an industrial county where pleas were open, and in a suburban court and another industrial county where pleas were closed, attorneys could and did judge shop. One of the lawyers explained how judge shopping entered into how he handled a difficult case and whether or not he would submit an open rather than the customary closed plea in this court.

I have a girl right now charged with armed robbery. First offense, eighteen years old. Walks into a bank with a gun and says, "Give me all your money." She gets about $1,200. As she's walking out of the bank, a security guard is coming in. He grabs her and takes the gun.

At her preliminary hearing, she just wouldn't talk to the assistant PD. He's trying to talk to her. And eventually he says, "A nice girl like you, why'd you do it?" "I was hoping somebody would shoot me." We looked into it more and found out she'd tried to commit suicide a couple of times—unsuccessfully, of course.

Now, in cases like that, because there was a gun involved, the DA is gonna go for eleven and a half to twenty-three months [in the county jail]. Now, I think by the time we really got down to negotiating, she'd already been in jail three months, and I said, "That's plenty for this girl."

I said to her, "Look, the DA's coming across with eleven and a half to twenty-three months. We can go to trial or we can try an open plea. If you try an open plea, it's all in the hands of the judge. He may give you eleven and a half to twenty-three, or he may give you more. He can give you five to ten years if he wants, or he can give you less. . . . It all depends on the judge we get." I was thinking of Judge ——— [a former prosecutor renowned for his stiff sentencing], because I'd never take her open in front of ———.

I told the prosecutor, "Here's what I'm gonna do. If I get the right judge, I'm gonna go open. If I don't, I'll take your deal." He says, "Okay."

See, an open plea gets him off the hook with the office. The office is always telling them, "You gotta go for time." This way he can go back and say, "Look, he took an open plea. The judge gave her three to six months. What do you want me to do?" An open plea gets him off the hook. He's done his job. Nobody can fault him. If the judge says, "Three months," who's gonna fight with him?

So [the deputy prosecutor] says, "Well, at least you know where I'm coming from." I said, "Yeah, I understand your position. If we get Judge ———, though, I'll take your deal. If we get somebody else, I'm gonna go open." [The deputy prosecutor] tells me, "I don't blame you."

The mechanics of judge shopping varied with the peculiarities of the courts' calendaring and scheduling procedures. For example, one court's trial terms lasted two weeks out of every four; cases stayed on each judge's trial docket for the entire term. Once the term ended, attorneys approached the court administrator to have certain of their unpled cases moved away from the originally assigned judge and placed on the dockets of other judges during the hiatus between trial terms. As one attorney explained:

> You wait until the case is off the docket. You have two weeks jury, two weeks off. You wait until the off week and then you just march in, when it's on nobody's docket, and say to Judge X, "Can we plead this case in front of you?" There's lots of ways of getting it in front of somebody else. I'll go to the court administrator and say, "You've had this on Judge Y's docket three times. How 'bout putting it somewhere else for a change?"

In another county, the central feature of its master calendar system—the "board"—was located in the case assignment room. This board listed all the cases that were first in line waiting for a courtroom, those on "standby" that would follow these cases, and then those cases without immediate court dates. When shopping for judges, skilled attorneys played the board by finding out where cases were in the queue, which courtrooms were about to open up, which ones were bogged down in trials, and which judges were looking for "short matters" or pleas.

> If you spend enough time in the assignment room, you can generally predict on a particular day who's sitting and who's free. . . . So my client might say, "Look, I'll plead." But I don't want to tell that to the DA until I find out what's happening in the assignment room. If Judge ——— sends down a message saying, "It's late in the day. We've got forty minutes. Send me a quick plea," I might say, "I think I just convinced my guy to take a plea."

*   *   *

You play it by ear. You have to see what the judge you don't want is doing. If he's in a long trial, you say, "Please put this case before the next available judge who's taking pleas." If you see that the judge you don't want is just about to conclude his trial, then maybe you won't ask to be put in for a guilty plea. You let it ride the board a bit more until he's engaged in something else, then ask to have it put in. You have to be flexible with guilty pleas, but if you decide to go to trial, there's not much you can do.

* * *

The name of the game is you've always gotta have a couple of cases that you're ready to throw to the . . . y'know . . . that you can get rid of or move around. You gotta be flexible. . . . I check in there twice a day; it's like going to the track. . . . By the way, you never tell the assignment people things at the last minute. You never leave them holding the bag. Always give them a little bit of notice. . . . Be nice to them.

* * *

You have to pick and choose. If you do it every case, you're dead. . . . Every now and then I'll need a favor. . . . The point is you can't do that all the time. That's why I don't do it on routine cases. . . . It has to count.

As with their other resources, attorneys rationed judge-shopping opportunities. A few basic rules of thumb guided their decision to judge shop.

- Use it, but don't abuse it.
- Be nice, cooperate.
- Maintain your credibility.
- Shop pleas, not trials.

The following comments made by members of another court's defense bar further illustrate these rules.

I have told the court administrator twice this term that there's no way I could appear before Judge ———. I try not to do that unless it's an absolute necessity.

* * *

The court administrator operates the kind of office where it's "I'll work with you as long as you work with me."

*   *   *

I don't want to lose my credibility. . . . I don't want every one of my guilty pleas to go before Judge X and then have Judge Y and Judge Z think, "What the hell, don't you like me?"

*   *   *

When you go to trial, you can't select your judge. You're just put on a wheel and you turn up in front of X, Y, or Z judge. . . . The [chief judge] keeps a pretty close watch on that, and I think you'll have some problems if you do try to do that.

One Against Two: When Judge Shopping Is Not a Bargain

In one autonomous county, judge shopping was not an advantage for the defense bar, because the district attorney determined which cases went before particular judges. The defense bar had little room for negotiations. Charge reductions were rare; even count drops were infrequent.[15] Guilty pleas were open, because the judges stoutly refused to listen to specific sentence recommendations. In addition, the judges refused to be drawn into guilty plea negotiations. Ballparking was uncommon; the judges discouraged informal chats about tentative pleas. The defense attorneys felt that the most they could hope for was to have the prosecutor remain silent at the time of sentencing. "Standing mute," which was a devalued currency in another court community, became a negotiable item of some importance to counsel in this court. The following comments by several attorneys highlight the straits of the defense bar in this community.

They're not gonna give you anything. It's as pure and simple as that. . . . With them, standing mute is a bargain, which they won't do a lot of times.

*   *   *

There's not a lot of meaningful plea bargaining here. When you come right down to it, they'll give you crumbs but rarely will they give you the cake.

15. Primary charge reductions occurred in less than 5 percent of the sampled cases in this court; the next highest was roughly 9 percent. Counts were dropped in less than 9 percent of the cases; the second highest was slightly more than 12 percent. For all nine courts, the average proportion of guilty pleas with some kind of charge reduction or change was 26 percent. See Nardulli, Eisenstein, and Flemming, *Tenor of Justice*, 247.

* * *

Their big deal is that they will stand mute at sentencing. Big deal! . . .
They don't give you much here. They really don't.

* * *

Interviewer: To what extent do judges involve themselves in plea
bargaining here?
Attorney: Rarely. Very rarely. . . . It's rarely done.

* * *

You're not gonna meet the judge in chambers and discuss possible
plea bargains. . . . What I'm saying is, I don't know of a single case in
which a judge has interjected himself into plea negotiations.

* * *

Attorney: The judges feel that they don't want to hear any num-
bers. "You're stepping into my territory now," they say.
They don't want to hear any numbers.
Interviewer: That makes your job tougher, doesn't it?
Attorney: It does.

Because the prosecutor's rigid position on guilty pleas reflected the
bench's wishes, the judges did not refuse pleas often, with one important exception, as many attorneys pointed out.

There's really not that many judges that will refuse an agreement if
it's presented to them. Although Judge ———, for one, will do it, . . .
Judge ——— will refuse agreements all the time. And then you just
have to take them to another courtroom.

This judge played a central role in the case assignment process.
Attorneys agreed that he was the most pro-prosecution judge on the
bench and its harshest sentencer. He demanded only "straight" guilty
pleas that offered no concessions to defendants. He also wanted serious
cases that captured media attention assigned to his courtroom. Several
attorneys confirmed the statement of one defense attorney: "I've been
in the prosecutor's office when the judge'll come prowling through
there saying, 'When are you gonna get me some big cases?'"
The prosecutor assigned cases to judges and thus governed the

judge-shopping process. According to one assistant prosecutor, open pleas frequently revolved around judge-shopping questions. "Yes," he confessed, "it's part of it, I would say, in about 35 percent of our bargains." Defense attorneys tried to avoid the one judge about whom they expressed concern when their cases called for it. Prosecutors recognized their edge over defense lawyers. As one assistant admitted, "It works advantages for us. There's no doubt about it." Another illustrated how the threat of placing a case before this judge benefited the prosecution.

> Assuming we have reached what we feel is a good bargain and the defendant says, "There's no way I'm taking this bargain. Forget it. I'll go to the jury," our next question is, "Fine. We're going before Judge ————." It happens all the time. He's our ace in the hole.

This same assistant also affirmed that leverage over case assignments helped in pretrial proceedings. "Evidentiary, search and seizure, and where the case law is split—y'know, it's not real clear-cut—we'll try to take it before a judge that is more [prosecution-oriented]." Defense attorneys knew where they stood. A public defender described a personal incident to make his point.

> I had a recent experience in which I presented an issue before a given judge. He ruled in my favor. Subsequently, all similar issues were directed away from him to another judge who is systematically in the [prosecution's] favor.

The defense attorneys' best way around these obstacles was Miscellaneous Court, or "Junk Court." This court was in session on Wednesdays of noncriminal trial weeks. At arraignment, conducted once a month, defense lawyers learned which judges would preside over this court and when. If attorneys felt the judge was acceptable, they asked at arraignment that particular cases be set for Junk Court. The other remaining cases went on the trial list to be scheduled for trial during the next trial term. A public defender explained the process of scheduling a case for Junk Court.

> Well, the best time to do it, I think, is at arraignment. If I'm doing this sort of scheduling sandbagging, I'd rather just go into arraignment where they just have two DAs. When the case comes up, they ask, "What do you want to do with this?" "Not guilty, trial by judge. Put it in Junk Court."

This option of moving directly into Miscellaneous Court gave attorneys a way of minimizing the sentences some of their clients faced. A hard-nosed prosecutor recognized how this option undermined his plans in certain cases.

> I'm assigned to a serious case, and I want to zap this guy. All of a sudden he goes to arraignment and he says he's gonna plead guilty on a certain date before a certain judge. When that happens, I might not see the case again.

Endgames and Sentencing

Closed pleas combined both disposition and sentencing. Open pleas led to another stage involving discussions about the sentence and review of the probation department's presentence report. In courts where sentencing stood apart from the guilty plea, some held conferences in chambers before courtroom pronouncements. "Chamberizing" gave defense attorneys a chance to talk about sentencing options informally and to work out compromises without the posturing that would be required in open court. Attorneys set aside formalities and used their credibility with judges when making pitches for their clients.

> If it's done in chambers, more facts emerge. I think the judge gets to know more. I think there's greater intensity of feelings and expression. You can be more honest. I can tell the judge, "Hey, this guy's an asshole, but he still doesn't warrant a prison sentence."

> You get a chance to prove your own reliability. If you concede your client ought to go to prison, if you do that many times, the judge sees you're pretty close to right in what you think about sentences for your clients. So when you say, "Judge, he absolutely deserves probation" or "He deserves a short term in jail," he'll give you some respect. I can be very honest and open with the judge. But if it's in the courtroom, all you can do is stress the positive.

In other courts, where open pleas were common but sentencing conferences in chambers were not, attorneys tried to talk to judges before sentencing as the need arose. Approaching judges in this way, however, required tact and knowledge of their different styles.

> I have gone in before sentencing to have a talk with the judge, but I do not do that with every judge. You know who you can talk to based

on their track record and who you can talk to rationally and above-board about something. I don't go into Judge W's chambers because he'll kick you out. But I can go to Judge X on occasion and Judge Y as often as I want to or Judge Z as I want. Now that's not saying that I'll get what I want, but they are open, and I know that I can talk to them as an individual.

Judicial quirks and oddities made grapevines flourish. The grapevine gave attorneys privy to its chatter useful inside information, as one attorney illustrated through an anecdote.

I had a case where the DA was arguing for a sentence to the state penitentiary. I told the judge, "I know you want to hammer my client, but let's hammer him in the county. If you send him to the state, Judge, it's out of your hands."

Now, this judge hates the parole board because it let some chick out who murdered her father. They've let her out twice now, and each time he writes the parole board.

When I said that he just looked up over his glasses and said, "I don't want to get into that discussion. I think we all know how I feel about the parole board." But that was it, y'know? He went for it. He loved it. He likes to keep his arm on a case plus he's scared to death the parole board's gonna do something nonsensical again.

Regardless of the nature of their pitch or whether attorneys had a chance to talk with judges before sentencing, the attorneys believed their words carried only as much weight as their credibility with the judges. They felt their standing with judges colored all aspects of the sentencing process. As one put it, "Superimposed on everything is your own credibility." Others agreed.

If you're able to push your point across, a lot of it has to do with the credibility you have as a defense attorney.

* * *

There are certain people that I represent that are going to prison, period. And they should. So for me to make a fool out of myself and ruin my changes to help someone else doesn't make any sense.

*   *   *

You know, with a guy that's a fifteen-time offender, I'm not gonna bring a priest in and have him say my guy's found the light. I'd be laughed out of the courtroom. It all goes to the respect that your colleagues and the judges have for you. . . . At sentencing they know that I'm not gonna waste their time.

Probation departments posed another contingency for attorneys. Their presentence reports (and, if they had made any, their sentencing recommendations) were the judges' only source of independent information about defendants and sentencing alternatives. One lawyer went so far as to claim:

The secret of sentencing is working with the probation people. You have to get along with them. You've got to deal with them on a human level. You don't go in and say, "Okay, I'm the lawyer and you've got to do this." You say, instead, "Listen. What I'd like to see . . ." You work on them, because the judges don't know your client and they have to rely on someone about him, and they rely on the probation department."

Another attorney related a lesson he learned about the probation department's importance in his court.

I had a case where the man had been given the maximum for possession with intent to distribute. He had been promised probation by his defense attorney. I picked the case up after sentencing. . . . I filed a motion for reconsideration of the sentence.

The judge refused to hear it. He wouldn't even give me a hearing date. Now, that's a little rough. So I went to the judge and I said, "Your Honor, I really need to discuss this with you." He said, "Go talk to [the chief probation officer]."

This was my first experience with [the probation chief]. So I talked to him and we got everything organized. The probation officer went to the judge personally. And I had the guy out in two days. I then had to start developing a relationship with [the chief], which makes life harder. Because not only am I dealing with the prosecutor and the judge, now I have to deal with probation.

See, the shocker was that I had not dipped into the grapevine to learn about the judges' practice of relying on [the probation officer], and so I got it full face without having been prepared. Which made it even worse, because everyone knew about the incident, including "up on the range," which is what they call the jail. It affects your reputation.

Attorneys tried to establish relations with probation officers that would lead to talks about their sentencing recommendations. As one attorney mentioned, "I make it a point to have coffee with the guys in the probation department. . . . Now, I don't mean to say that I spend my whole time working people, but if they know me and I know them, then we can work better together."

In addition, defense counsel encouraged their clients to put their best foot forward during their interviews with probation officers.

I tell them to be absolutely, totally straight. "If they catch you in a lie," which I've seen happen, "they'll screw you."

* * *

The way the defendant comes across in the interview is the most important aspect of the report. If they come across unfavorably, then they're going to get an unfavorable recommendation. If they come across favorably, they're gonna get a favorable recommendation. . . . So I tell them, "If you insist on your innocence, then you're not gonna accomplish anything. As a matter of fact, it's gonna cause more difficulty for me." I tell them, "Don't make any excuses. Don't qualify it. Just tell them you did it. It was a mistake; it was dumb, period."

* * *

I tell them, "If you walk in with a cocky attitude or an 'I'm not sure I even did it' look, you deserve the probation report you will likely get." I pound it into them that they're trying to make two impressions: one, "I did it," and two, "I won't do it anymore." If they don't hit it off with the probation officer, they make my job significantly worse.

For coaching to return dividends, congenial relations between the attorneys and probation officers were necessary. Attorneys also cozied up to probation officers because they feared that prosecutors were contacting the officers. A lawyer said, "If I know which person it is, I can call them and make suggestions, as I'm sure the prosecutor does, and in fact as police officers sometimes do." Another attorney complained that, with the advent of a new, more aggressive prosecutor, "They're writing letters to the probation officer recommending stiff sentences. . . . They never really did that much before."

Interviewer:	Does that mean you're going to talk to the probation officer more after the guilty plea?
Attorney:	I haven't before, but as of yesterday I'm gonna start doing it. Because the last two sentences I've had—ten to twenty and seven to fourteen—I noticed in both presentence reports there's a big letter from the district attorney's office. . . . I'm gonna start doing the same thing, speak up for the guy a little bit, do something.

Summary

From a defense attorney's perspective, an ideal mix of courthouse policies would include closed pleas, concessions involving both primary charge reductions and count drops, and opportunities for judge shopping. Closed pleas reduce uncertainties and enhance client control. Closed pleas, along with primary charge reductions and count drops, introduce the flexibility in sentencing needed to do justice. And the option of placing particular cases before specific judges lessens the chance that a judge will refuse to accept the plea, to the embarrassment and possible regret of the attorney. The least ideal circumstances will include open pleas, symbolic concessions, and no control over which judges would hear which cases.

None of the defense attorneys in the nine courts labored under either of these sets of circumstances. Their work environments were complex mixtures of conflicting local practices that at times left them uncertain about how to plead a case, worried about their client's reactions to possible sentences, and concerned about what the judges would do. Uncooperative prosecutor's offices, of course, made the attorneys' work more difficult. Routine cases did not necessarily raise these problems, and routine dispositions were thus generally acceptable to defense lawyers. In nonroutine matters, however, the attorneys broke these routines. Their craft consequently included both the reproduction of courthouse routines and knowing when and how to deviate from these routines.

Estimating the frequency with which attorneys found it necessary to work around courthouse routines is a risky venture. However, it is likely that attorneys representing defendants in serious felony cases, such as robbery, rape, arson, and murder, because of the higher stakes and the loosening of sentencing norms, most often tried to free themselves of courthouse conventions and constraints. For the nine courts, such cases equaled 20 percent of all guilty pleas.[16]

16. Nardulli, Eisenstein, and Flemming, *Tenor of Justice,* 361.

Conclusions

Introduction

The craft of justice combines both politics and work. Politics shapes the boundaries of adversarial conduct in courtrooms. It molds the patterns of status and influence in the courthouse. What happens in courtrooms cannot be separated easily from what goes on in the conference rooms, chambers, offices, and corridors of courthouses. Craft is practical knowledge of how others perform their work and of the relationships involved in this work. It combines personal experiences with the lessons learned by others so that legal practitioners can organize their work and manage their relationships, all of which makes their craft highly contextual. Accordingly, because courtroom work is performed in stratified court communities within a political and policy context of bounded adversarial relationships, what is regarded as "common sense" in one court community may not be regarded as such in another. In this way, common sense, the interpretation and use of experience and folklore, becomes the court community's local culture.[1]

Courtroom Work and Variations in the Craft of Justice

The courtroom craft of assistant prosecutors and defense attorneys varied greatly with the particular mix of policies that existed in the court community. Both sets of actors in all nine courts, however, shared a common concern for their professional reputations because their reputations signaled to others the kinds of persons with whom they were dealing. These actors were not impoverished in their information about each other. They had histories of prior encounters and the grapevine kept them (as well as the court community at large) up-to-date about who had done what to whom lately. The function of this

1. Clifford Geertz, *Local Knowledge: Further Essays in Interpretative Anthropology* (New York: Basic Books, 1983).

informational system was to encourage conformity or adherence to the court community's norms and way of doing things.[2]

Craft is a practical skill. It is iterative and experiential. New members learn what works in their particular courthouse, watch how others do their jobs, and listen to the tales, both happy and sorry, of others. This process of imitating others becomes a matter of "social proof" in which conformity to what is common sense in the court is evidence of the correctness of certain kinds of behaviors.[3] For example, even though the incentives and positions of private and public attorneys differed, the ways in which they handled cases with respect to preliminary hearings or motions were often similar as a matter of conformity to local professional norms. The grapevine, of course, is a constant source of proofs and second-hand evidence about the consequences of non-conformity.

Reputations were largely a matter of responsiveness and credibility, both of which helped create the foundation for cooperation. Responsiveness combined the qualities of trustworthiness, accommodativeness, predictability, and amiability. Credibility, on the other hand, included trial competence, which could be translated into courtroom victories and could affect sentencing outcomes.[4] Since reputations for cooperation tended to prevail within the courts, new members were likely to adopt a similar strategy, believing that this was the key to acceptance and to being treated well. Thus, newcomers in the court communities, despite sometimes questionable trial skills, were seen by others as being responsive.

The bind for assistant prosecutors in establishing credible working relations with judges and defense attorneys was that they were employees and representatives of the chief prosecutor. These two considerations could clash. For assistants who worked in offices with stiff guilty plea policies, it meant learning how to slip around these restrictions without jeopardizing their jobs. Judges often extended helping hands, which created bonds of gratitude but also indebtedness. Assistant prosecutors had to recognize that a fine line separated responsiveness from subservience and needed to learn that part of their craft was

2. Robert Axelrod, "The Evolution of Norms," *American Political Science Review* 80(December 1986):1095.

3. Axelrod, "Evolution of Norms," 1105.

4. For example, in cases with more serious charges, prosecutors with more punitive attitudes who were ranked as having greater trial competence than defense attorneys had a positive impact on sentences in guilty plea cases. See Peter F. Nardulli, Roy B. Flemming, and James Eisenstein, "Unraveling the Complexities of Decision Making in Face-to-Face Groups: A Contextual Analysis of Plea-Bargained Sentences," *American Political Science Review* 78(December 1984):912.

knowing when and how to use their authority to draw this line. The assistants, then, had to learn how to manage relationships in the courtroom to meet often conflicting demands.

The specifics of the assistants' courtroom craft was not the same from one court to the next. With respect to tasks, for example, some deputy prosecutors had to manage the dockets of judges, while others did not shoulder this burden. Some assistants handled cases from their inception to their conclusion, while others did not have to concern themselves with preliminary hearings and only had to prepare cases once they reached the circuit court. The discretion to perform these tasks also varied as a reflection of office policies; some assistants had few options at hand when dealing with cases, while others had access to many levers. Another difference reflected the assignment policies of the prosecutor offices and the number of defense attorneys in the courthouse.

While some assistants worked in front of the same judges week after week, prosecuting whatever cases came before the judges, and dealt with only a handful of defense attorneys, other deputies followed cases from one judge to the next and prosecuted cases involving larger numbers of attorneys. The fewer and more stable the participants were that assistants had to face on a daily basis, the easier and more certain managing relations in the courtroom was. The craft of assistant prosecutors, then, could be relatively simple or relatively complex, depending on the array of tasks for which they were responsible, the discretion they were given to do this work, and the number of judges and attorneys with whom they had to interact. The narrower the task assignment was, the greater the discretion, and the fewer and more familiar the judges and attorneys were, the simpler the craft of assistant prosecutors.

Defense attorneys largely accepted the circumstances they faced in the courthouse. Their craft was shaped by concerns over efficiency, adherence to professional norms, minimizing any regrets for their actions, and being effective, given the realities of the courthouse. In many cases, these concerns were incompatible.

For example, attorneys frequently cited the professional rule of thumb that the preliminary hearing should never be waived. Yet expeditious alternatives, such as early guilty plea agreements and access to prosecutor files, and economic considerations induced attorneys to waive these hearings. On the other hand, client control problems and the possibility of motions at later stages were countervailing factors that encouraged attorneys to request that the hearings be held. These considerations, combined with a concern for maintaining credibility within the courthouse, led defense attorneys to ration their legal resources. They were reluctant to "paper" the court with motions. Furthermore, motions, like preliminary hearings, offered few tangible returns or benefits.

Trial decisions, while they involved similar kinds of considerations as motions, included uncertainty about "trial penalties." In this instance, second guesses and folklore discouraged attorneys from advising their clients that the gamble of a trial was worth the risk. Common sense about the risk of trials, however, lacked strong empirical foundation in most of the courts.

The guilty plea work of attorneys differed according to the mix of court and prosecutor policies. These contexts, plus the court community's going rates, created "routines" that eased the vexing problem of uncertainty that defense attorneys sought to solve. Part of the defense attorneys' craft was to reproduce these routines. The other part, however, was knowing when and how to avoid the routine handling of nonroutine cases.

In "open plea" courts, attorneys tried to gain some assurance from the judges about sentences in cases where the stakes were high and the going rate was unsettled or unclear. When attempting to "close" these pleas, attorneys observed courthouse etiquette that shielded the judges from impressions that they "plea bargained." In "closed plea" courts, attorneys gambled on open pleas before understanding judges in order to undercut the prosecutor's plea offer. The perceived risks of open pleas were reduced if attorneys could judge shop. They were further reduced when attorneys had credible relations with probation officers and if they planned their endgames by coaching their clients on how to behave during interviews with probation officers. The upshot is that the content of the craft of defense varied with whether guilty pleas typically were open or closed, whether judge shopping was an option, and whether prosecutor policies permitted charge concessions.

The courtroom craft of judges was influenced by the calendaring, docketing, and assignment policies of their courts. The judges, of course, had a voice in the selection of these policies. Their courtrooms, moreover, remained more or less their personal fiefs. They decided how they wanted to use their time in the courtroom, and in courts with individual calendars they picked scheduling options that suited their tastes and their views of how these options affected attorneys. Judges policed guilty pleas in their courtrooms in a variety of ways. Their mix of policing methods reflected individual concerns over preserving the appearance of judicial neutrality, retaining their sentencing prerogatives, and ensuring the expeditious movement of cases. The extent to which judges practiced similar courtroom crafts depended in some measure on the level of consensus within the bench; the more collegial the court, the more likely it was that judges followed roughly similar routines in their courtrooms.

The working craft of judges, like that of prosecutors, varied in complexity with the array of tasks they handled. Judges in courts with individual calendars and who heard both civil and criminal cases had more diverse job demands requiring more complicated ways of managing their work than judges who sat on benches with master calendars and presided over specialized dockets. Furthermore, as with prosecutors, the judges' ability to manage relations and uncertainty in their courts increased with the stability and hence the familiarity of the attorneys who appeared before them.

The content of court craft, then, varied. More important, these variations were largely a result of the policy decisions made by the sponsoring organizations within the court community. Within the specific context created by these policies, individual differences emerged, but the complexities involved in organizing work and the uncertainties that needed to be managed reflected the particular mix of policies prevailing in the courthouse.

Political Craft and Varieties of Court Communities

Court communities are constructed by their members. The central characteristics of a court community—its status and influence structure, its technologies for processing cases, its grapevine and norms governing interpersonal relations—evolve through the actions and interactions of courthouse participants. These characteristics lend stability and conservatism to the courthouse. Court craft reproduces and reinforces these characteristics much of the time because it is an iterative, experiential, and practical body of skills based on knowing what works. The community's members learn by doing and by following the lead of others. If something works, they continue doing it. However, the community's characteristics, as well as its working crafts, ultimately reflect the interplay of organizational and institutional interests within the courthouse, and it is this interplay that is most likely to lead to changes in the craft of justice.

The political craft of justice turns attention to the role of the sponsoring organizations and their institutional relationships within the court community. While the working craft of the participants is to a large extent internal to the community, the political craft of the major actors is complexly shaped by both internal and external factors. Figure 1 locates the nine counties in terms of the prosecutors' organizational styles and the social organization of the benches. The counties are then identified according to their sociopolitical type and by the characteris-

Prosecutor's Organizational Strategy

Social Organization of Court	Bureaucratic Weapon	Efficient Firm	Reactive/Proactive Clan
Collegial		Autonomous[4]	Industrial [2] Industrial [3] Industrial [4] Autonomous[3]
Competitive	Suburban [2]		
Conflictual	Suburban [1]	Autonomous[4]	Suburban [1]

Higher ◄──────────────────────────► Lower
Likelihood of Prosecutorial Dominance

Characteristics of Defense Bar:

1. Lower concentration of defense bar; lower proportion of public paid cases. Both counties had public defenders.

2. Lower concentration of defense bar; higher proportion of public paid cases. Both counties had assigned counsel.

3. Higher concentration of defense bar; lower proportion of public paid cases. Both counties had public defenders.

4. Higher concentration of defense bar; higher proportion of public paid cases. All three counties had public defenders or contract attorney offices.

Figure 1. Varieties of criminal court communities.

tics of the criminal defense bars (i.e., public defender versus assigned counsel or contract attorneys, whether the defense bar was concentrated or diffuse, and whether indigent cases were a high or low proportion of defense work). Figure 1 also indicates the likelihood that the court community was dominated by the prosecutor's office or by the bench. This figure highlights the variety of court communities in the nine counties. If the various combinations of factors are considered, it also points to the potentially complex array of court communities that might be identified if information were available for the roughly 425 circuit courts in the United States with four or more judges in 1987.

The court communities that were most alike were those of the declining industrial counties. The three benches were collegial, and the prosecutors ran their offices like clans. However, two of the prosecutors were conservators while the third was a reformer who tried to give his office a proactive rather than reactive orientation. The defense bars were also different. In one county, the court classified a large proportion of the felony defendants as being indigent and, through its assignment program, distributed these cases to a large, diffuse defense bar. The other two counties had public defenders, and the markets for criminal lawyers were more concentrated. However, they differed in that indigent defense work was a smaller proportion of the market in one than in the other.

The other counties did not form such tidy clusters. And even the cluster formed by the industrial counties was not homogeneous, as it included an autonomous county with many of the features of the industrial communities—a collegial bench, a prosecutorial clan, and a concentrated criminal defense bar. While no simple pattern emerged for the other counties, a rough association, marked by some notable exceptions (as in the case of the aforementioned autonomous county), can be discerned among the courthouse styles of prosecutors, their organizational strategies, and the type of county.

The two insurgent prosecutors who made their offices into bureaucratic weapons were both elected from suburban counties. But the other suburban prosecutor took a conservator role and ran his office like a reactive clan. Two of the three courthouse reformers who organized their offices into efficient firms were located in autonomous, middle class counties, although the office in the other autonomous county was a reactive clan. And two of the three DA offices in the industrial counties were headed by conservator prosecutors and arranged like reactive clans. This pattern seems consistent with claims that prosecutors' offices reflect the social and cultural patterns of their local communities.[5] From a cross-sectional perspective, conservative, suburban counties appear to choose prosecutors with aggressive, no-holds-barred, crime-fighting programs while middle-class, good-government counties pick chief prosecutors who manage their offices with businesslike efficiency and working class communities elect DAs with more relaxed styles.

One difficulty in inferring ties between local community and prosecutorial style is that this cross-sectional perspective ignores the histories of the counties. The predecessors of the two suburban insurgents, for example, ran their offices more like clans, and they knuckled under to bench demands. Furthermore, one of the insurgents, after two contentious, strife-torn terms, was toppled in a reelection bid by the

---

5. Joan Jacoby, *The American Prosecutor: A Search for Identity* (Lexington, Mass.: Lexington Books, 1980), 47.

same political forces he successfully fought when he first ran for prosecutor. Furthermore, the office in one of the autonomous counties had been a reactive and unprofessional clan before a reformer prosecutor took over the reins. And, as a final example, in one of the industrial counties, two candidates with reformer styles had preceded the conservator who was the incumbent at the time of the fieldwork for this study.

A second difficulty is that this cross-sectional perspective slights the internal incentives that prompt prosecutors to adopt a particular courthouse style. The insurgents and reforming prosecutors picked approaches that reflected their views and perceptions of how the court community operated and whether challenges to the status quo would violate their common sense of what the position of the prosecutor's office in the court community should be.

It may be that these exceptions merely prove the rule; perhaps the styles and strategies of succeeding prosecutors, although they may fluctuate and differ, "average out" over time. Thus, suburban counties more often have insurgent DAs who organize bureaucratic weapons than do autonomous counties that, most of the time, prefer reform-oriented prosecutors who take pride in running efficient offices, while industrial communities are satisfied with low-key prosecutors who don't make waves and won't rock the boat. Accordingly, the example of the chief prosecutor in one of the industrial counties, who started out a reformer and ended up a conservator and who decided not to seek reelection after he lost the support of the Democratic party and other local power brokers, may illustrate this "self-correcting" process in which prosecutorial styles and policies are kept in line with local community expectations. However, with only nine counties and a handful of years as the bases for observing the link between local communities and prosecutor offices, this issue cannot be resolved conclusively.[6]

A similar ambiguity surrounds the apparent relationship between

6. The literature on this link is surprisingly slim, if not virtually nonexistent, especially when compared to the many studies of judicial elections that have been done (although none have looked at the impact of elections on the judicial organization of trial courts), and more particularly when the pivotal role of the prosecutor is considered. Jacob devotes little more than a page or so in his book on the politics of crime in ten large cities to contrast the political positions and activities of the prosecutors over a thirty year period. See Herbert Jacob, *The Frustration of Policy: Responses to Crime in American Cities* (Boston: Little, Brown and Company, 1984), 121–22. Two other relevant studies, although they are not comparative and cover shorter periods of time, which limits their ability to address the issue raised here, are Herbert Jacob, "Politics and Criminal Prosecution in New Orleans," in James R. Klonoski and Robert I. Mendelsohn, eds., *The Politics of Local Justice* (Boston: Little, Brown and Company, 1970), 132–48, and Stuart A. Scheingold and Lynne A. Gressett, "Policy, Politics, and the Criminal Courts," *American Bar Foundation Research Journal* 1987(Spring–Summer 1987):461.

the social organizations of the benches and the types of counties. It may be that the important factor was the size of the courts and not the sociopolitical characteristics of the local communities. For example, all three industrial counties, plus two of the autonomous counties, had collegial benches. In contrast, the social organizations of the three suburban courts were either competitive or conflictual.

The smaller size of the courts in the industrial and autonomous counties may be one factor encouraging collegiality, although that was no guarantee of it, as the example of the conflictual four-judge court in the third autonomous county suggests. Elections, retirements, resignations, and new judgeships all can upset the internal equilibrium of courts, but their effects can be magnified on small benches of four or five judges. Still, the smaller courts tended to be collegial, and the suburban courts, which in contrast were larger, were either competitive or conflictual; consensus may fall victim to diversity as courts increase in size with the populations of their local jurisdictions. Moreover, even a dominant political party with some control over the selection of judges may not muffle dissenting or rancorous voices on the bench. In two of the suburban counties where the Republican party reigned, the judges nevertheless were divided among themselves along political lines. To this should be added the potentially disruptive effects of expansions in the benches, which increases not only the number of persons who will participate in the governance of the court but the odds of further diversity as well.

In smaller jurisdictions, the courts grew less rapidly, if at all. The homogenizing effects of political party recruitment may be less important than the common social, business, and professional ties that link members of the bar in smaller counties and that extend to include the judges on the bench. Elections for judges are not without their risks, but the chances of facing a challenger (which, of course, did not exist in the retention elections in two of the states) and failing to win another term are not high. A judge may remain on the bench for a very long time. Thus, mutual recognition by the handful of judges on each bench of the fact that they very likely will be together for a number of years may stifle the urge to be a maverick or to complain openly about a fellow judge who is.

Dominance within the court community reflects the organization of the courts and of prosecutors' offices. Dominance is one means of enforcing or maintaining different ways of disposing of cases. It is also a means of effecting changes in the balance between cooperation and conflict or maintaining it. Figure 1 indicates that prosecutorial dominance occurred when the DAs exploited the bureaucratic potential of their offices. Judicial dominance in the court community typically existed where prosecutors were conservators and ran their offices like clans.

Insurgent prosecutors seek to change the habits of craft in the courthouse, and they are prepared to live with more adversarial relationships within the court community. Their success depends on whether they can gain an advantage over the bench and defense bar. Prosecutors, it has been noted several times, have valuable resources for this effort. But their success may be transitory or only partial. One of the suburban prosecutors remained in office for two terms. When he sought a third term, he failed to win in his party's primary. His truculence and unwillingness to compromise rallied the defense bar and its supporters in the Republican party to back the candidate the DA had defeated in his first campaign. The other suburban county offers a contrasting example. The court community could not dislodge the prosecutor because he assiduously sought to make himself a pivotal figure within his political party and a popular official within the county. He remained in office for three terms and, after running for a statewide position, decided to retire, handing over the office to his longtime confederate and first assistant, who subsequently became DA. With respect to disposition of cases, the prosecutors attained some of their goals and changed the ways the courts had traditionally processed felonies (which, it might be added, include the adjustments judges and defense attorneys had to make to circumvent policy restrictions in both court communities). From the standpoint of status and influence within the communities, the prosecutors succeeded in making their offices the dominant forces in the counties.

Judges, of course, may have the upper hand over prosecutors, as illustrated by the autonomous county where the judges' preferences concerning guilty plea clearances by the prosecutor changed the disposition process. Furthermore, this county provides an example of a judge-dominated alliance with the prosecutor's office, aimed at regulating the guilty plea process through the prosecutor's control over judge shopping. Dominance also can maintain the status quo, as indicated by the obdurateness of the chief judge in an industrial county regarding changes in his favored docketing practices. The status and influence structures of courthouse communities, therefore, highlight the role that dominance plays in supporting courthouse norms and the way in which struggles over dominance lead to changes in these norms and crafts.

The overall pattern suggested by Figure 1 is that when prosecutors fail to take advantage of their organizational and institutional resources, the judges by default have an edge over the prosecutors, as long as the benches remain reasonably consensual. Prosecutors who do exploit the bureaucratic potential of their office are likely to be the dominant actors within the court community, given the institutional weaknesses of judges as a collective body. The defense bar usually remains at best a potential silent partner or ally of the bench in these struggles for status and influence.

Legal Pluralism in American Trial Courts: A Concluding Thought

American courts are complex. The craft of justice is varied. Efforts to capture in a few words, a couple of contrasting examples, or a simple classification the many significant differences in how craft is practiced and in how local courts structure themselves are doomed to failure. The evidence from nine courts in three states makes this point abundantly clear. Yet nine courts, let alone two or three, were not enough to fully explore the contours of legal pluralism in America's courts. This study and its companion volumes are initial mappings of this complicated terrain. They point the way to thinking about courts so that complexity is recognized and taken into account.

The craft of justice and court communities share a circular relationship. Craft helps to build and sustain the court community as its members seek to establish careers and to succeed in the courts. Uncertainty about work and relationships is to be avoided, and much of craft is aimed at learning how to reduce it. Reputations, routines, and hence predictability bubble up from day-to-day encounters over cases to contribute to the "common sense" of the courtrooms and courthouse. In turn the stratified structure of the court community and its grapevine and gossip about reputations encourage conformity to these emergent norms and definitions of craft . . . at least for a time.

The stability of these meanings of craft is rarely complete. External events disrupt the organizations and institutional relations that hold these meanings in place. Internally, the fact that the functionally interdependent but institutionally autonomous actors continually make decisions with potentially negative effects on other members batters away at the foundation of the status quo. Within the court community, dissatisfied prosecutors or ambitious judges may choose to employ the institutional power available to them to change matters, setting in motion decisions that may alter the procedures underlying the working craft of the courtrooms.

Court communities are not only complex, then, but in a state of potential or actual flux as autonomous changes arise out of the interplay of external and internal events and out of the work and politics in the communities. Variations in the craft of allocating time, organizing work, and managing relationships inevitably occur. The members and organizations making up the court community thus are continuously involved in the selection and retention of these variations. Legal pluralism emerges within and among courts through interactions of community and history, politics and professionalism. The next stage toward an understanding of legal pluralism in America's trial courts should recognize not only the broad diversity of craft and community that prevails in the courts, but the importance of knowing how often they change.

Appendix A. Characteristics of the Nine Research Sites and the Interviews

The identities of the nine courts' locations have been obscured whenever possible in this book. This was done for two reasons. First, assurances of anonymity were given the prosecutors, judges, and lawyers who cooperated in this research. Because of the focus of this book, these assurances would have been hollow promises if the sites had been named during the course of discussing the craft of justice in their courts. Second, the purpose of this book was not to describe and compare the localities, but to use the empirical data collected in this project to illustrate more general patterns that emerged from the analysis. It is very possible, given the scope and detail of this research project, to lose sight of the forest by concentrating on the contrasts and similarities of specific trees. At this point, however, it would not be inappropriate to sketch brief profiles of the nine research sites. Figure A.1 presents the locations and some of the major characteristics of the nine counties that served as research sites for this book.

The three suburban communities in this study were the counties of DuPage in Illinois, Oakland in Michigan, and Montgomery in Pennsylvania. All three counties are parts of larger metropolitan areas. DuPage is located next to Chicago, Oakland is next to Detroit, and Montgomery shares a border with Philadelphia. These counties are conservative, Republican, and wealthy, and have relatively small minority populations. The three industrially declining communities were St. Clair, Saginaw, and Erie, located, respectively, in Illinois, Michigan, and Pennsylvania. These counties are less politically conservative than the suburban counties, more Democratic, and poorer and have generally larger minority populations. The autonomous counties were Peoria, Kalamazoo, and Dauphin. They are not part and parcel of metropolitan

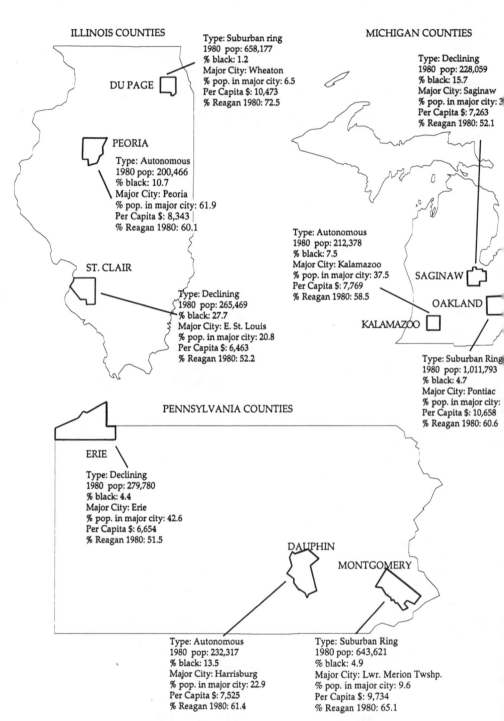

ILLINOIS COUNTIES

Type: Suburban ring
1980 pop: 658,177
% black: 1.2
Major City: Wheaton
% pop. in major city: 6.5
Per Capita $: 10,473
% Reagan 1980: 72.5

DU PAGE

PEORIA

Type: Autonomous
1980 pop: 200,466
% black: 10.7
Major City: Peoria
% pop. in major city: 61.9
Per Capita $: 8,343
% Reagan 1980: 60.1

ST. CLAIR

Type: Declining
1980 pop: 265,469
% black: 27.7
Major City: E. St. Louis
% pop. in major city: 20.8
Per Capita $: 6,463
% Reagan 1980: 52.2

MICHIGAN COUNTIES

Type: Declining
1980 pop: 228,059
% black: 15.7
Major City: Saginaw
% pop. in major city: 3
Per Capita $: 7,263
% Reagan 1980: 52.1

Type: Autonomous
1980 pop: 212,378
% black: 7.5
Major City: Kalamazoo
% pop. in major city: 37.5
Per Capita $: 7,769
% Reagan 1980: 58.5

SAGINAW

OAKLAND

KALAMAZOO

Type: Suburban Ring
1980 pop: 1,011,793
% black: 4.7
Major City: Pontiac
% pop. in major city:
Per Capita $: 10,658
% Reagan 1980: 60.6

PENNSYLVANIA COUNTIES

ERIE

Type: Declining
1980 pop: 279,780
% black: 4.4
Major City: Erie
% pop. in major city: 42.6
Per Capita $: 6,654
% Reagan 1980: 51.5

DAUPHIN

MONTGOMERY

Type: Autonomous
1980 pop: 232,317
% black: 13.5
Major City: Harrisburg
% pop. in major city: 22.9
Per Capita $: 7,525
% Reagan 1980: 61.4

Type: Suburban Ring
1980 pop: 643,621
% black: 4.9
Major City: Lwr. Merion Twshp.
% pop. in major city: 9.6
Per Capita $: 9,734
% Reagan 1980: 65.1

Figure A.1. Locations and characteristics of the research sites.

complexes, like the suburban ring counties, but they also do not suffer from the kinds of economic ills that afflict the declining communities. The autonomous counties were Republican, relatively prosperous, and politically conservative.

These counties, as the information in Figure A.1 indicates, were not sets of identical triplets. They differed among themselves in various ways that warrant brief attention. DuPage and Montgomery were typical upper-class, white, bedroom suburbs located on the edge of large cities. The GOP dominated local politics in these counties, but the party was fractured and divided in DuPage, while it was cohesive and centralized in Montgomery. Oakland was slightly more diverse socially and economically, and this diversity spilled over into its politics.

Large sections of Oakland were filled with expensive housing purchased by affluent white families during the sixties and seventies. But parts of the county were developed after World War II, when Detroit's automobile boom filled pay envelopes and propelled union workers into newly constructed housing north of the city's borders. A fairly large black population lived in Oakland's largest city, Pontiac, where the county seat and courts were once located and where the Pontiac and GMC Truck and Coach assembly plants until recently provided jobs. Democrats thus had a reasonable shot at public office. The county commissioners were made up of eleven Democrats and sixteen Republicans at the time of the fieldwork. The sheriff was a Democrat, and the previous prosecutor had been a Democrat. Oakland's Republican party organization was vigorous and active, but it was not as monolithic or as dominant as the GOP in Montgomery or DuPage.

The autonomous counties of Peoria and Kalamazoo held many things in common, except that Peoria had once been riddled with vice and corruption. Political reform after World War II scrubbed Peoria's government clean. Both communities had strong middle-class orientations with conservative, Republican inclinations and a sense of civic pride bordering on boosterism. The political parties, despite the ballot preferences of the voters, did not dominate county politics in Peoria or Kalamazoo. Dauphin differed in that its major city and county seat, Harrisburg, is also the capital of Pennsylvania. Dauphin, in part because of this fact, had a larger minority population than the other autonomous counties. The Republican party was also much stronger in Dauphin and wielded considerable influence over courthouse politics.

East St. Louis, one of the poorest and most economically depressed cities in the United States, is located in St. Clair County. East St. Louis is predominantly black; the rest of St. Clair County is white. The population outside East St. Louis is better off economically, although St. Clair as a whole is a working class county. Racial violence and political corruption are part of St. Clair's history. Political reform never came to the county, and the Democratic party held sway over the county government as it has for generations. Similar kinds of divisions existed in Saginaw, although its politics were not like St. Clair's.

Saginaw's economy depended on the automobile industry in the city and farming in the rest of the county. The Saginaw river divided the city of Saginaw. On one side of the river were sections of the city with slums rivalling those in Detroit, a downtown on the skids, and a struggling area of large homes built by long-gone lumber barons who grew rich during Michigan's timber boom in the late 1800s. On the other side, across the river, where the circuit court was located, were areas redolent of small town America. Conservative German Lutherans lived in one section of the county, while in the center of the city, blacks, poor whites, and Hispanics survived amid backroom gambling parlors and after hours drinking "clubs." The two parties were competitive in this situation, each drawing their votes from different parts of the county, although the Republicans tended to come out on top most often. Political reform had also touched both city and county government. Rampant corruption and partisan favors on the scale practiced in St. Clair did not exist.

Relatively few blacks lived in Erie, but like St. Clair and Saginaw it also struggled to make do with a declining, lackluster economy. Erie was largely white ethnic and working class. The Democratic party dominated politics in the city. Voters outside the city tended to cast their ballots for the Republican party, but for a long time they could not match the totals tallied in the city by the Democrats. In the late 1970s the county government gained a home rule charter. After this reform, Republicans broke the hold Democrats had on elected county offices. The county administrator, for example, came from the ranks of the GOP.

The differences that made each county distinctive should not obscure the many fundamental similarities that characterized each triplet of counties. The sharp contrasts that separated the suburban ring counties from the others made the differences between DuPage, Oakland, and Montgomery pale in significance. The same can be said about the declining industrial counties and the autonomous communities.

Table A.1 provides information about the number of interviews that were conducted in each of these counties. Virtually every interview was tape-recorded and later transcribed. All of the prosecutors and judges handling felony cases when the fieldwork began were interviewed, as well as all assistant public defenders assigned to criminal cases in the circuit courts. However, in the case of Oakland, which had fourteen

TABLE A.1. Number of Interviews by Role and Court.

	Prosecutors	Judges	Defense Attorneys
Illinois			
DuPage	16	7	23
Peoria	7	3	13
St. Clair	7	4	19
Michigan			
Oakland	18	8	19
Kalamazoo	13	4	13
Saginaw	12	4	13
Pennsylvania			
Montgomery	12	7	24
Dauphin	9	6	16
Erie	9	5	16
Total	103	48	155

judges, the need for an adequately sized sample of felony cases for each judge restricted the interviews to one of the two "teams" of seven judges that rotated the criminal docket between them. A select number of "regular" private attorneys and court-appointed lawyers were also interviewed. Thus, the "universe" of public defenders was interviewed, while a nonrandom sample of private or court-assigned "regulars" was interviewed. Court records of appearances and word of mouth were used to identify these regulars.

The transcribed interviews totaled over nine thousand pages of text. The contents of these interviews were analyzed, broken down, and identified according to grids in which the major relevant role activities of the person interviewed were cross-referenced by the individual's relationships with others in the court community. For defense attorneys, for example, this grid included such activities as getting started in the profession, decisions about preliminary hearings, motions, guilty pleas, trials, and sentencing. The second part include the attorney's relations with judges, prosecutors, clients, probation officers, other defense lawyers and the local bar, the police, and local politicians. The various parts of the interviews were then sorted and categorized according to these grids. After this process was completed for all of the interviews, the contents of the categories were examined for patterns while taking into account the characteristics of the individual court communities. These excerpts became the basic data from which the crafts of judges, prosecutors, and attorneys were reconstructed.

Appendix B. Publications Based on the Nine-Court Project

This book is the concluding work of one of the largest, most intensive, comparative studies of America's criminal courts ever undertaken. The project generated two multivolume reports, several articles, and two other books. For readers who want to review these studies or who wish to assess the project in its totality, this appendix pulls together the various items into a single list. The paper presented at the Annual Meeting of the Law and Society Association in 1979 is for the most part the proposal submitted to the National Institute of Justice and outlines how the project was originally designed and conceived. Papers presented at other conferences are not included in this list, since most were ultimately published. The unpublished 1979 paper describing the project is available from the authors.

Conference Paper

"Explaining and Assessing the Pretrial Process: A Comprehensive Theoretical Approach and Operationalized, Multi-Jurisdictional Application." Paper presented at the Annual Meeting of the Law and Society Association, San Francisco, California, 10–12 May 1979.

Government Reports

Explaining and Assessing Criminal Case Dispositions: A Comparative Study of Nine Counties, Final Report. 5 vols. Washington, D.C.: National Institute of Justice, U.S. Department of Justice, 1982 (Grant 79-NI-AX-0062).

Sentencing as a Socio-Political Process: Environmental, Contextual, and Individual Level Dimensions, Final Report. 2 vols. Washington, D.C.: National Institute of Justice, U.S. Department of Justice, 1983 (Grant 81-IJ-CX-0027).

Books

The Contours of Justice: Communities and Their Courts. Boston: Little, Brown and Company, 1988.
The Tenor of Justice: Felony Courts and the Guilty Plea Process. Urbana: University of Illinois Press, 1988.

Journal Articles

"The Political Styles and Organizational Strategies of American Prosecutors: Examples from Nine Courthouse Communities." *Law and Policy,* 12(January 1990):25–50.
"The Timing of Justice in Felony Trial Courts." *Law and Policy,* 9(April 1987):179–206.
"Client Games: Defense Attorney Perspectives of Their Relations with Criminal Clients." *American Bar Foundation Research Journal* 1986(Spring):253–77.
"Insider Justice: Defense Attorneys and the Handling of Felony Cases." *Journal of Criminal Law and Criminology* 77(Summer 1986):379–417.
"Criminal Courts and Bureaucratic Justice: Concessions and Consensus in the Guilty Plea Process." *Journal of Criminal Law and Criminology* 76(Winter 1985):1103–31.
"Unravelling the Complexities of Decision-Making in Face-to-Face Groups: A Contextual Analysis of Plea Bargained Sentences." *American Political Science Review* 78(December 1984):912–28.
"The Societal Costs of the Exclusionary Rule: An Empirical Assessment." *American Bar Foundation Research Journal* 1983(Summer):585–607.

Index

Craft, as metaphor for behavior in courts: aspects of craft, 5–6; links between micro- and macro-levels of analysis, 7–9; mixed-motive relationships and prosecutors' advantages over others, 9; relation of craft to routine, 4–5, 9; stability of craft in court communities, 203–5

Defense attorneys: conception of role of public defender organization, 135–37, 157–58; economics of private practice, 144–47; financial problems of indigent defense work, 147–49; politics of indigent defense work, 149–57; relationships in court community, 137–39; reputation, importance of, 139–42; reputation, elements of, 142–44; variations on standard role conception, 158–62
Denzin, Norman, 15 n.25
District Attorney. *See* Prosecutors

Efficient firms. *See* Organizational strategies of chief prosecutors
Eich, William, 69 n.2
Eisenstein, James, 4 n.6, 8n, 10 n.12, 14 n.19, 15 n.22, 16 nn.26–29, 18 n.32, 23 n.2, 74 n.3, 81 nn.4–5, 99 n.7, 103 n.8, 106 n.4, 118 n.9, 163 n.2, 172n, 186 n.15, 194 n.16, 196 n.4

Feeley, Malcolm, 4 n.6
Fenno, Richard, 15 nn.23–24, 17 n.31
Fishman, James, 23 n.2
Flemming, Roy, 3 n.4, 10 n.12, 13 n.15, 14 n.19, 15 n.22, 16 nn.26–29, 18 n.32, 25 n.5, 74 n.3, 81 n.4, 103 n.8, 106 n.4, 118 n.9, 135 n.2, 151 nn.9–10, 163 n.2, 165 n.6, 172n, 186 n.15, 194 n.16, 196 n.4
Flood, John, 163 n.3

Geertz, Clifford, 195 n.1
Gibson, James, 3 n.4
Gressett, Lynne, 25 n.4
Guilty pleas: defense attorneys and, 173–94; judges and, 112–29; trial prosecutors and, 59–65

Hellman, Arthur, 79 n.1
Heumann, Milton, 4 n.5, 164 n.4

Howard, J. Woodford, 3 n.2, 80 n.2, 84 n.6

Jacob, Herbert, 3 n.3, 4 n.6, 8n, 23 n.2, 25 n.4, 38 n.9, 81 n.5, 99n, 202n
Jacoby, Joan, 13 n.14, 24 n.4, 38 n.10, 201n
Janis, Irving, 171 n.10
Judge shopping, 182–89
Judges. *See* Courtroom craft of judges; Social organization of judges in trial courts
Judicial politics and policy disputes, 100–104

Kadish, Sanford, 9n
Kahneman, Daniel, 171 n.9
Kimberly, John, 39 n.11
King, Kamla, 14 n.20
Kunen, James, 135 n.1

Legal pluralism in American trial courts, 1, 205–6
Lermack, Paul, 33n
Levin, Martin, 13 n.17, 14 n.21
Lochner, Philip, 144 n.6

Mann, Kenneth, 144 n.5
Mather, Lynn, 4 n.7, 12n
Maynard, Douglas, 4 n.5
McDonald, William, 105 n.1
McIntyre, Lisa, 135 n.1, 137n, 152n, 157n
Merry, Sally Engle, 1n
Mintzberg, Henry, 39 n.11
Mohr, Lawrence, 15 n.25, 25 n.6
Motions challenges by defense attorneys, 168–71
Myers, Martha, 13 n.18

Nardulli, Peter, 3 n.3, 10 n.13, 14 n.19, 15 n.22, 16 nn.26–29, 18n, 74n, 81 n.4, 103n, 106 n.4, 118n, 163 n.2, 168n, 172n, 186n, 194n, 196 n.4
Neubauer, David, 4 n.6, 25 n.4
Nisbett, Richard, 171 n.9

O'Brien, David, 80 n.2, 105 n.2
Organizational strategies of chief prosecutors: bureaucratic weapon, case study of, 40–43; efficient firm, case study of, 43–44; link between court-

University of Pennsylvania Press
Law in Social Context Series

Roy B. Flemming, Peter F. Nardulli, and James Eisenstein. *The Craft of Justice: Politics and Work in Criminal Court Communities.* 1992

Joel F. Handler. *Law and the Search for Community.* 1990

Robert M. Hayden. *Social Courts in Theory and Practice: Yugoslav Workers' Courts in Comparative Perspective.* 1991

Richard Lempert and Joseph Sanders. *An Invitation to Law and Social Science.* 1989

Candace McCoy. *The Politics of Plea Bargaining: California's Proposition 8 and Its Impact.* 1993

Joseph Rees. *Reforming the Workplace: A Study of Self-Regulation in Occupational Safety.* 1988

Jeffrey A. Roth, John T. Scholz, and Ann Dryden Witte, editors. *Taxpayer Compliance, Volume I: An Agenda for Research.* 1989

Jeffrey A. Roth, John T. Scholz, and Ann Dryden Witte, editors. *Taxpayer Compliance, Volume II: Social Science Perspectives.* 1989

This book was set in Baskerville and Eras typefaces. Baskerville was designed by John Baskerville at his private press in Birmingham, England, in the eighteenth century. The first typeface to depart from oldstyle typeface design, Baskerville has more variation between thick and thin strokes. In an effort to insure that the thick and thin strokes of his typeface reproduced well on paper, John Baskerville developed the first wove paper, the surface of which was much smoother than the laid paper of the time. The development of wove paper was partly responsible for the introduction of typefaces classified as modern, which have even more contrast between thick and thin strokes.

Eras was designed in 1969 by Studio Hollenstein in Paris for the Wagner Typefoundry. A contemporary script-like version of a sans-serif typeface, the letters of Eras have a monotone stroke and are slightly inclined.

Printed on acid-free paper.

A volume in the Law in Social Context Series.

Roy B. Flemming is Professor of Political Science
at Texas A&M University. He is the author of
*Punishment Before Trial: An Organizational
Perspective of Felony Bail Processes,* and is currently
preparing for publication *Who Wins in America's
Trial Courts?: Explorations in Law, Politics, and
Institutions.* Peter F. Nardulli is Professor of
Political Science at the University of Illinois. He
is the author of *The Constitution and American
Political Development: An Institutional Perspective.*
James Eisenstein is Professor of Political Science
at Pennsylvania State University. He is the
author of *Politics and the Legal Process.* Flemming,
Nardulli, and Eisenstein are the authors of *The
Contours of Justice: Communities and Their Courts*
and *The Tenor of Justice: Criminal Courts and the
Guilty Plea Process. The Craft of Justice* is the final
book in the trilogy that began with these
volumes.